The Progressive Heritage of the Bauhaus

On the Origins of an East German Bauhaus Collection

The Progressive Heritage of the Bauhaus
On the Origins of an East German Bauhaus Collection

Published for Bauhaus Dessau Foundation
by Wolfgang Thöner and Claudia Perren

Text: Wolfgang Thöner in collaboration
with Christin Müller-Wenzel

Contents

Introduction

Today, the collection of the Bauhaus Dessau Foundation comprises more than 50,000 objects and documents relating to the history of the Bauhaus from 1919 to 1933, predominantly covering the Bauhaus Dessau from 1925 to 1932 as well as the history of how the institution was received, particularly in East Germany from 1945 to 1989. In its very heterogeneity, the collection reflects the diversity of the historical Bauhaus. Along with sketches from the preliminary course, from architecture classes and from the various workshops, and in addition to a rich photographic archive, its treasures include original furnishings, lamps, and textiles as well as domestic utensils from the metal, carpentry, and weaving workshops, visual artworks, and documents of all kinds. Together they show the school to have been a formative actor in Dessau at a time of enormous cultural, social, and economic upheaval.

The collection not only features highlights of Bauhaus design; it also allows nuanced insight into the processes that led to their creation. While the Bauhaus Dessau Foundation collection was started in the 1970s, the developments leading up to it go back much further. This book returns to those early years of "collecting Bauhaus." It describes and analyzes the institutional and curatorial processes in the German Democratic Republic (GDR) that led to the collection being established, processes that would have been impossible without the involvement of various personal networks, some of which dated back to the beginnings of the GDR.

This was not a traditional museum or collection project: politically and ideologically, the Bauhaus was an often highly fraught phenomenon, which makes illuminating its background especially important. Without some kind of public interest and appreciation, the collection could never have been established and then consolidated. Several factors had to come together here: a research focus—ultimately interdisciplinary in scope—on the achievements and products of the Bauhaus, not just for safeguarding the material but also for setting standards of evaluation; the presence of collecting and art-market structures related to the Bauhaus; and, of course, a general appreciation for the institution as well as the research and collecting activities devoted to it. All these led to sustained, politically sanctioned public interest, eventually generating an impetus to establish an institution that would address issues of contemporary concern in a manner similar to the historical Bauhaus of 1919–1933.

When the Bauhaus left Dessau in 1932, unlike its departure from Weimar in 1925, no Bauhaus collection was left behind. Apart from documents in the municipal archive and several works in the Anhaltische Gemäldegalerie (Anhalt Art Gallery Dessau) that had survived Nazi iconoclasm, nothing was accessible to the public. Small collections, some documents and objects were held solely in private hands. Following a brief, hopeful intermezzo of a more positive reception between 1945 and 1947, public ignorance of the Bauhaus returned to Dessau. Only a handful of Bauhauslers (Bauhaus associates and graduates), art historians, designers, and museum workers sought to keep its memory alive. After a few tentative steps, a breakthrough came in 1966, when a rehabilitation of the Bauhaus was contemplated for the fortieth anniversary of its opening in 1967. Some considered building up a collection, or even reopening the Bauhaus as a design school. Nothing came of these plans. Still, the anniversary brought with it the first comprehensive overview of the Bauhaus in Germany, displayed in the state gallery in Dessau's Georgium under the title "Moderne Formgestaltung. Das fortschrittliche Erbe des Bauhauses" (Modern Design: The Progressive Heritage of the Bauhaus). Over five hundred objects in private ownership or state collections were put on display. Due to a lack of interest among the East German political elite, the exhibition had little impact. Only the processes culminating in the establishment of the Wissenschaftlich-Kulturelles Zentrum (WKZ: Scientific-Cultural Center) in 1976 forged new links to the Bauhaus, which had been active in Dessau from 1925 to 1932 as an art and design school.
No other twentieth-century school of this kind has attracted such attention or become as synonymous with the most diverse phenomena, ranging from architecture to design, from the visual arts to pedagogy. And none has been so ideologically contested. In order to understand what is special about a Bauhaus collection, it is necessary to first give

an impression of the attention received by the Bauhaus and of the controversy surrounding this institution. This is addressed in the first chapter, which summarizes findings in the history of ideas, sociology, political science, and cultural studies, as well as research specific to art, design, and architecture. The unique significance of the Bauhaus can only be understood by investigating how and why different views of the Bauhaus emerged and what these views were based on.

The third part of this book deals with the history of the collection's acquisitions. On September 25, 1976, the first commercial exhibition devoted exclusively to the Bauhaus opened in Leipzig. The WKZ was given first option on purchases. As a result, 170 of the exhibits ended up in Dessau. From the five ensuing Bauhaus sales exhibitions at the Galerie am Sachsenplatz, several hundred additional works found their way into the Dessau Bauhaus collection. A small team, initially advised and supported by the Weimar Bauhaus circle, was expanded starting in 1983 with the appointment of research fellows at the WKZ Bauhaus Dessau. They began researching, exhibiting, and purchasing in their own right. Close contacts with Bauhauslers and their descendants were established and nurtured. This is how the estate of Reinhold Rossig (1903–1979) came to the WKZ Bauhaus Dessau in the late 1970s. Through Lutz Schöbe's research on the work of Franz Ehrlich (1907–1984), the estate of this significant architect enriched the Dessau collection starting in the mid-1980s. The Bauhaus Dessau acquired the estate of Carl Fieger (1893–1960) in 1988 and parts of the estate of Hannes Meyer (1889–1954) in 1989. The following year, the estate of Konrad Püschel (1907–1997) was added to the collection.

This book builds upon earlier research. The first collection catalogue, compiled by colleagues in the collection department of the former Bauhaus Dessau and published in 1988, offered only a limited selection. Much the same could be said of *Bauhaus Dessau: The Collection*. In 2004, *bauhaus objekte* became the first extensive publication to offer more than just texts on the history of the collection, presenting over five hundred objects on CD-ROM. Right on time for the opening of the permanent exhibition *Versuchsstätte Bauhaus. The Collection*, the collection catalogue *Bauhaus Dessau. The Collection* was published in September 2019.

With regard to regional and other networks, we were able to draw upon research from the Bauhaus Dessau Foundation and the Bauhaus-Universität Weimar as well as research carried out by Uta Karin Schmitt for the 1967 exhibition.

We have drawn heavily upon the 1967 exhibition catalogue and the catalogues of the Bauhaus sales exhibitions held between 1976 and 1983 at the Galerie am Sachsenplatz in Leipzig. Transfer of ownership papers held in the Bauhaus Dessau Foundation from 1977 onwards were accessed and utilized, as were letters and other documents from the estates of Bauhauslers such as Konrad Püschel, Marianne Brandt (1893–1983), Franz Ehrlich, and Hannes Meyer.

It was my great fortune that Christin Müller-Wenzel, a young researcher from Halle (Saale), was able to contribute the two central sections on the Galerie am Sachsenplatz. She is responsible for the chapters "The Galerie am Sachsenplatz in Leipzig and its Bauhaus-related activities" (1975–1983) (pp. 57–67) and "First acquisitions: The Bauhaus exhibitions at the Galerie am Sachsenplatz" (pp. 81–87).

Very special thanks to the Ernst von Siemens Kunststiftung, which generously supported this project.

Claudia Perren
Director and CEO of the Bauhaus Dessau Foundation

Wolfgang Thöner
Head of the Collection the Bauhaus Dessau Foundation

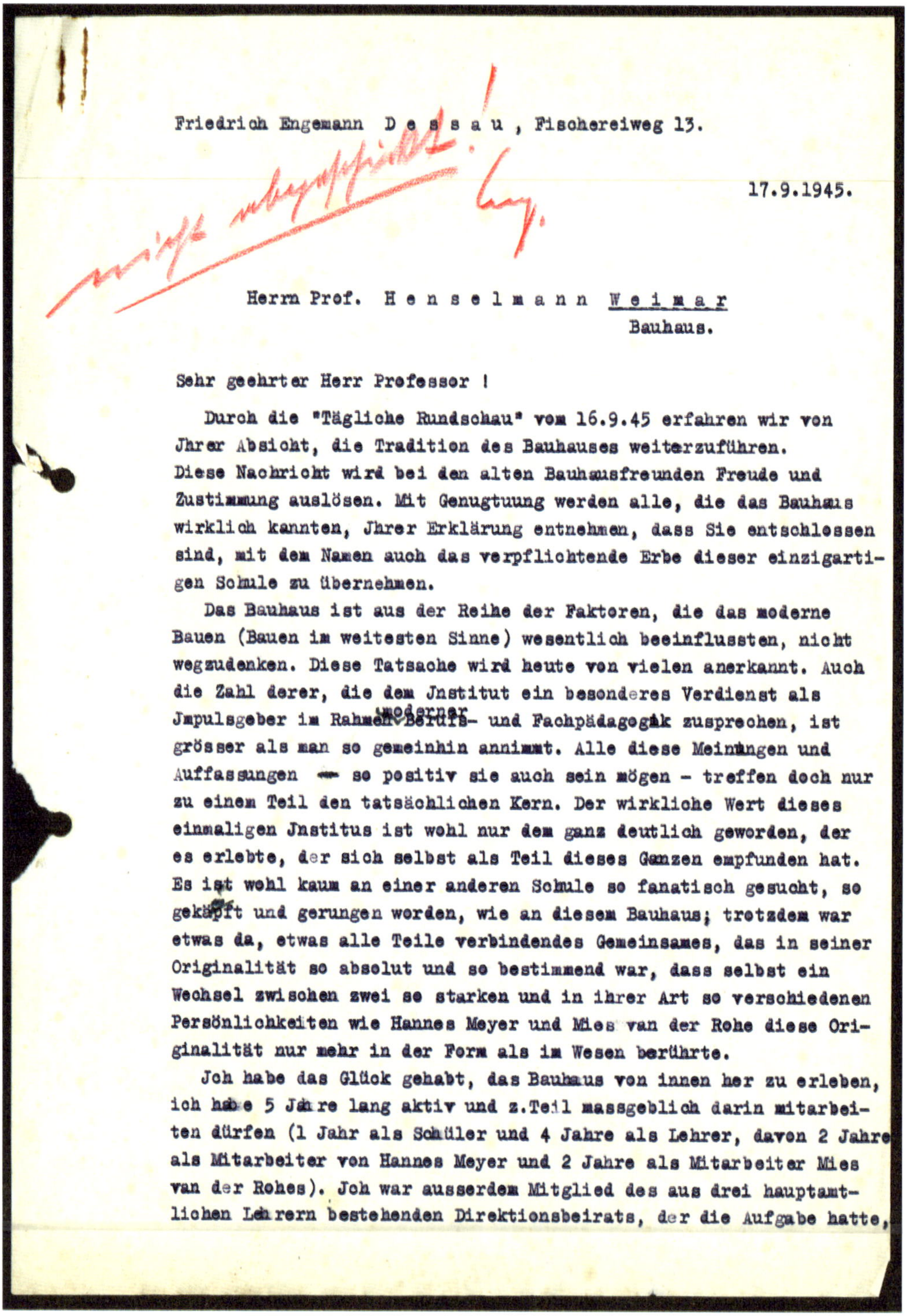

Friedrich Engemann D e s s a u , Fischereiweg 13.

17.9.1945.

Herrn Prof. H e n s e l m a n n W e i m a r
Bauhaus.

Sehr geehrter Herr Professor !

Durch die "Tägliche Rundschau" vom 16.9.45 erfahren wir von Jhrer Absicht, die Tradition des Bauhauses weiterzuführen.
Diese Nachricht wird bei den alten Bauhausfreunden Freude und Zustimmung auslösen. Mit Genugtuung werden alle, die das Bauhaus wirklich kannten, Jhrer Erklärung entnehmen, dass Sie entschlossen sind, mit dem Namen auch das verpflichtende Erbe dieser einzigartigen Schule zu übernehmen.

Das Bauhaus ist aus der Reihe der Faktoren, die das moderne Bauen (Bauen im weitesten Sinne) wesentlich beeinflussten, nicht wegzudenken. Diese Tatsache wird heute von vielen anerkannt. Auch die Zahl derer, die dem Jnstitut ein besonderes Verdienst als Jmpulsgeber im Rahmen moderner Berufs- und Fachpädagogik zusprechen, ist grösser als man so gemeinhin annimmt. Alle diese Meinungen und Auffassungen — so positiv sie auch sein mögen – treffen doch nur zu einem Teil den tatsächlichen Kern. Der wirkliche Wert dieses einmaligen Jnstitus ist wohl nur dem ganz deutlich geworden, der es erlebte, der sich selbst als Teil dieses Ganzen empfunden hat. Es ist wohl kaum an einer anderen Schule so fanatisch gesucht, so gekämpft und gerungen worden, wie an diesem Bauhaus; trotzdem war etwas da, etwas alle Teile verbindendes Gemeinsames, das in seiner Originalität so absolut und so bestimmend war, dass selbst ein Wechsel zwischen zwei so starken und in ihrer Art so verschiedenen Persönlichkeiten wie Hannes Meyer und Mies van der Rohe diese Originalität nur mehr in der Form als im Wesen berührte.

Jch habe das Glück gehabt, das Bauhaus von innen her zu erleben, ich habe 5 Jahre lang aktiv und z.Teil massgeblich darin mitarbeiten dürfen (1 Jahr als Schüler und 4 Jahre als Lehrer, davon 2 Jahre als Mitarbeiter von Hannes Meyer und 2 Jahre als Mitarbeiter Mies van der Rohes). Jch war ausserdem Mitglied des aus drei hauptamtlichen Lehrern bestehenden Direktionsbeirats, der die Aufgabe hatte,

Fig. 1 Friedrich Engemann, letter to Hermann Henselmann on the planned restart of the Bauhaus in Weimar, first page (not delivered), September 17, 1945

1 The reception of the Bauhaus in East Germany, 1945–1990

As probably the most influential design institution of the twentieth century, the Bauhaus had a presence in East Germany—that is, the Soviet Occupation Zone (1945–1949) and its successor state, the German Democratic Republic (GDR, 1949–1990)—not just in its diverse intellectual and material legacy, denounced as hostile at one extreme and celebrated as progressive at the other, but also through the activities of its former teachers and students. This legacy was not confined to experts and an interested public, as was the case in West Germany before 1968. It was always a politically contentious affair, inseparably linked to fundamental questions of culture and lifestyle—or in GDR parlance, "the socialist way of life."[1]

The Bauhaus was more heterogeneous and open (and thus also less "professional" in its sometimes rank experimentation) than comparable institutions. The school was renowned for developing and applying innovative teaching methods; it worked in the fields of architecture, urban planning, landscaping, industrial and graphic design, and the various arts, from painting, drawing, and sculpture to stage performances and the new media; it was at once a forum for theoretical debate and the producer and marketer of its own wares. The Bauhaus always saw itself as part of an international avant-garde, consciously positioning itself in an ever-expanding interdisciplinary network. For this reason, it is often impossible to tease out a specific way the Bauhaus was received from a more general reception of modernism, which could extend all the way from avant-garde tendencies to "mainstream internationalism."[2] When investigating a discourse in which reference is made to the Bauhaus, consideration must always be given to what was intended in any particular instance. An inquiry into the East German reception of the Bauhaus is thus always bound to the question of the unique character of GDR modernism, a modernism that distinguished itself as much from Bauhaus ideas as from its West German counterpart.

The force field that held together "such differently oriented forces," as Paul Klee (1879–1940) had put it in 1921,[3] was also vaguely characterized with reference to an "idea." The reception has long grappled with this Bauhaus idea. In 1923 Walter Gropius (1883–1969), the school's founder, was already writing of the school's "idea and structure."[4] Speaking three decades later in the United States, Mies van der Rohe (1886–1969), third director of the Bauhaus from 1930 to 1933, likewise described the Bauhaus as an idea, since "only an idea had the power to spread so far."[5] And one of the first Bauhaus scholars in East Germany,

1 Lothar Kühne, "Zum Begriff und zur Methode der Erforschung der Lebensweise," in: *Weimarer Beiträge. Zeitschrift für Literaturwissenschaft, Ästhetik und Kulturtheorie* 8, Berlin/Weimar 1978.

2 Werner Oechslin, "Mainstream-Internationalismus oder der verlorene Kontext," in: V. Lampugnani (ed.), *Die Architektur, die Region und der Ort. Regionalismen in der europäischen Stadt,* Munich 2000, 98.

3 "I welcome the fact that such differently oriented forces are working together in our Bauhaus. I also approve the conflict between these forces if its effect is evidenced in the final outcome." Paul Klee, "Stellungnahme zu einer Umfrage am Bauhaus, Dezember 1921," in: Hans M. Wingler, *Das Bauhaus. 1919–1933 Weimar Dessau Berlin und die Nachfolge in Chicago seit 1937,* Bramsche 1962, reprint of the 2nd expanded edition of 1968, Cologne 2005, 60.

4 Walter Gropius, *Idee und Aufbau des Staatlichen Bauhauses*, Weimar 1923.

5 Ludwig Mies van der Rohe, "Speech for the 70th birthday of Walter Gropius on May 18, 1953 in the Blackstone Hotel in Chicago," quoted in: Sigfried Giedion, *Walter Gropius,* Stuttgart 1954, 20.

Lothar Lang, saw a distinction between the "idea" of the Bauhaus and its "reality."[6] Another, far more popular, line of reception is that of a distinctive Bauhaus style.[7]

In East Germany, a variously motivated reception of the Bauhaus was an important component of discourses on national and international tradition and identity, on (life) styles and aesthetic ideologies, as well as on social, economic, and political conditions. Until the mid-1960s, such discourses were still dominated by the generation that had participated in 1920s debates or had experienced them firsthand. Scholarly or critical approaches to the history, theories, and other products of the Bauhaus were still in their infancy. From the mid-1960s, however, a new generation began researching the Bauhaus while simultaneously reexamining the Bauhaus's diverse creative legacy through the prism of present-day concerns. In doing so, they sought to reactivate that legacy as a "living heritage," both institutionally and in their own design work. If 1968 was the year that paved the way for a lastingly positive view of the Bauhaus in West Germany, one that extended far beyond specialist discourse to leave its mark on official state cultural policy, the equivalent year for East Germany was 1976.

Reception of the Bauhaus in the Soviet Occupation Zone and the early GDR (1945–1950)

In Germany's Soviet Occupation Zone, a wide range of approaches to art and design was possible in the immediate postwar years. As in Germany's western occupation zones, the Bauhaus was frequently regarded as a phenomenon untainted by fascist ideology and even as a victim of Nazi dictatorship; the new society emerging from the rubble could therefore build upon its accomplishments. This image was due in large part to the way in which the culture of the modernist avant-garde, especially its art and architecture, had been stigmatized by the Nazi regime as "degenerate." In addition, art and architecture in Nazi Germany were often represented as having been free from avant-garde influences. For all the "blood and soil" ideology, the architectural reality in highly industrialized Nazi Germany was far more complex. There was a "Bauhaus modernism in National Socialism"[8] in which Bauhauslers had played an important role. They continued to do so in East and West Germany after 1945, with "biographical connections" that persisted through all the upheavals of those years.[9]

6 See Lothar Lang, *Das Bauhaus. Idee und Wirklichkeit*, Berlin 1965.
7 Regina Bittner, "Der Bauhausstil als Lebensstil?," in: Regina Bittner (ed.), *Bauhausstil. Zwischen International Style und Lifestyle*, Berlin 2003, 26–37.
8 Winfried Nerdinger (ed.), *Bauhaus-Moderne im Nationalsozialismus. Zwischen Anbiederung und Verfolgung*, Berlin 1993.
9 Werner Durth, *Deutsche Architekten. Biographische Verflechtungen 1900–1970*, Stuttgart 2001.

In East Germany, schools of architecture and design that consciously modeled themselves on the Bauhaus were reopened or newly established after 1945. Former Bauhauslers had a hand almost everywhere. The fresh start at Weimar's Hochschule für Baukunst und bildende Künste (Academy of Architecture and Fine Arts, today's Bauhaus-Universität) was associated with names like Hermann Henselmann (1905–1995), a modernist architect who may not have been at the Bauhaus himself but who emphasized his links to the school, Peter Keler (1898–1982), and Gustav Hassenpflug (1907–1977).[10] In Dessau, Hubert Hoffmann (1904–1999) sought to reopen the Bauhaus, convening a planning committee to that end. Mart Stam (1899–1986), Marianne Brandt, and Selman Selmanagić (1905–1986) spearheaded efforts in Dresden and Berlin-Weissensee, while Walter Funkat (1906–2006), among others, worked in Halle's Burg Giebichenstein, later the Hochschule für industrielle Formgestaltung (Academy of Industrial Design). References to Bauhaus design concepts can be found in projects by former students such as Franz Ehrlich, whose involvement in Dresden's postwar architectural planning was aimed not at rebuilding the city within its old limits but at developing it as an urban landscape. The "planning collective" under Hans Scharoun (1893–1972) worked on a similar concept of a city made up of living modules. Berlin, too, was to be set back into its glacial valley landscape. One of the collective's members was Bauhausler Selman Selmanagić, who a few years later, as rector of the art academy in Berlin-Weissensee, attempted to realize the Bauhaus ideal of interdisciplinary collaboration across all fields of art and design. Even before the GDR was founded in 1949, such developments frequently met a premature end as they ran up against an anti-modernist political tendency that had become entrenched early on. Supported and partly initiated by Soviet cultural officers, the principles of "socialist realism" were given massive political backing as the sole legitimate criteria for art and design.

The Bauhaus as a "phenomenon hostile to society" (1951–1955)

For architects and town planners in East Germany, the "Sixteen Principles of Town Planning," published in 1950, became the lodestar for everything they did.[11] The rejection of Bauhaus ideas, seen as irreconcilable with these principles, culminated in the so-called formalism debate. In the "fight against formalism in art and architecture," leading SED (Socialist Unity Party) politicians regarded "modernist" design and planning methods and the "modernist style" as an affront to the approved "national traditions." From 1950 onwards, architecture was conceived as an especially effective ideological tool for educating the "new human being."

10 Klaus-Jürgen Winkler, "Bemerkungen zur Bauhausrezeption an der Weimarer Hochschule unmittelbar nach dem Krieg," in: *Wissenschaftliche Zeitschrift der Hochschule für Architektur und Bauwesen Weimar* 38, series A, 1992, issue 5/6, 277–286.

11 See Simone Hain, "'Von der Geschichte beauftragt, Zeichen zu setzen': Zum Monumentalitätsverständnis in der DDR am Beispiel der Gestaltung der Hauptstadt Berlin," in: Romana Schneider und Wilfried Wang (eds.), *Macht und Monument. Moderne Architektur in Deutschland 1900 bis 2000*, Ostfildern-Ruit 1998, 189.

Naturally, the specific situation of the Cold War played a crucial role here. In West Germany, the "International Style," closely associated with the Bauhaus, was promoted (along with other trends) as a truly democratic architecture for the free Western world. Modern architecture was often seen as a stylistic problem by those opposed to functionalism. In the socialist countries, by contrast, internationalism was construed in line with Soviet orthodoxy as the creation of similar social and political conditions, with emphasis being placed on "national traditions." The concept of the International Style had been developed in 1932 by historians at New York's Museum of Modern Art.[12] The United States now presented itself as the homeland of modernism.[13] Now this supposedly American brand of modernism was to be reintroduced into Western Europe in general, and West Germany in particular, under American leadership. In the GDR, this view was directly repudiated in a book co-authored by Bauhauslers.[14] The dominant discourses in East and West concurred solely in spurning a narrowly defined functionalism.

The return to classicism, to local details and traditional models, was intended to anchor the radical social and political changes taking place in the GDR in a familiar setting. Bauhaus became a convenient label for the array of modernisms—from constructivism to the "International Style"—that by 1951 at the latest had been deemed unacceptable. Their "lack of beauty" and "artistic worthlessness" condemned them as "formalist," if not "cosmopolitan-imperialist." Even Hermann Henselmann had changed his tune: "By dissolving all the normative categories which elevate a building to a work of art," he wrote in 1951, "the theory of constructivism (also known as functionalism) leads inevitably to cosmopolitanism."[15] In his contribution to the anti-Bauhaus literature, Kurt Liebknecht went into architectural details, contrasting the sheer glass walls of modern buildings with the Gothic window. The latter furnished a model for "the new type of dwelling, which is an expression of our democratic order ... and a symbol of 'Stalinist care for mankind.'"[16]

Walter Ulbricht cited the FDGB school in Bernau—a project of the second Bauhaus director, Hannes Meyer, that had recently undergone a controversial extension—as an "expression of cosmopolitan building." This educational facility, typical of a "Bauhaus style" that had "continued to have a significant influence after 1945," could "just as well be located in Africa or America." It "practically scoffed at the interests of the workers who will be trained there to become functionaries of our democratic order and whose money paid for its construction."[17] The Bauhaus style had to be "clearly recognized as a phenomenon hostile

12 Henry-Russell Hitchcock and Philip Johnson, *The International Style*, New York/London 1995 (first published as *The International Style: Architecture Since 1922*, New York 1932), 29.

13 See Elizabeth Mock (ed.), *In USA erbaut. 1932–1944*, New York 1944 / Bremen 1948.

14 Deutsche Bauakademie, *Handbuch für Architekten*, Berlin 1954.

15 Hermann Henselmann, "Der reaktionäre Charakter des Konstruktivismus," in: *Neues Deutschland*, December 4, 1951, quoted in: Andreas Schätzke, *Zwischen Bauhaus und Stalinallee. Architekturdiskussion im östlichen Deutschland 1945–1955,* Braunschweig/Wiesbaden 1991, 147.

16 Kurt Liebknecht, "Hohes oder breites Fenster?," in: *Neues Deutschland*, March 20, 1952, quoted in: Schätzke, 155.

17 Walter Ulbricht, "Address to the People's Chamber on October 31, 1951," quoted in: Schätzke, 145.

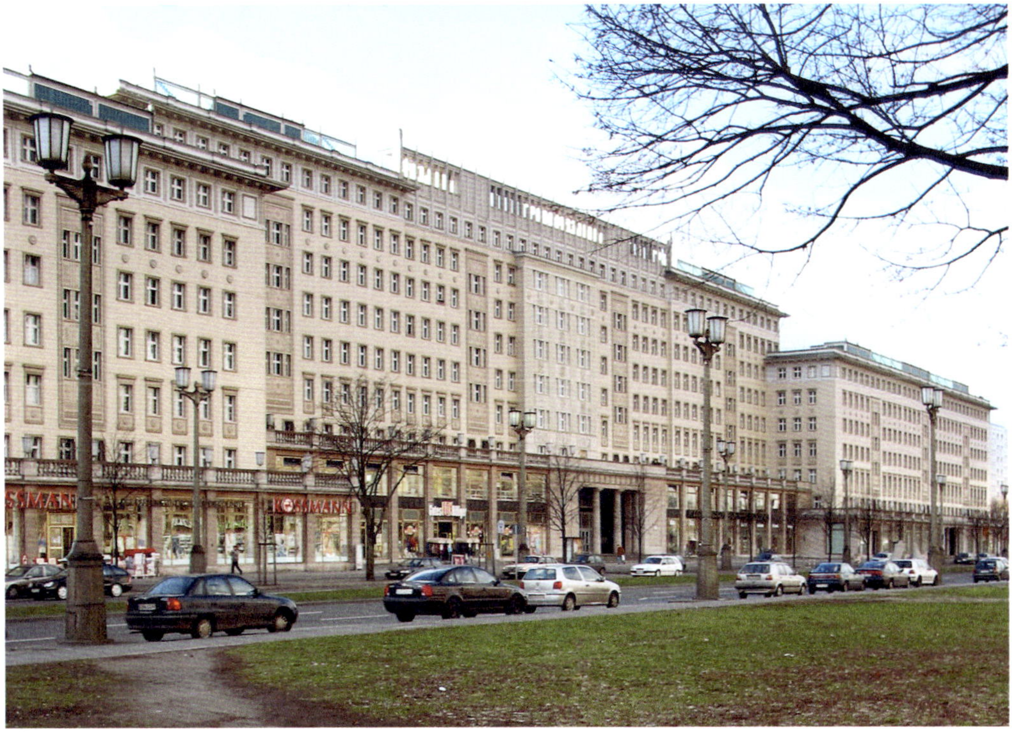

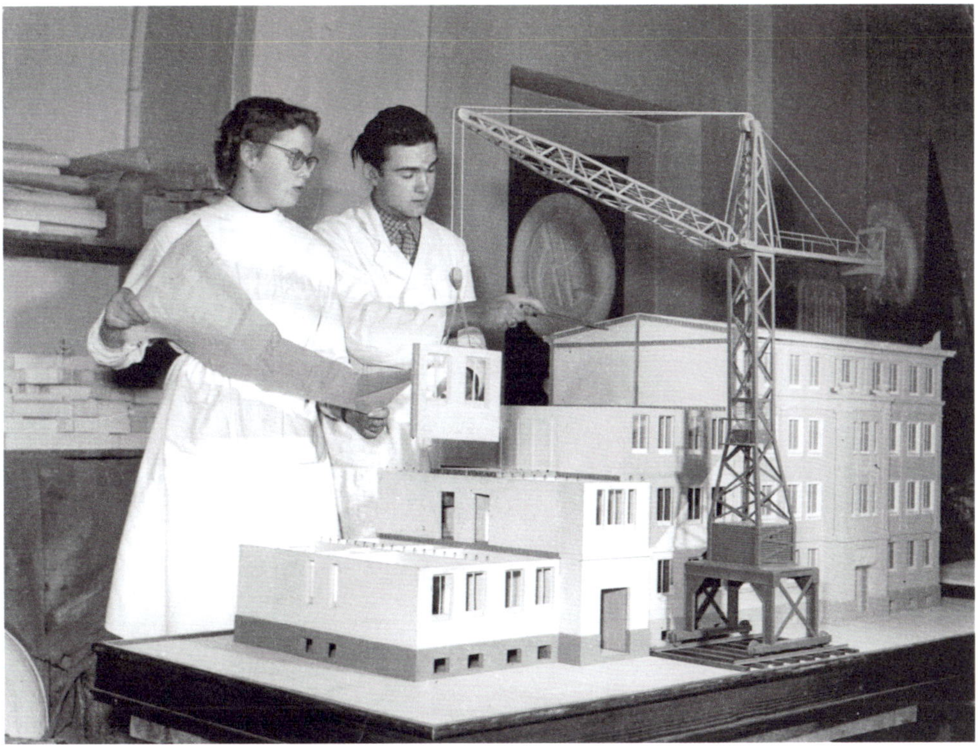

Fig. 2 Richard Paulick (with Erich Rank), Block C, Stalinallee, Berlin, 1952–53
Fig. 3 Carl Fieger with a member of the collective from Deutsche Bauakademie, model of test building, Berlin-Treptow, November 10, 1954

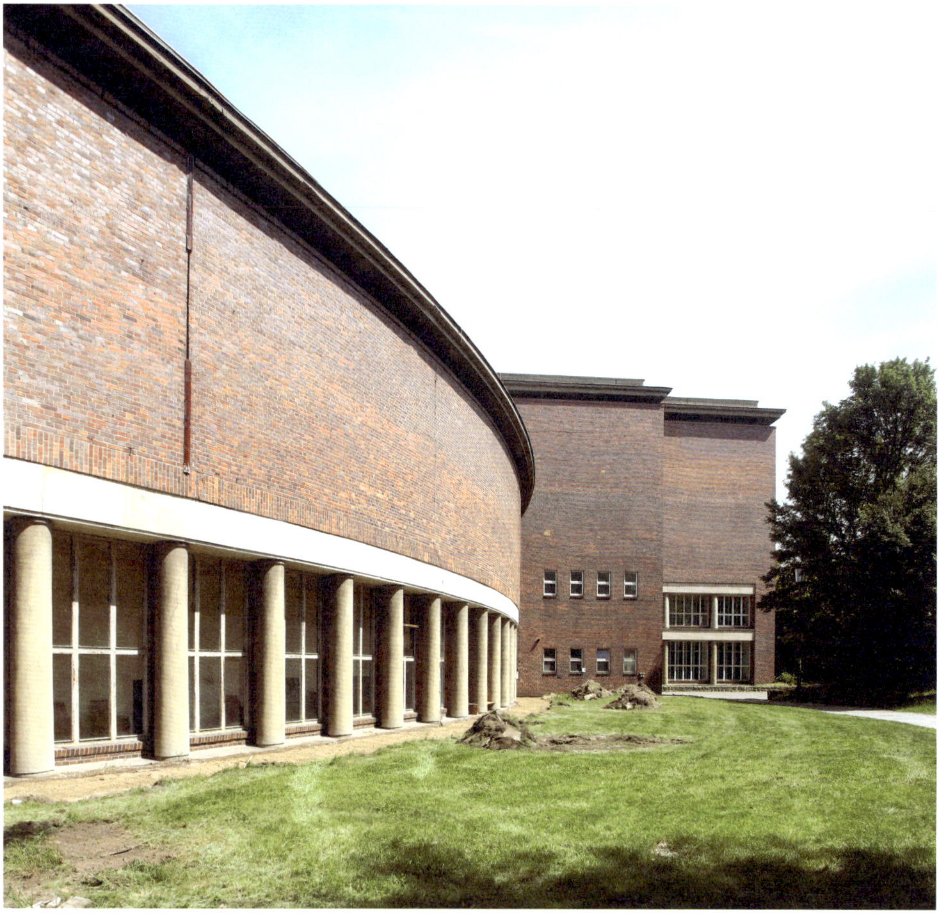

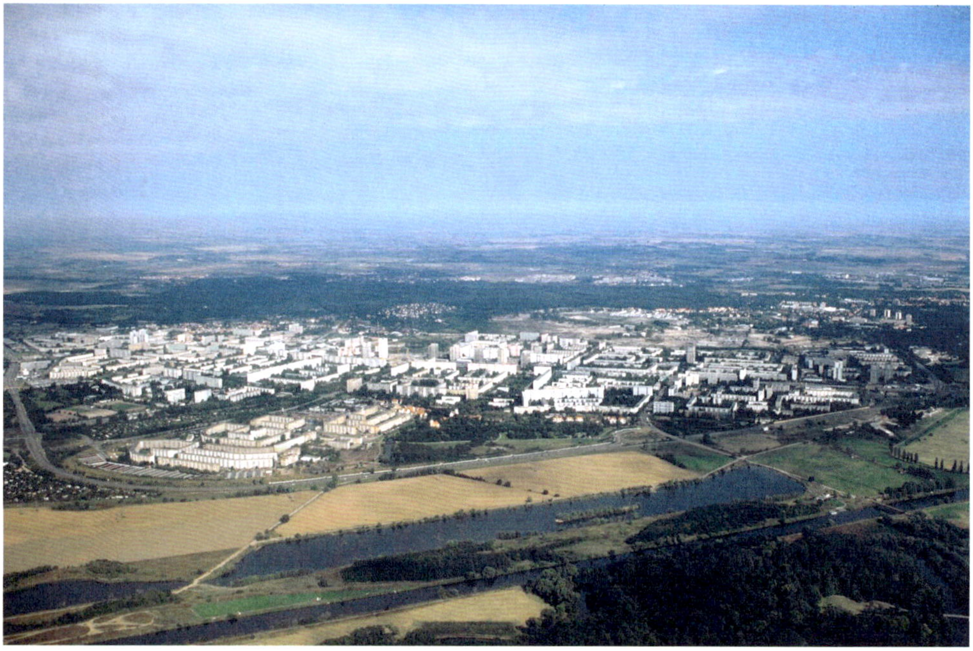

Fig. 4 Franz Ehrlich (with collective), radio broadcast building complex Berlin-Nalepastraße, 1951–56
Fig. 5 Richard Paulick (with collective), Halle-Neustadt, 1963–68

to society" (*volksfeindliche Erscheinung*) since it denied "the need to creatively apply the most progressive elements of the national architectural heritage, claiming that ideas cannot be shaped in architecture, and that priority in architecture be given to purpose, function, construction. This was taken so far that Hannes Meyer, one of the last directors of the Bauhaus, asserted that we could no longer speak of the art of building, only building in general."[18]

Grand representative boulevards—in the sense of the officially endorsed "national traditions"—now sprung up in the centers of the GDR's larger cities. None was more imposing than the Stalinallee, built between 1951 and 1959. Bauhausler Richard Paulick (1903–1979) had a hand in planning it, as did Hermann Henselmann and Hans Hopp. Paulick and Carl Fieger also made first attempts at using industrialized building methods in Berlin, ornamented with classicist decor.[19]

Notwithstanding the struggle over "national traditions," there were other, less obvious, ways of reconnecting with Bauhaus ideas. One example is Franz Ehrlich's broadcasting building in Berlin (1951–1956). Writing in 1996, Dieter Hoffmann-Axthelm attested it a "specific functionalism" situated "neither on the highway of modernism nor on the byway of national style."[20]

The reception of the Bauhaus in the period of the "New Economic System of Planning and Management" (1955–1970)

The change in building policy in the late 1950s was due primarily to economic constraints. It was announced in a speech given by Nikita Khrushchev in December 1954 criticizing Stalinist architectural doctrines and calling for the thoroughgoing industrialization of construction processes. The "fight against constructivism" was to go on, but it would now no longer be waged with "architectural decorations and aesthetic embellishments."[21] Since the GDR government had also abandoned German reunification as a short-term goal, "the demand for the development of a socialist architecture with pan-German ambitions had lost political relevance."[22] The presidium of the Deutsche Bauakademie (German Academy of Architecture) was still concerned, however, that a "false interpretation of the Khrushchev speech" might "open the floodgates to functionalism and constructivism."[23] Reflection on industrial construction thus only partly eased restrictions on design—the historicism of national traditions

18 Walter Ulbricht, "Address to the People's Chamber on October 31, 1951," quoted in: Schätzke, 144.
19 See Wolfgang Thöner und Claudia Perren (eds.), *Carl Fieger. Vom Bauhaus zur Bauakademie*, Bielefeld/Berlin 2018.
20 Dieter Hoffmann-Axthelm, "Eine Entdeckungsreise. (II) Bauten von Franz Ehrlich," in: *Bauwelt*, vol.26, 1996, 1538.
21 Nikita Khrushchev, "Building Better, Cheaper, and Faster: Address to the All-Unions Building Conference in Moscow on December 7, 1954," quoted in: Schätzke, Zwischen *Bauhaus und Stalinallee*, 159.
22 Thomas Topfstedt, "Nachbetrachtungen," in: Schätzke, 170.
23 Schätzke, 162.

was superseded by the no less ideological technicism of prefabricated building.

Functionalism and the Bauhaus began to be reappraised and rehabilitated from 1961 onwards, during the brief episode of the "New Economic System of Planning and Management," when a higher value was placed on science and technology as well as on modern management methods. Research findings since the late 1990s suggest that modern architecture in the Soviet Occupation Zone and the GDR should "not merely be measured against the yardstick of worldwide modernism" but needs to be understood as a "contribution in its own right."[24] Yet in wavering between "fixation and delimitation,"[25] the GDR still took its cue from corresponding developments in West Germany, particularly in the field of architecture. It can thus also be understood as a "catch-up modernism."[26]

Particularly with regard to the Bauhaus, it is important to note that there were two sides to "East German modernity." On the one hand, the GDR was a modern society insofar as industrialization and certain areas of social development were concerned; on the other, many of the institutional and political prerequisites for modernity were lacking, particularly those conducive to an autonomous legal system and the formation of democratic conditions. Wolfgang Engler has shown how, in the period from the building of the Berlin Wall in 1961 to the Prague Spring of 1968, GDR citizens were offered a "suite of measures" that were "primarily economic in motivation" in a state-sanctioned "modernization from above." Besides promoting the "new economic policy," these initiatives also advanced the "effective equality of the sexes in employment, family and everyday life" as well as a highly developed legal system.[27] In his view, this "modernization" was paralleled by the evolution of architecture and design in these years, largely shaped by Bauhauslers.[28] Engler has demonstrated in his studies that the tension between the two sides was often reflected in individuals: "The eclectic group of experts was positioned between below and above. Neither completely beholden to the all-powerful state nor striving unambiguously for emancipation, it filled in the spectrum of modernization variants. One would be sorely mistaken to reduce East German modernity to the administrative-technocratic format that it also came in."[29]

All this left its mark on the building industry, regarded as relatively inefficient. In this context, the experiences and ideas of the 1920s New Building movement—and with them the Bauhaus—attracted renewed interest. The preeminent project of those years was the building of Halle-Neustadt from 1961 to the early 1970s. Its chief architect from 1963 to 1969 was Richard Paulick. With this project, he reconnected with a modernism that was already passé. In the West, in particular, a new generation of architects criticized the concepts

24 Andreas Butter and Ulrich Hartung, *Ostmoderne. Architektur in Berlin 1945–1965*, Berlin 2004, 10.
25 Peter Müller, *Symbolsuche. Die Ost-Berliner Zentrumsplanung zwischen Repräsentation und Agitation*, Berlin 2005.
26 Gabi Dolff-Bonekämper and Hiltrud Kier (eds.), *Städtebau und Staatsbau im 20. Jahrhundert*, Munich/Berlin 1996, 39.
27 Wolfgang Engler, "Die ostdeutsche Moderne. Aufbruch und Abbruch eines partizipatorischen Gesellschaftsprojektes," in: Karl-Siegbert Rehberg, Wolfgang Holler, and Paul Kaiser (eds.), *Abschied von Ikarus. Bildwelten in der DDR – neu gesehen*, Cologne 2012, 29–39, here 29.
28 Rehberg, 35.
29 Rehberg, 37.

of modernism; postmodernism increasingly rejected the Bauhaus from the late 1970s.[30]

The reevaluation of the Bauhaus led in the GDR, and especially in Dessau, to the first measures to preserve Bauhaus buildings for posterity. Attitudes to the Bauhaus were far from uniform, however: until 1976, Hannes Meyer was denounced for having denied architecture the character of art, while recent buildings by Walter Gropius and Ludwig Mies van der Rohe were considered exemplary. Until the late 1970s, the visual arts produced at the Bauhaus, and abstract art in particular, were also considered problematic.

The focus of the confrontation between the political systems now shifted away from competition in the domain of culture towards living standards, as defined by consumption. Design, in particular, was all but exempted from ideologically fraught discussions of art. This allowed attention to shift to the responsibility of designers in all disciplines to the human environment as a whole, with the example set by the Bauhaus playing an important role.[31]

Serious scholarly work on the Bauhaus also got underway. *Das schöpferische Erbe des Bauhauses* (The Creative Legacy of the Bauhaus), a book by Soviet writer Leonid Pažitnov, appeared in German in 1963.[32] The translation was published by the Institute for Applied Art, subsequently the Amt für industrielle Formgestaltung (AiF, Bureau of Industrial Design). In the mid-1960s, the first monographs on the Bauhaus by GDR authors appeared and the first exhibitions were held.

The Bauhaus as inspiration: The change in reception of the Bauhaus after 1971

The criticism directed at Halle-Neustadt and similar projects points to a concerted effort at eliminating the housing problem—a declared national objective from 1971 until 1990—by means of prefabricated construction reduced to a few bare prototypes. The increasingly crisis-ridden East German economy hardly permitted any other options. The profession of architect became one-dimensional, in stark contrast to the generalist approach taken by the Bauhaus.

It may seem paradoxical that the Bauhaus's rehabilitation in the GDR came at this very moment of incipient postmodern critique in the West and monotonously modernist, impoverished construction in the East. For some theorists and practitioners, the Bauhaus (and by extension functionalism as well, demonized until the late 1950s) became a source of inspiration for a harmoniously organized society.[33]

30 Wolfgang Pehnt, *Das Ende der Zuversicht: Architektur in diesem Jahrhundert. Ideen – Bauten – Dokumente*, Berlin 1983.

31 See Siegfried H. Begenau, *Funktion – Form – Qualität. Zur Problematik einer Theorie der Gestaltung*, Berlin 1967, 69.

32 See Leonid Pažitnov, *Das schöpferische Erbe des Bauhauses*, Berlin 1963.

33 Thomas Topfstedt, "Nachbetrachtungen," in: Schätzke, *Zwischen Bauhaus und Stalinallee*, 170.

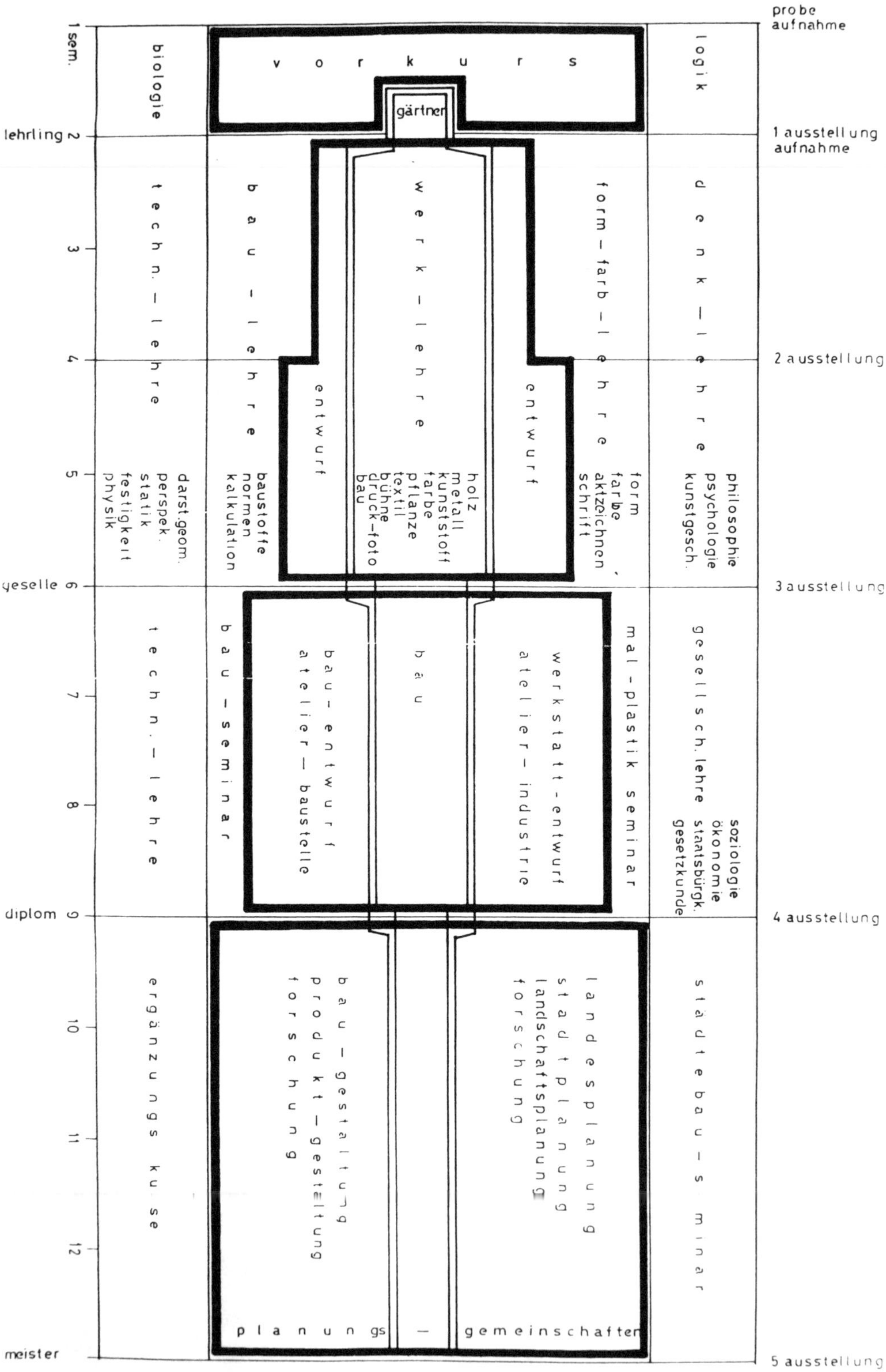

Fig. 6 Hubert Hoffmann, planned teaching scheme for the Bauhaus Dessau to be reopened, 1946

2 From the beginnings of Bauhaus studies to the establishment of the WKZ Bauhaus Dessau in 1976

Hubert Hoffmann and efforts to establish a new Bauhaus (1945–1947)

Despite the vehemence of the campaigns directed against the Bauhaus since 1933, its memory was still kept alive in some circles in postwar Dessau. This began with Bauhauslers themselves (both students and teachers), who maintained an active presence in various ways. The episode is also instructive with respect to the history of the collection, since the leading actors were already conceptualizing the different strands of Bauhaus reception and working on bringing them together, anticipating what would eventually happen after 1976: along with the reestablishment of a proactive, interventionist institution, there were cultural activities offered to a general public, reflections on conserving or restoring Bauhaus buildings, and proposals for a Bauhaus exhibition that might provide the nucleus for a future archive or museum.

In the weeks after April 21, 1945, when units of the US Army marched into Dessau, only a few Bauhauslers still remained in the city—besides the painter and illustrator Carl Marx (1911–1991), probably only the architects Friedrich Karl Engemann (1898–1970) and Carl Fieger as well as the artists and designers Max Ursin (1909–1997) and Rolf Radack (biographical dates unknown). When Germany was split into four occupation zones, Dessau found itself in the Soviet Occupation Zone from May 1946. The local Bauhauslers all saw this situation as an opportunity. They presumably experienced the collapse of the Nazi state as personal liberation and looked forward to renewing their links to the Bauhaus in a more or less direct way. Carl Marx expressed this sense of a new beginning with great clarity: "In 1945, the lights went back on and hope returned."[34]

The Bauhauslers living in Dessau in 1945 were all still young and energetic enough to be able to feel the thrill of a fresh start: Carl Marx was the youngest at 35, Max Ursin only a year older, Hubert Hoffmann, the moving spirit behind all the attempts to reestablish the Bauhaus, was 41, Friedrich Karl Engemann 47, Hinnerk Scheper (1897–1957) 48, and Carl Fieger, the oldest, was 52 at the time. After 1945, they were joined by other Bauhauslers: stage designer Georg Neidenberger (1907–1964), architects Wilhelm Jakob Hess (1906–1982), Fritz Pfeil (1909–1965), Adolf Menge (1905–unknown), and Willi Stamm (1905–1973), as well as photographer and illustrator Kurt Stolp (1904–1981). Apart from Carl Fieger and Hinnerk Scheper, they all belonged to the Dessau student generation. Wilhelm Jakob Hess, Carl Marx, Fritz Pfeil, and Max Ursin had studied under Ludwig Mies van der Rohe; Friedrich Karl Engemann, Adolf Menge, Georg Neidenberger, and Kurt Stolp had also attended the school during the Hannes Meyer era; and only Hubert Hoffmann had begun his studies when Walter Gropius was still director. This unique Bauhaus community, the like of which would never again be seen in East Germany, existed for only a few short months between 1945 and 1947.[35]

To many of those in Germany and throughout the world who viewed the Bauhaus as a positive contribution to a new culture, the school's products and mission were far from

34 Bauhaus Dessau Foundation (ed.), ... *das Bauhaus zerstört 1945–1947 das Bauhaus stört ...*, Dessau 1996, 52.

obsolete. Brutally interrupted by Nazi dictatorship, the Bauhaus had again become a living presence. The alumni in Dessau were not the only ones soon calling for the school to be reestablished. On November 12, 1945, one outsider wrote an anonymous letter to the *Bernburger Volksblatt* welcoming the renaming of the square in front of the Bauhaus Building as "Bauhausplatz" three days earlier. The writer connected this with hopes for "the Bauhaus's imminent return" and warned the "petty-minded": "There is still Bauhaus wallpaper, likewise Bauhaus furniture, and 'Bauhaus' has become a familiar concept."[36] Decades later, Max Ursin recalled seeing a United States Information Service poster in November 1945 in Hannover inscribed with the words: "If all Germany invented this century was the Bauhaus, it would still have made an invaluable contribution to the world!"[37]

All these efforts would have remained piecemeal, and drawn only a handful of Bauhauslers to Dessau, had not Fritz Hesse, who in 1925 had already been pivotal in providing the Bauhaus with a new home in Dessau following its closure in Weimar, once again become the city's mayor in the summer of 1945. Hesse thought it only natural that as part of the reconstruction effort, consideration should be given to reestablishing the Bauhaus in Dessau and providing it with administrative support. Appointed mayor by the Soviet military administration, he got in touch with Hubert Hoffmann, involved in town planning in Magdeburg at the time, to offer him a position with the public works department in Dessau. At the same time, he revealed to him his plans to have the Bauhaus reopened.[38] In December 1945, Hoffmann became Baurat (chief government architect) in Dessau and moved into an apartment at Bauhausplatz 6, located directly opposite the Bauhaus. For several months, this was also the official address of the newly established Bauhaus secretariat. Hoffmann proceeded to make contact with fellow Bauhauslers Friedrich Karl Engemann, Carl Marx, Rolf , and Max Ursin, all of whom were living in Dessau at the time.

In summer 1945, architect Hermann Henselmann was already planning to bring back the Weimar school under the name "Bauhaus: Academy for Architecture and Creative Work Made by Hand and Machine." When Fritz Hesse got wind of this from a newspaper report, his reaction was swift. In a letter dated

35 The precise course of developments leading up to the collapse of the Bauhaus project, including the roles of all those involved, is described and analyzed by Svenja Simon in her essay "Der Versuch der Wiedereröffnung des Bauhauses in Dessau nach 1945," in: Bauhaus Dessau Foundation, ... *das Bauhaus zerstört* (= n. 34), 8–33. In 1996, the author of this volume played a part in conceptualizing and researching the book and exhibition on this topic. Svenja Simon's key findings will be followed here. See also the essay in the same book: Dirk Manzke, "(Vier Nachsätze) zur versuchten Wiedereröffnung des Bauhauses in Dessau nach 1945," Bauhaus Dessau Foundation, ... *das Bauhaus zerstört* (= n. 34), 86–88.

36 *Volksblatt Bernburg*, November 12, 1945, Stadtarchiv Dessau-Roßlau, SB 62, sheet 31.

37 Bauhaus Dessau Foundation, ... *das Bauhaus zerstört* (= n. 34), 7.

38 Hubert Hoffmann had studied architecture at the Bauhaus Dessau from 1926 to 1929. In the early 1930s he was commissioned by Walter Gropius, together with Wilhelm Jacob Hess and Cornelius van der Linden, to produce a detailed "analysis of the Dessau area" and a general development plan based on the analysis. Both were presented to an audience of international experts at the famous and momentous fourth congress of the CIAM (Congrès Internationaux pour l'Architecture Moderne) in 1933. Hubert Hoffmann was thus intimately acquainted with the state of affairs in Dessau.

September 23, 1945, he reminded Henselmann of everything the Bauhaus had achieved in Dessau between 1925 and 1932, particularly those buildings "still known to this day as Bauhaus buildings."[39] The name Bauhaus was "inseparably associated with the city of Dessau." Hesse referred to his own efforts on the school's behalf and the personal consequences of his engagement. He now even included the townspeople in his identification with the Bauhaus and Dessau: "Through all this, we Dessauers believe we have served the Bauhaus with great distinction." As a trained lawyer, he indicated that he had made an agreement with the last Bauhaus director, Ludwig Mies van der Rohe, giving him the exclusive right "to employ the term 'Bauhaus' and exercise all rights pertaining thereto." Hesse had no doubt, he informed Henselmann, that Mies van der Rohe would "acknowledge the Dessau institution its due right to the name 'Bauhaus'" and that Walter Gropius would also "support such a declaration."

After Joost Schmidt (1893–1948) and Gustav Hassenpflug, Bauhauslers still active in Ber-lin, had thrown their weight behind Hesse, Henselmann replied, conceding the name to Hesse. He nonetheless urged cooperation and proposed the idea of three Bauhaus institutes in Weimar, Dessau, and Berlin. In October 1945, Hesse was also contemplating reusing the municipally owned Bauhaus Building for the future school. It had undergone makeshift repairs after sustaining wartime damage and was currently housing a number of schools. The ultimate collapse of all these plans was precipitated by the SED victory in communal elections in Dessau on September 8, 1946, when Hesse was replaced in office by the Soviet-educated Karl Adolphs, a man adamantly opposed to all such schemes.

As early as January 1946, a first Cultural Week was organized with concerts, theatrical performances and an exhibition involving Bauhauslers Carl Marx, Rolf Radack, and Max Ursin. In the same month, Hoffmann put out a call for an international Bauhaus exhibition, scheduled to open on September 1, 1946. The exhibition was intended to "give an overview of the achievements of individual Bauhaus members over the past dozen years."[40] For Hoffmann, the Kulturbund zur demokratischen Erneuerung Deutschlands (Cultural Association for the Democratic Renewal of Germany) provided a vehicle for cultivating an informed public discourse that would pave the way for a future Bauhaus. Through the Kulturbund, he also organized exhibitions on the problems of reconstruction, on current projects of freelance architects in Dessau, and on the competition to build a new station forecourt.

For Hoffmann, however, the key institutions leading to a new Bauhaus were the Bauhaus planning committee and the Bauhaus workshops. The new Bauhaus was to arise from a process combining regional politics with the network of Bauhauslers. As Hoffmann wrote in 1946: "The planning committee has the task of carrying out scientific-artistic and technical research for planning in the region of Saxony. The Bauhaus thus becomes a laboratory that makes available the equipment for practical

39 Fritz Hesse, letter to Hermann Henselmann, Dessau, September 23, 1945, Stadtarchiv Dessau-Roßlau, SB/02, sheet 25–26.

40 Hubert Hoffmann, typewritten manuscript on the "Bauhaus exhibition 1946," 1946, Hubert Hoffmann Archive.

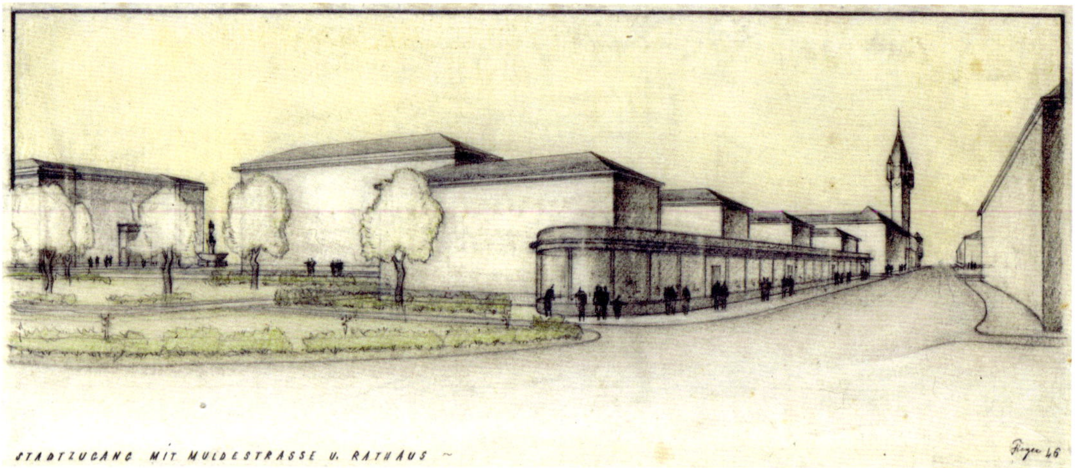

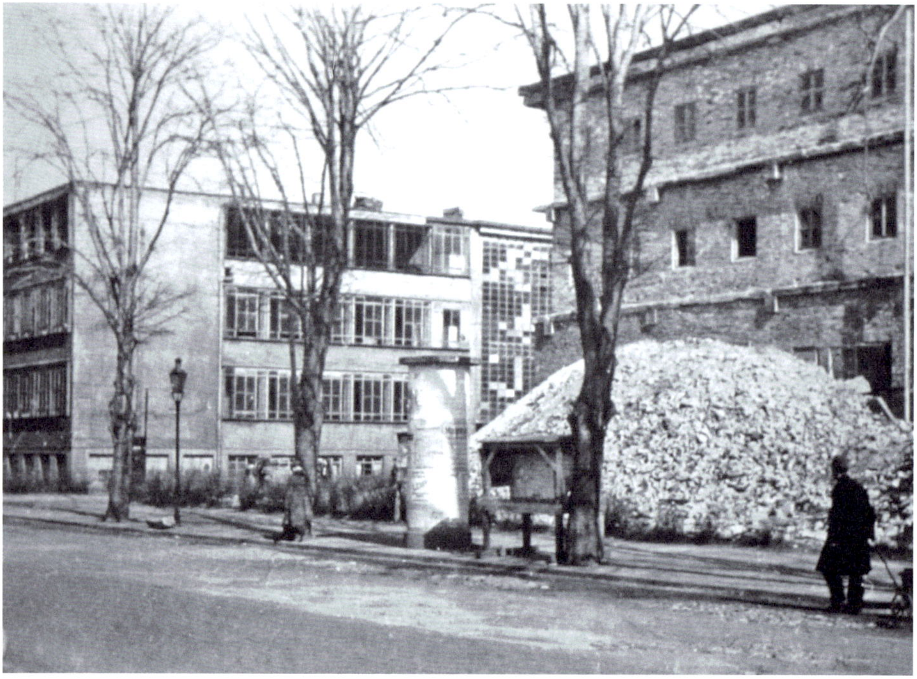

Fig. 7 Carl Fieger, extension of the Dessau Town Hall (perspective), pencil and colored pencil on tracing paper, 1946
Fig. 8 The destroyed Bauhaus Building, 1945–46

planning work."[41] As a "semi-bureaucratic body, at once a research and training institute," it was to form "the preliminary stage for a yet to be established Bauhaus," which Hoffmann termed an "Academy of Planning and Design."[42] Hoffmann made contact with Bauhaus émigrés, corresponding with Walter Gropius, among others. A list, probably drawn up in 1946 or 1947, gives an idea of the personnel he had in mind, which included not only Bauhauslers. Alongside those mentioned earlier, it includes the names of Fritz Winter (1905–1976), Josef Albers (1888–1976), Max Bill (1908–1994), Wilhelm Wagenfeld (1900–1990), Eduard Ludwig (1906–1960), Gerhard Weber (1909–1986), Franz Ehrlich, and Otto Lindig (1895–1966).[43]

Following the SED victory in the elections, political and hence also cultural conditions in the city changed. The decisive factor, however, was that Hoffmann's activity as a provincial planner in Lithuania between 1942 and 1944 had come to light in the course of denazification proceedings (in this connection, his alleged Nazi Party membership was also held against him), leading to his summary dismissal in March 1947. His membership in the SED was also canceled. Yet Hoffmann refused to concede defeat. In the summer of 1947, he founded the so-called Torhaus GmbH in hopes of reviving the Bauhaus workshops. And as late as January 8, 1948, he was still discussing his plan of attack with Hans Scharoun and Wilhelm Wagenfeld, seeking contact with the workshops of Burg Giebichenstein in Halle as well as industry groups in Wolfen.[44] Hoffmann only left Dessau when all these efforts proved in vain, probably in 1949. The reestablishment of the Bauhaus did not happen.

Friedrich Karl Engemann, a former student and then teacher at the Bauhaus, now senior instructor at the local trade school, had been tasked by Fritz Hesse in September 1945 with developing new ideas for vocational training in the construction industry. Engemann's initial concept foresaw, among other things, an introductory class modeled on the Bauhaus preliminary course. What he envisaged was not yet a revived Bauhaus, merely an institute specializing in the building industry reformed along Bauhaus lines. In a paper from February 1946, Engemann emphasized his "old, unshakeable belief in the correctness of the Bauhaus idea."[45] In November 1946, his proposals were set out in a municipal administrative document that also renamed the planned workshops for apprentices in the construction industry "Bauhaus workshops." These were to be organized into eight different domains: construction, woodwork, metalwork, color, textiles, printing, pottery, and "garden and landscape."[46] Engemann's name had appeared in Hoffmann's list of "teaching personnel for the Bauhaus" under the carpentry workshop as a "teacher of secondary subjects." In a letter to Hesse from

41 Hubert Hoffmann, *Denkschrift zur Bildung einer Planungsgemeinschaft und des Lehrinstituts Bauhaus*, July 30, 1946, Archive of the Bauhaus Dessau Foundation, Nachlass Engemann.
42 Hoffmann, *Denkschrift*.
43 Reproduced in: Bauhaus Dessau Foundation (ed.), *... das Bauhaus zerstört* (= n. 34), 19.
44 Hubert Hoffmann, document in letter to Walter Gropius, February 11, 1948, Gropius Papers, Houghton Library, Harvard University.
45 Friedrich Karl Engemann, *Gedanken zum Neuaufbau des Gewerblichen Berufs- und Fachhochschulwesens*, February 1946, Archive of the Bauhaus Dessau Foundation, Nachlass Engemann.
46 Engemann, *Gedanken*.

October 1946, Hoffmann additionally recommended him as a suitably qualified caretaker for the war-damaged Bauhaus Building. Hoffmann saw in Engemann "the right personality, one that is at home in the school's affairs and needs while commanding the required breadth in practical matters and, what is more, a familiarity with the unique tasks and obligations of the Bauhaus."[47]

The painter and graphic designer Carl Marx, who had made an artistic fresh start in 1945 and kept his head above water with advertising work, had been friends with Hubert Hoffmann since their student days. In 1946 there were plans for Carl Marx to join the painter and graphic designer Rolf Radack in setting up workshops for commercial art and photography in the Masters' Houses.[48]

Max Ursin also appeared on Hoffmann's list of teaching staff for a future Bauhaus. Parallel to Engemann's endeavors to develop a Bauhaus doctrine, he took on responsibility for the Bauhaus workshops. A carpentry workshop was set up in the orangery of Schloss Luisium, with Ursin receiving lodging in the building as its director. Among other things, the workshop manufactured furniture for domestic use, lamps, jewelry, and ceramics, which Ursin sold in a low rise building in the Kavalierstrasse until his departure from Dessau in 1949.[49]

Hinnerk Scheper, director of the Berlin Office of Monuments since 1945, temporarily moved to Dessau in 1946 at Hubert Hoffmann and Fritz Hesse's initiative. In a letter to Walter Gropius from January 12, 1946, Hoffmann reports of his efforts on behalf of the Bauhaus, which included drawing on the talents of former Bauhauslers. "Several are already active here," Hoffmann writes, mentioning Scheper along with Neidenberger, Fieger, Marx, Ursin, and Radack.[50]

In 1946, Scheper certainly played a part in drawing up what Hoffmann calls "reconstruction plans for the Gropius House and the two destroyed Masters' Houses."[51] In the same year, Scheper photographed the patched-up Bauhaus Building, and his advice was also sought on the color scheme for the Crystal Palace, the Anhalt theater and Schloss Wörlitz.[52] As late as 1948, Scheper was still applying for heritage listing for the Bauhaus Building and the Masters' Houses. In a paper from February 11, 1948 on the "restoration of the Bauhaus and the Masters' Houses Settlement of the Bauhaus," co-authored with Hubert Hoffmann, he stated: "After attempts to restore the Masters' Houses with the help of the Junkers directors proved unavailing, I took steps to ensure that the city of Dessau regained possession of all the Masters' Houses Settlement … On December 29, 1947, in a conversation about Bauhaus buildings with Ministerialrat Schubert, head of the state heritage office in Halle, it was agreed that the latter would provide funds for restoring the buildings, under the condition that these

47 Hubert Hoffmann, letter to Fritz Hesse, October 20, 1946, Archiv Hubert Hoffmann.

48 See note 44.

49 See Andreas Butter, *Die unsichtbare Bauhausstadt. Eine Spurensuche in Dessau*, Leipzig 2013, 122–125.

50 Hubert Hoffmann, letter to Walter Gropius, Dessau, January 12, 1946, Gropius Papers, Houghton Library, Harvard University.

51 Hoffmann, letter to Walter Gropius, Dessau, January 12, 1946.

52 Renate Scheper, *Foto: Hinnerk Scheper. Ein Bauhäusler als Bildjournalist in Dessau*, Beiträge zur Stadtgeschichte 13, Dessau 1991, 33.

buildings would be put to a use roughly in keeping with their former purpose... On January 14, 1948, a discussion took place with Professor Scheper, heritage officer for Greater Berlin and director of the Institute for the Preservation of Monuments within the Academy of Sciences. Prof. Scheper is in agreement with the aforementioned arrangements, pledges his support and is keen to share his own plans for the Bauhaus Building."[53] This campaign also ended in defeat by 1949 at the latest.

Carl Fieger, a former colleague at Walter Gropius's architectural bureau, had resumed work as a freelance architect in 1945. He was also a member of the Dessau urban planning committee. From 1946, he made plans for Dessau's reconstruction and supplied designs for buildings around the town hall. There was surely some communication with Hubert Hoffmann and Hinnerk Scheper about their conservation efforts.

Other Bauhauslers likewise lived and worked in Dessau after the war but were evidently not involved in efforts to revive the school. They included civil engineer Ernst Gülzow (1911–1992), office worker Walter Pannier (1908–1978), teachers Walter Puff (1904–1984) and Heinrich Weitsch (1912–2012), the former master of craft of the carpentry workshop, Karl Bökenheide (1883–1957), and his son Heinrich. The last two ran a cabinet-making shop in Elisabethstrasse until the 1970s.[54] The continued presence of these Bauhauslers ensured that a substantial body of Bauhaus-related objects, artworks and documents remained in Dessau in private hands; from 1976 onwards, many of these assets found their way directly or indirectly into the Dessau Bauhaus collection.

The community of Bauhauslers in Dessau, which had begun with such high hopes in 1945, collapsed once Fritz Hesse and Hubert Hoffmann, its guiding spirits, had left town. Very few Bauhauslers remained in Dessau. The only one to command a national reputation was Carl Marx, bound by lifelong friendship to his fellow student, Hubert Hoffmann. Of the many projects that failed to catch on, only one bore belated fruit: the Dessau Bauhaus exhibition planned for 1946, which might have been the catalyst for a Bauhaus collection, led in 1949 to an exhibition that reunited many of those involved in the failed bid to revive the Bauhaus. A collaborative project between East and West, its point of reference was Berlin, not Dessau, although Bauhauslers from Dessau were also represented. The exhibition, mounted in Berlin-Neukölln by the Greater Berlin magistracy and the Deutscher Werkbund (German Association of Craftsmen), was called "22 berliner bauhäusler stellen aus" (22 berlin bauhauslers exhibit); the catalogue is a unique testament to the way the Bauhaus was received in the immediate postwar period.[55]

53 Hubert Hoffmann, document in letter to Walter Gropius, February 11, 1948 (= n. 44). Junkers was an important manufacturer of aircraft and aircraft engines based in Dessau.—Translator's note.

54 See Butter, *Die unsichtbare Bauhausstadt* (= n. 49), 20, 105–107 and the compact biographies on pp. 170–186.

55 *22 berliner bauhäusler stellen aus. Katalog der Ausstellung "veranstaltet vom amt für kunst des magistrats von groß-berlin und der gemeinschaft der berliner bauhäusler unter dem protektorat von dr. adolf jannosch und dem deutschen werkbund,"* Berlin 1950.

Friends of the Bauhaus: The Harksen family in Dessau and their circle (1945–1976)

For many years after 1949, no concerted moves were made by those Bauhauslers still living and working in Dessau to reconnect with the Bauhaus at an institutional level. The Bauhaus was thus all but absent from official cultural life until the late 1950s. Yet beneath the surface, influence continued to be exerted by a local network that had had its origins in the Bauhaus years and that had barely played a part in the earlier activities of Hubert Hoffmann and his colleagues. In contrast to the direct interventions in urban planning, architecture, and design favored by Hoffmann and his circle, this local network, mainly comprised of former members of the "Friends of the Bauhaus" association, was largely centered on art. The most important members came from the Harksen family, whose services to the artistic and cultural history of the former province of Anhalt and its capital, Dessau, cannot be overstated.[56] They shall therefore be introduced individually here.

Two generations of the Harksen family were active in Dessau: Hans Harksen (1897–1985), Julie Harksen (1898–1980), Marie-Luise Harksen (1901–1990), and Sibylle Harksen (1931–1999). Hans Harksen had studied German literature and economics, among other things. In 1929, while working in the tax office of the city of Dessau, he had developed an enthusiasm for the Bauhaus and had joined the "Friends of the Bauhaus." He also did important work fostering links between the city and the Bauhaus. At the same time, he began amassing his own private Bauhaus collection. Hans Harksen developed a particularly close relationship with Wassily Kandinsky (1866–1944). This close contact with the Bauhaus was held against him when the city of Dessau terminated his employment in 1933. He found work in the commercial sector in Dessau and later in Berlin. In 1945 he returned to Dessau and was appointed municipal treasurer by the reinstated mayor, Fritz Hesse.

Yet with Hesse's departure, Harksen lost his position and was made director of the city archive instead. In this role, he launched initiatives that went far beyond his official responsibilities. These included carrying out research in art and cultural history, editing the *Dessauer Kalender* (Dessau Calendar) (from 1958) and leading a number of working groups and societies dedicated to the history of Anhalt. He became Dessau's most important chronicler while also specializing in the history of the workers' movement and industry in the region. The Bauhaus played a significant role throughout. In numerous lectures and articles, and also by making available his small Bauhaus collection, Hans Harksen helped maintain an interest in the Bauhaus for a select circle of art lovers. He mainly shared his findings with the public at the Gemäldegalerie Schloss Georgium (Georgium Art Gallery), a former château where Hans Harksen's sister, Julie Harksen, and his wife, Marie-Luise Harksen, were both employed.

Julie Harksen had studied art history and had been involved since 1928 with the Anhaltische Gemäldegalerie, founded just a year

56 Most of the information about the Harksen family is taken from the following book: Stadt Dessau – Amt für Kultur, Tourismus und Sport (ed.), *Dessau, das Bauhaus und die Familie Harksen*, Dessau 2003, particularly the contributions by Reinhard Melzer.

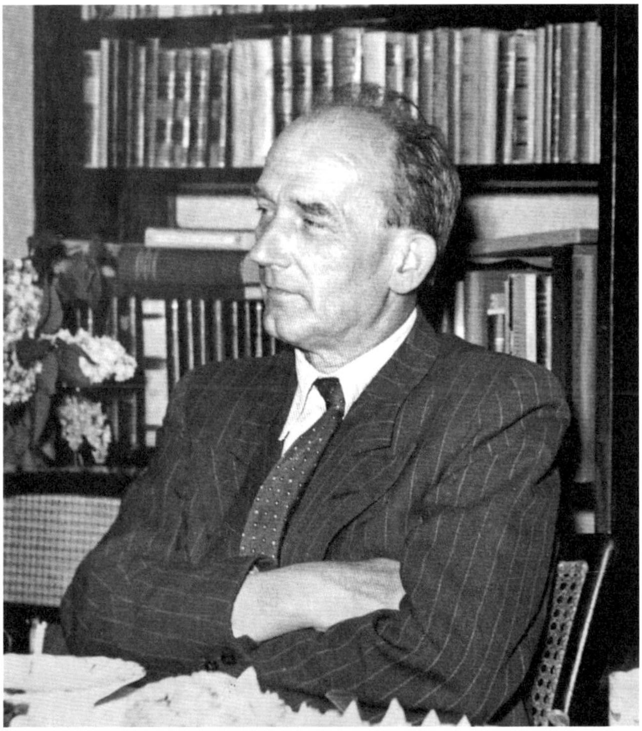

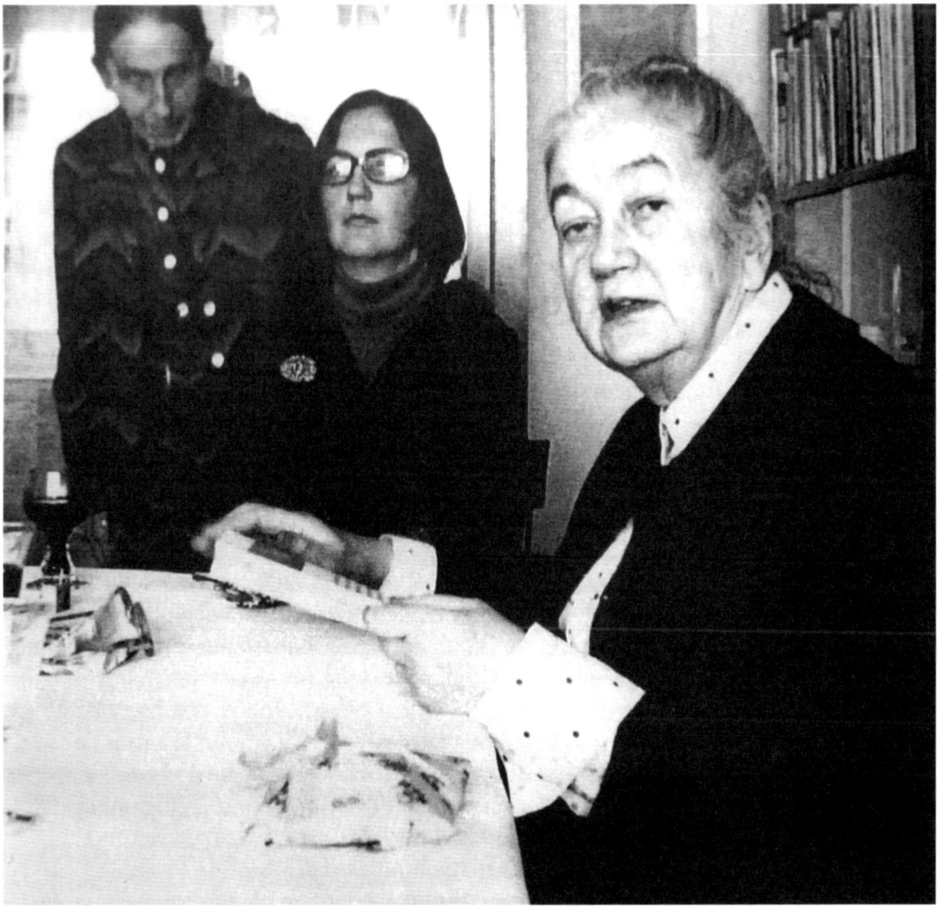

Fig. 9 Hans Harksen, 1960s
Fig. 10 Julie Harksen, Sibylle Harksen, and Marie-Luise Harksen, 1970s

earlier. Together with her sister-in-law, she had been entrusted by the gallery's then-director and state heritage officer, Ludwig Grote, with the task of compiling the first inventory. At war's end, Julie Harksen became director of the former Anhaltische Gemäldegalerie. Supported by a few colleagues, and from 1950 by the art historian Ingrid Ehlert, she was instrumental in retrieving and collating the gallery's extant and evacuated holdings. In 1948 the gallery was reestablished in Schloss Mosigkau, before being relocated two years later to the Palais Bose in the Johannisstrasse. Given that most of the gallery's artistic treasures had been transferred to the USSR, the exhibition displayed mostly educational charts. In 1958 many of the paintings and other artworks confiscated by the Soviets were finally returned to Dessau, allowing the gallery—now renamed Staatliche Galerie Dessau (State Gallery Dessau)—to be reopened in 1959.

Julie Harksen served as director of the Staatliche Galerie Dessau, Schloss Georgium, until 1961. Marie-Luise Harksen, née Schmidt, had married Hans Harksen in 1931. The trained art historian began working at the Anhaltische Gemäldegalerie in 1928 and supported Ludwig Grote in writing his book *Land Anhalt* (The Province of Anhalt). From 1931 she worked mainly as a curator of monuments to catalogue Anhalt's artistic heritage. She was also actively involved in conservation work after 1945. Sibylle Harksen, the daughter of Hans and Marie-Luise Harksen, grew up in a culturally stimulating household in which Bauhaus art was also a continual presence. She followed in her parents' footsteps, becoming an art historian and helping rebuild the gallery from 1948. Upon graduating, she became an assistant at the Martin-Luther-Universität in Halle.

In the late 1950s, the Harksens became acquainted with Hans Maria Wingler. The founder of the Bauhaus Archive, originally located in Darmstadt, Wingler had made his way to Dessau in the late 1950s after making contact with the archives in Weimar. He was particularly taken with the work of Carl Fieger, who died in Dessau in 1960. In early 1961 he wrote to Fieger's widow requesting loans for a Fieger exhibition at the Bauhaus Archive in Darmstadt. One of the first exhibitions mounted by the Bauhaus Archive thus came there from Dessau. In the flyer for the exhibition, Fieger was acknowledged for his architectural achievements, while in discussions of the exhibition he was dubbed the "romantic of objectivity," among other things.[57] The exhibition toured several West German towns as an extension to an exhibition on Walter Gropius before crossing the recently built Wall to return to Dessau in 1964.

Hans Harksen wrote in the *Dessauer Kalender* in 1965: "The Gemäldegalerie Schloss Georgium arranged the loan through the Ministry of Culture, and an agreement was reached with Frau Fieger that an exhibition would be held in Dessau before the works were dispatched. It ran from May 10 to June 18, 1961 in Schloss Georgium under the title 'Carl Fieger – Architekturzeichnungen und Entwürfe' (Carl Fieger: Architectural Drawings and Sketches). The Dessauer Kulturspiegel published an article on it in the June 1961 edition titled 'Carl Fieger – ein Vorkämpfer der Baukunst unserer Zeit' (Carl Fieger: A Pioneer of

57 J. L. Reith, "Romantiker der Sachlichkeit. Carl Fieger, der Zeichner und Architekt des Bauhaus-Kreises," in: *Die Welt*, May 17, 1961.

the Architecture of our Time) by Ingrid Ehlert. Written in collaboration with Frau Dora Fieger, it provided a highly instructive picture of the life and impact of Carl Fieger. The drawings and sketches were then sent on to Darmstadt …"[58]

In this article from 1965, Hans Harksen, like Karl-Heinz Hüter and Konrad Püschel before him in Weimar, advocates setting up a Bauhaus museum in Dessau: "It is to be hoped that Carl Fieger's drawings and sketches will be bought for an eventual Bauhaus museum in Dessau. Consideration should also be given to purchasing Fieger's house at Südstrasse 6, with lifelong rights of use granted the current proprietors. In addition, one or several houses in the Gropius estate that are still largely in their original condition would have to be purchased and fitted out with their original interior furnishings, assuming these are no longer intact."[59]

The influence of the Harksen family, which extended far beyond their professional duties, also led to the recruitment of newcomers to the Bauhaus circle. In 1957, then nine-year-old Helmut Erfurth became a member of a working group initiated and led by the Harksens. Erfurth recalls joining the Bauhaus circle via a philately club led by a former Junkers employee: "Four times a year all the committees came together … and on one such occasion a thin-looking man approached me there. He said to me: 'I know your mother; she was involved with the Bauhauslers, too, through the weaving workshop in the country women's vocational training center,' and he asked me whether I wanted to come along to the working party he was organizing for young friends of the Bauhaus."[60]

Even at that time, Helmut Erfurth had some familiarity with the Bauhaus: "How did I come across the Bauhaus? Actually, it's been with me since I was born. My parents had a bedroom designed and built by Heinrich Bormann. … My parents already had a connection to the Bauhaus. My mother through the country women's vocational training center, which was partly here, too. My father attended the local technical schools back when they were still in the Mauerstrasse and then when they … were here at the Bauhaus … which must have been around 1927."[61]

According to Erfurth, there were "interdisciplinary links" between groups of technicians, doctors, artists and craftsmen, especially in the Ziebigk district. "I can remember as a child how the old Junkers people used to meet regularly. I should mention that my father was an old Junkers engineer. That was here in Ziebigk in the 'Erholung' [pub]. There were many old Ziebigk folk, including craftspeople, with stories to tell about the Bauhaus. There was also the Leopold Fischer estate where Bauhauslers were living. I'll give you an example: … Carl Marx, the painter, from the Knarrberg. His father had been a foreman at Junkers … He turned up every now and again to drink a beer in company. There was actually a purpose to the club; people met there to talk to each other after the war … so they helped each

58 Hans Harksen, "Zur Carl-Fieger-Ausstellung in Darmstadt," in: *Dessauer Kalender* 1965, quoted in: Stadt Dessau – Amt für Kultur, Tourismus und Sport (ed.), *Dessau, das Bauhaus und die Familie Harksen*, Dessau 2003, 55.
59 Harksen, "Zur Carl-Fieger-Ausstellung in Darmstadt."
60 Helmut Erfurth in conversation with Wolfgang Thöner, Dessau, June 18, 2018.
61 Erfurth conversation. Heinrich Bormann studied at the Bauhaus Dessau in the late 1920s.

other out ... I can still remember seeing first-rate drawings by way of my wife's relatives: one of my uncles was a qualified barber at the 'Sieben Säulen,' and when we ... once visited him for a family anniversary, I was amazed to see little pictures by Oskar Schlemmer and also a fine watercolor by Feininger."[62]

Erfurth asked his uncle how he came by the pictures: "And he said: Quite simply, the artists came and ... couldn't afford the haircut so they paid for it with a little picture. That was standard practice back then ... That's also how the WKZ got hold of a watercolor by Feininger, from Aken; it used to hang in the passageway there. I was working in the furniture combine. I saw it and said: That looks like a Feininger. And the carpentry shop owner confirmed it: ... 'Yes, my father made the furniture for Feininger's music room' ... and it [the watercolor] then came to the WKZ via Schulz, the art dealers."[63]

This informal fellowship transcended ideological borders: "The other important thing is that party loyalties in Ziebigk were mixed. There were the young socialist workers, my father, Marx and others from the SPD. There were also a number of communists there, the kind later described as so-called salon communists. And then there were conservative groups as well, although you couldn't call them right-wing or nationalist, the kind of people who always appreciated solid craftsmanship."[64]

Erfurth also recalls gatherings that went beyond such social exchanges: "We mostly met at the Harksen family's place ... There was a wonderful 1919 Klee etching hanging in the corridor: *Zerstörung und Hoffnung* (Destruction and Hope) ... As a young man, Harksen had worked part-time in the Bauhaus education department, guiding visitors through Dessau and through the Bauhaus Building—I heard that from Marianne Brandt—and he had also been in Gropius's private architectural studio and helped out with the accounts there, since he had a good head for finances. And because he was so artistically engaged—through his family, of course, and through his sister and also his later wife, Marie-Luise—they knew the artists, and I can remember ... books from Kandinsky with personal inscriptions, Schlemmer pictures with personal dedications ... Julia, his sister, had a very delicate voice. She tried to explain a whole series of pictures to us, including their composition, ... with reference to classical pictures, and then she brought in examples from the Baroque or Dürer. That really opened my eyes. ... Hans Harksen then guided us through Dessau, not just the Bauhaus; it was also about the town's history, so he took us to the Employment Office [the Gropius-designed Arbeitsamt] a few times—the union was based there at the time—and he explained how it was built."[65] Altogether, there were twelve to sixteen youths in this working group, including the future painter Hans Stein.

Erfurth also met Carl Fieger: "With my father we visited Carl Fieger in 1957/58 in his house at Südstrasse 6 ... A quiet, calm, but absolutely modest man who never drew attention to himself. We were there with Dr. Harksen, who practically had to force him to say a word. He spoke very well, but modestly and in a low-pitched voice. [There was] always

62 Erfurth conversation.
63 Erfurth conversation.
64 Erfurth conversation.
65 Erfurth conversation.

also respect for Gropius."[66] Before the Wall was built in 1961, such excursions also led to Berlin, to the "Onkel Toms Hütte" estate or the Interbau exhibition in the Hansa district. The visitors met other Bauhauslers such as Richard Paulick and Edmund Collein (1906–1992) in Berlin, or Friedrich Engemann and Walter Funkat in Halle (Saale). Gertrud (1903–2000) and Alfred Arndt (1898–1976) also came over from West Germany to visit the Carl Fieger exhibition in Dessau in 1961.

The teaching of Konrad Püschel and first publications on Bauhaus history at the Hochschule in Weimar (1952–1970)

Undoubtedly the most important promoter and networker for the reception of the Bauhaus in the GDR until 1976, with a particular focus on the second Bauhaus director, Hannes Meyer, was Konrad Püschel. He had studied at the Bauhaus Dessau between 1926 and 1930 under all three Bauhaus directors and had worked with Hannes Meyer at the building site for the ADGB Trade Union School building in Bernau. He had also joined Hannes Meyer in emigrating to the Soviet Union. In 1948, Püschel was appointed lecturer at the Hochschule für Architektur und Bauwesen (Academy for Architecture and Construction) in Weimar. Even at times when the Bauhaus was out of favor with the authorities, he drew upon experiences from his Bauhaus years in his teaching and discussed questions concerning the Bauhaus with interested students.[67] In 1964, Püschel and his students compiled a thick dossier on the Bauhaus Building as the basis for its imminent restoration, which he was not alone in calling for. In 1967, he lent items from his Bauhaus period for the first-ever Bauhaus exhibition in the GDR, held in Dessau.[68] Püschel had also established contact with former Bauhaus students and corresponded with them regularly; 1947 saw him writing to Hannes Meyer and his wife, Lena Meyer-Bergner (1906–1981). From the early 1970s, at the latest, he was in constant contact with the latter, a fellow Bauhaus graduate. In 1954, immediately after she was widowed, Lena Meyer-Bergner began seeking allies for a publication and exhibition on her husband, first in Switzerland and then in West Germany.[69]

Official research on the Bauhaus got underway in Weimar with a different cast of characters and in different contexts. The formal occasion was preparations for the hundredth anniversary of the Hochschule für Architektur und Bauwesen in 1960.[70] In 1957, the school's Senate decided to set up a committee to carry out research and present its findings in a publication and an exhibition. Konrad Werner Schulze, Professor for Architectural History, was placed in overall charge of the project, while his assistant Karl-Heinz Hüter, who had just published an overview of the Hochschule's history, oversaw the content. Planning for the

66 Erfurth conversation.
67 Konrad Püschel, *Wege eines Bauhäuslers. Erinnerungen und Ansichten*, Dessau 1996, 111.
68 Püschel, *Wege eines Bauhäuslers*, 127.
69 See Lena Meyer-Bergner, letters to Kay Kulmala and others, Archive of the Bauhaus Dessau Foundation.
70 Norbert Korrek and Christiane Wolf, *Das Internationale Bauhaus-Kolloquium in Weimar 1976–2016. Ein Beitrag zur Bauhaus-Rezeption*, Weimar 2016, 13. This publication documents the exhibition of the same name held at the Bauhaus-Universität Weimar in 2016.

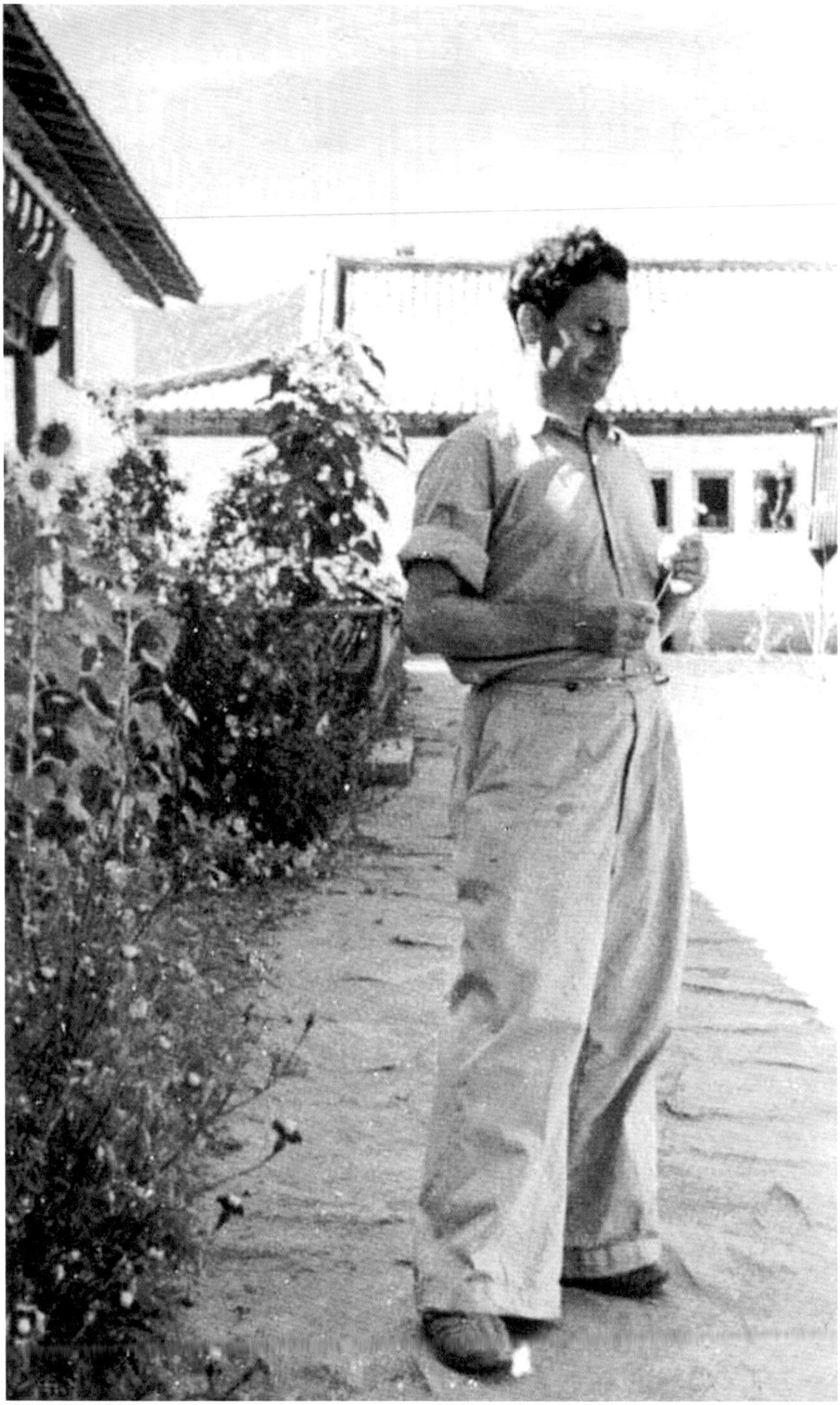

Fig. 11 Konrad Püschel in Hamhung, North Korea, around 1955

exhibition was entrusted to Peter Keler (1898–1982), another professor at the Hochschule and former Bauhaus student.

The first outline of the publication was submitted on March 25, 1958. It makes clear that all the phases of the institution's history were to be given consideration, including the Bauhaus period from 1919 to 1925. Remarkably, the paper states that "a publication on the Bauhaus as a whole, i.e. the Weimar and Dessau periods" was also "in preparation in Frankfurt/M." "Prominent scholars and artists from throughout Germany and abroad" would be called upon for contributions. Karl-Heinz Hüter, who was to deliver the section on the School for Applied Arts under Henry van de Velde (whom he was researching for his dissertation at the time), envisaged a collaboration with West German art historian Hans Maria Wingler. This plan foundered on the ideological objections of SED party leaders at the Hochschule, who clearly looked askance at cooperation with the West. In the time remaining, a presentation of the Hochschule's history from the "Marxist standpoint" was no longer possible. In particular, the Bauhaus and the Hochschule under Paul Schultze-Naumburg (1930–1945) were seen as problematic. The Senate complied with the recommendation and called off the centennial celebrations. Only the Staatliche Kunstsammlungen zu Weimar (Weimar State Art Collections) put on an exhibition in 1960 to mark the founding of the Weimar art school a hundred years earlier. In the exhibition catalogue, director Walther Scheidig discussed the Bauhaus but confined himself in the exhibition itself to the visual art of painters Lyonel Feininger (1871–1956), Wassily Kandinsky, Paul Klee, Oskar Schlemmer (1888–1943), and Gerhard Marcks (1889–1981).[71]

From October 1964, the Hochschule in Weimar had plans to extend an invitation to Walter Gropius. "The invitation was subsequently linked to the proposal that he be conferred an honorary doctorate. Reginald R. Isaacs, who was in Weimar in July 1964 researching his Gropius monograph, acted as go-between. Because the State Secretariat for Higher and Technical Education requested that 'nothing be undertaken in the matter,' Keler was forced to conclude by the end of 1965 that the 'entire Bauhaus question ... has yet to be resolved at a central level.'"[72] As with similar efforts in Dessau (described on the following pages), a formal invitation to Gropius was never issued.

Surely stirred to action by the Bauhaus exhibition in Stuttgart, the Senate of the Hochschule decided in the summer of 1968 to commemorate the Bauhaus's fiftieth anniversary. A large-scale exhibition was planned in conjunction with the Kunstsammlungen zu Weimar, for which the research assistant in the Theory and History of Architecture department, Adalbert Behr, produced a 200-page manuscript. Although the project never got off the ground, Behr's text provided a basis for further research.[73]

Several exhibition projects were realized in Weimar: in 1967, the Kunstsammlungen zu Weimar and the Helsinki Academy of Art jointly organized a traveling exhibition on the Weimar Bauhaus.[74] Two years later, the Kunstsammlungen zu Weimar drew upon its own holdings to mount the exhibition "Bauhaus Weimar 1919–1925. Arbeiten der Werkstätten

71 Korrek and Wolf.
72 Korrek and Wolf, 33.
73 Korrek and Wolf, 38ff.

für Holz, Keramik, Metall und Textilien der Weimarer Periode des Bauhauses" (Bauhaus Weimar 1919–1925: Works from the Wood, Ceramics, Metal, and Textiles Workshops from the Weimar Period of the Bauhaus);[75] and in 1970 it organized another Bauhaus exhibition in cooperation with the National Museum in Stockholm, focusing almost exclusively on art produced at the Bauhaus Weimar.

The Bauhaus Building is added to the protected monuments list (1964)

The reevaluation of the Bauhaus was also evident from 1962 onwards in the efforts made by the city of Dessau to restore the Bauhaus Building. On June 20, 1964 Karlheinz Schlesier, Dessau city architect at the time, synthesized earlier resolutions into a "plan for the reconstruction of the Bauhaus in Dessau."[76] The belated engagement with a previously unloved tradition was motivated primarily by a desire to improve the GDR's reputation among experts and abroad. In 1964 Walter Gropius's American biographer, Reginald R. Isaacs, journeyed to the GDR to interview Bauhauslers like Richard Paulick, speak with historians, and lay the groundwork for a visit from Walter Gropius. This proposal led to a conference on October 29, 1964 at the Haus des Lehrers on Berlin Alexanderplatz involving Hans Hopp, president of the German Architects' Federation, representatives of the Ministry of Culture, historians Kurt Junghanns and Karl-Heinz Hüter, the Curator General of the GDR, and Bauhausler Peter Keler, among others. Gropius's wish to visit Dessau and Weimar, in particular, "met with assent and there was willingness to consider an invitation."[77] There was clearly still no accepted Party line on the Bauhaus: "Since an invitation to Prof. Gropius presupposes we take an unambiguous stance on the Bauhaus, the Ministry of Culture, the Deutsche Bauakademie, and the Hochschule für Architektur und Bauwesen Weimar need to work together expeditiously, drawing on the materials already at hand, to come up with a position statement."[78] A second resolution was made: "The Ministry of Culture, the Halle Regional Council, and the Dessau City Council will commence large-scale reconstruction work on the Bauhaus in Dessau in 1965."[79] An expert opinion submitted by the Deutsche Bauakademie, written by Kurt Junghanns in November 1964, emphasized that the Bauhaus and the Bauhaus Building were not just important as socialist heritage, but had worldwide significance as a "historic memorial to the institution and an artistic monument from the early period of contemporary

74 Korrek and Wolf, 41.
75 Jutta Hörnig (ed.), *Bauhaus Weimar 1919–1925. Arbeiten der Werkstätten für Holz, Keramik, Metall und Textilien der Weimarer Periode des Bauhauses*, Weimar 1969. Additionally, there were two exhibitions in 1967 and 1968 on the work of *Grete Reichardt*: Museum für Kunsthandwerk Leipzig und Städtische Kunstsammlungen Karl-Marx-Stadt (ed.), Grete Reichardt, Karl-Marx-Stadt 1967; Staatliche Museen zu Berlin – Kunstgewerbemuseum Ost-Berlin and Thüringer Museum Eisenach (eds.), *Grete Reichardt, Erfurt-Bischleben – Weberin, Walter Gebauer, Bürgel/Thüringen – Keramiker, Günther Laufer, Eisenach – Kunstschmied*, Eisenach/Berlin 1968.
76 Stadt Dessau, Stadtbauamt, Stadtarchitekt Karlheinz Schlesier, *Konzeption für die Rekonstruktion des Bauhauses in Dessau*, June 20, 1964, Stadtarchiv Dessau, SB/68.
77 Karlheinz Schlesier, memorandum for file from October 31, 1964 on the conference on October 29, 1964, private archive.
78 Schlesier memorandum.
79 Schlesier memorandum.

architecture." Neglecting this heritage would risk "provoking bafflement and concern in the capitalist and socialist camp, and especially drawing criticism from architects in the GDR."[80]

Junghanns further referred to the support the Bauhaus had received from leftist forces, particularly the German Communist Party. The Bauhaus had been "attacked and in 1933 dissolved by the same reactionary wing of the German bourgeoisie that today pretends to promote progress and German culture by supporting historical research into 1920s architecture and protecting the buildings of that era."[81] This was unacceptable: "Neglecting the works of important 1920s architects would play into the hands of German monopoly capitalism."[82]

In appraising the role of the Bauhaus as an instigator of current developments, Junghanns adopted the pattern of reception that would prevail until the late 1970s: the "new objective formal language" the Bauhaus had introduced to architecture and design could be appreciated as an important stimulus "in the transition phase to industrial construction methods and the struggle to recognize the modular construction system as the basis of a socialist architecture," whereas the "cultivation of abstract art and the architectural excesses influenced by it" should be rejected as "negative consequences of capitalism."[83]

Walter Gropius would revisit his old haunts in Dessau and Weimar neither in 1965 nor in the years that followed; the restoration of the Bauhaus Building would have to wait another ten years. Yet at least some Bauhaus buildings were now heritage listed, research into the Bauhaus had received fresh impetus, and the idea of establishing a Bauhaus collection was still in the air.

80 Transcript of the expert opinion drafted by Kurt Junghanns for the Deutsche Bauakademie, addressed to the German Architects' Federation, November 23, 1964, on the *Inclusion of the Bauhaus building in the list of centrally administered architectural monuments*, Stadtarchiv Dessau, SB 68.

81 Junghanns, *Inclusion*.

82 Junghanns, *Inclusion*.

83 Junghanns, *Inclusion*.

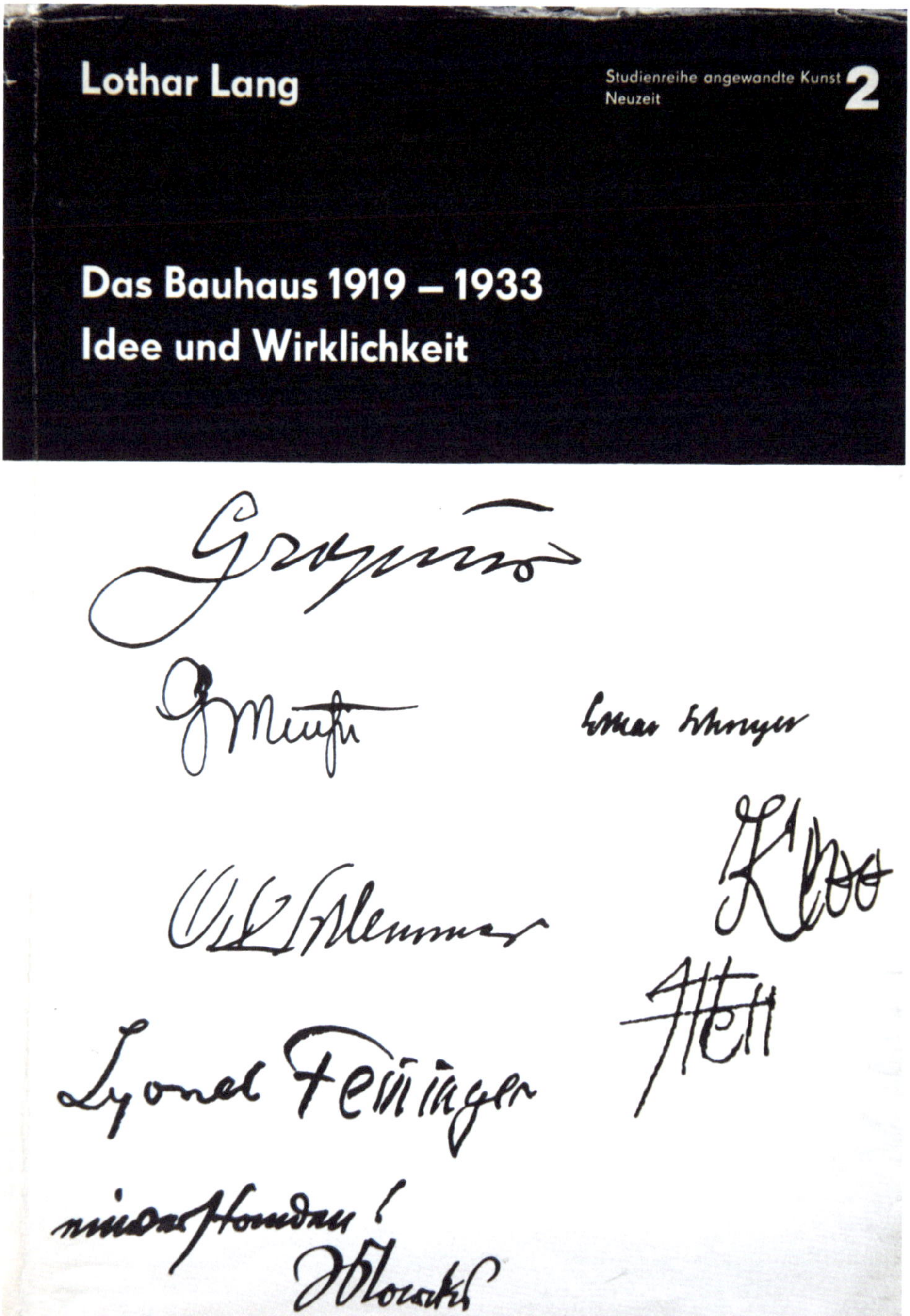

Fig. 12 Cover of the publication: Lothar Lang, Das Bauhaus 1919-1933. *Idee und Wirklichkeit*, Berlin, 1965

First books on the Bauhaus (1965–1966)

Scholarly engagement with the Bauhaus in the GDR, and a resulting stream of publications, did not get underway until the late 1950s. The key sites for research that went beyond studies on individual aspects or individuals to consider the institution as a whole, including its unique characteristics and contemporary relevance, were Weimar and Berlin.

Karl-Heinz Hüter was the first such scholar in the GDR. From 1956, he worked on a study on the hundred-year history of the Weimar academy that also dealt with the Bauhaus and arrived at findings that effectively called into question the official stance on the school that had hitherto prevailed. This was only possible because, for all the Bauhaus's diversity, Hüter attested it a fundamentally socialist orientation.

In 1963, a German translation of a booklet by Russian author Leonid Pažitnov was published by the Institut für angewandte Kunst (Institute for Applied Art), which was the forerunner to the Zentralinstituts für Formgestaltung (Central Institute for Design) and later Amt für industrielle Formgestaltung (Bureau of Industrial Design): *Das schöpferische Erbe des Bauhauses 1919–1933* (The Creative Legacy of the Bauhaus, 1919–1933). The positive reception of the Bauhaus's achievements in the Soviet Union made it easier for historians in the GDR to approach this topic. Indeed, in the editor's foreword to this publication, art historians and artists were explicitly invited to share their views. Nonetheless, Hüter's "Study of the Sociopolitical History of a German Art School" (the subtitle of his book on the Weimar Bauhaus) was not able to appear until 1973, despite having been completed in 1967: Hüter was accused of having sent the manuscript to Walter Gropius.[84] The most high-profile critic of the Bauhaus until the 1960s was Herbert Letsch, who condemned the Bauhaus for its anti-humanist, coldly technical aesthetic.[85]

The most important books on the Bauhaus to appear before Hüter's study were Lothar Lang's *Das Bauhaus. Idee und Wirklichkeit* (The Bauhaus: Idea and Reality, Central Institute for Design, Berlin, 1965) and Diether Schmidt's *Bauhaus. Weimar 1919–1925. Dessau 1925–1932. Berlin 1932–1933* (Verlag der Kunst, Dresden 1966). Lothar Lang's Bauhaus study, the first full-length monograph on the history of the Bauhaus in the GDR, was reissued in a second, expanded edition in 1966. Lothar Lang, an art historian by training, used the space opened up by Pažitnov to reclaim the Bauhaus as a creative heritage for socialism. In the form of an historical overview, he describes the school's development from its beginnings in Weimar via the Dessau period to its end in Berlin. The Dessau period is presented as the decisive phase, since through the transformation of an "abstract constructivism into concrete functionalism" effected at the time,[86] the groundwork was laid for socialist architecture and industrial design.

The artistic ideas of individual Bauhaus masters in their respective areas of expertise stand at the center of Lang's book. He blames

84 See Karl-Heinz Hüter, Das Bauhaus in Weimar. Studie zur gesellschaftspolitischen *Geschichte einer deutschen Kunstschule*, Berlin 1973.

85 See Herbert Letsch, "Zur Frage des Klassencharakters der ästhetischen Konzeption des Bauhauskonstruktivismus," in: *Wissenschaftliche Zeitschrift der Hochschule für Architektur und Bauwesen Weimar* 2, 1959/1960, 143–149.

86 Lothar Lang, *Das Bauhaus 1919–1933. Idee und Wirklichkeit*, Berlin 1965, 62.

"the work of several abstract painters who were active at the Bauhaus" for earlier reservations and the reticence of Marxist art historiography on the subject of Bauhaus history.[87] He then elegantly shifts to the increasingly positive voices of Marxist scholars.

In his review of Lang's book for the specialist journal *form + zweck* (form + purpose),[88] S. H. Begenau commended it for introducing an institution that, for the first time, "made the human environment as a whole—and an industrially produced environment at that—the object of design based on an awareness of man's overall responsibility to society. This achievement, above all, is worthy of appreciation."[89] The abstract art produced at the Bauhaus remained a "problematic case," including for Lang; it could only be justified as a basis for instruction. Lang (along with Diether Schmidt) considered Walter Gropius and Ludwig Mies van der Rohe the most important Bauhaus directors and architects for a socialist society; as in the formalism debate of the early 1950s, Hannes Meyer was reproached for having denied architecture's artistic nature.

In 1966 a relatively slender volume by art historian Diether Schmidt was published under the title *Bauhaus. Weimar 1919–1925. Dessau 1925–1932. Berlin 1932–1933.*[90] Over fifty five pages, Schmidt offers a mostly factual account of Bauhaus history. The book's publication by the Verlag der Kunst in Dresden indicated that in this case, at least, a wider public was being addressed. Schmidt's verdict on earlier criticism of the Bauhaus in the GDR is remarkably forthright: "The correct idea that one could not simply keep going in 1945 at the point where the Nazis had forced one to stop in 1933 was quite mechanically used to condemn all twentieth-century artistic traditions as 'formalism.' ... In defiance of the historical facts, it was claimed that the so-called 'Bauhaus style' had its origins in the United States of America, and was thus the 'legitimate offspring of American cosmopolitanism.'"[91]

According to Schmidt, contemporary problems, such as the necessary industrialization of construction, demanded that these positions be revised. Schmidt makes the following point in his introduction: "The time has come for the artist to enter into a harmonious relationship with society, for society no longer to isolate him from social life, supported by a centuries-old cult of genius proclaiming the value of making 'fine art' that serves no purpose, but rather to accept and integrate him as an equal productive force. This point in time was what the Bauhaus masters fervently wished for and worked towards. The ideas of the Bauhaus, which resemble the utopian anticipation of socialist conditions, demonstrate their artistic productivity in socialism and are realized with its help."[92] Diether Schmidt agrees with Lang that the Dessau period of the Bauhaus is particularly important and of acute contemporary relevance, albeit only under Walter Gropius and Ludwig Mies van der Rohe: Hannes Meyer's "latent hostility to art"[93] is still chalked up against him.

87 Lothar Lang, *Das Bauhaus 1919–1933*, 14–15.
88 Siegfried H. Begenau, *Funktion – Form – Qualität. Zur Problematik einer Theorie der Gestaltung*, Berlin 1967, 69.
89 Siegfried H. Begenau, *Funktion – Form – Qualität*, 43.
90 Diether Schmidt, *Bauhaus. Weimar 1919–1925. Dessau 1925–1932. Berlin 1932–1933*, Dresden 1966.
91 Schmidt, 7.
92 Schmidt, 47.
93 Schmidt.

The Bauhaus exhibition in Dessau, 1967

The Bauhaus had thus returned to public awareness at several levels. Ideological objections were not just reined in; rather, the Bauhaus was now seen by many as a precious heritage and as an institution that had much to teach present and future generations. The network of Bauhaus devotees in Dessau started preparing an exhibition, co-organized by a number of previously mentioned figures active in Weimar, Dresden, Leipzig, and Berlin. Ingrid Ehlert, director of the Staatliche Galerie Schloss Georgium, and Julie Harksen, director of the Dessauer Kunstsammlungen, were jointly responsible for conceptualizing the exhibition.[94] Whereas the Bauhaus connection had still been practically hushed up in the 1961 exhibition devoted to Carl Fieger, it was now possible to display a broad cross-section of the school's work.

The rehabilitation of the Bauhaus had proceeded apace. Indeed, the school could now even be cautiously commended to the powers that be as a source of inspiration. The secretary of the Kulturbund (Cultural Association) in Dessau, Lilo Lacroix, wrote in 1965: "We regard the Bauhaus as productive cultural heritage. We are particularly interested in the area of industrial design, but beyond that, of course, in all facets of progressive artistic creativity associated with the Bauhaus."[95] She also had ideas about how the Bauhaus was to be managed in the future. She wanted it to be a "cultural center for Dessau, for interested foreigners and for art students."[96]

Thus emboldened, in 1965 a group made up of members of the Bauhaus circle around Hans Harksen and the Kulturbund set about organizing the exhibition, initially planned to open in December 1966, the fortieth anniversary of the opening of the Dessau Bauhaus Building. Alongside Julie Harksen and Ingrid Ehlert, the catalogue mentions art historian Diether Schmidt, the Bauhauslers Hajo Rose (1910–1989) from Leipzig, Marianne Brandt from Karl-Marx-Stadt, and Konrad Püschel from Weimar, as well as Dessau locals Hans Harksen and Wolfgang Paul, an architect who had studied under Konrad Püschel (among others) in Weimar. Hajo Rose, who lived and worked in Leipzig as a commercial artist and exhibition designer, advised the organizing committee on exhibition and catalogue design. He also got them in touch with Marianne Brandt and Paul Citroen (1896–1983) in the Netherlands. Richard Paulick stayed more in the background when it came to arranging loans, while several Bauhauslers such as Franz Ehrlich did not even put in an appearance. As they assembled the exhibition, a desire to establish a Bauhaus collection awakened among those involved. The most important point was naturally the organization

94 The decisive impulse for the exhibition project came from Hans Harksen. He first had to convince his sister Julie, who did not share his enthusiasm for the Bauhaus. I have Reinhard Melzer to thank for this information (conversation on October 19, 2018).

95 Quoted in Uta Schmitt, "'Ein gutes Beginnen ... Was wird weiter geschehen?' Die ersten Bauhaus-Ausstellungen in der DDR," www.kunsttexte.de, 1/2010. This text, with extensive commentary and references to secondary material, is the most comprehensive publication on the topic apart from Reinhard Melzer's text from 2003. See Reinhard Melzer, "Moderne Formgestaltung, das fortschrittliche Erbe des Bauhauses. Eine Ausstellung in der Staatlichen Galerie Dessau Schloss im Jahre 1967," in: Stadt Dessau – Amt für Kultur, Tourismus und Sport (ed.), *Dessau, das Bauhaus und die Familie Harksen*, Dessau 2003, 27–31.

96 Schmitt, "Ein gutes Beginnen."

Museum des Kunsthandwerks Leipzig
Staatliche Kunstsammlungen Dresden
Galerie Neue Meister – Kupferstich-Kabinett
Staatliches Museum für Photographie Dresden
Staatliche Galerie Moritzburg Halle
Staatliche Kunstsammlungen Weimar – Schloßmuseum
Städtische Textil- und Kunstgewerbesammlung
Karl-Marx-Stadt
Universitäts- und Landesbibliothek Dessau
Frau Margarete Baitz, Dessau
Frau Marianne Brandt, Malerin und Bildhauerin, Karl-Marx-Stadt
Frau Dora Fieger, Dessau
Frau Hilde Freihammer, Dessau
Herr Gerd Gruber, Plauen
Herr Hans Hamisch, Dipl.-Arch., Dessau
Frau Dr. Julie Harksen, Direktor der Staatlichen Kunstsammlungen Dessau
Herr Dr. Hans Harksen, Stadtarchivar, Dessau
Familie Harksen, Roßlau
Herr Hellmut Hochbaum, Kunsthandwerker, Dessau
Herr Professor Keler, Weimar
Herr W. P. Koch, Dessau
Frau Annemarie Lange-Wimmer, Berlin
Herr Professor Karl Müller, Halle
Herr Günter Miska
Herr Richard Rieseler, Elektro-Ing., Dessau
Herr Konrad Püschel, Dipl.-Arch., Dozent, Weimar
Herr Hajo Rose, Gebrauchsgraphiker, Leipzig
Frau Grete Reichardt, Kunsthandwerkerin, Erfurt-Bischleben
Herr Reinhold Roßig, Berlin
Frau Charlotte Schmidt-Rom, Dessau
Frau Magdalene Schulke, Kunsthandwerkerin, Dessau
Herr Professor Selman Selmanagic, Berlin
und andere Künstler und Kunstsammler.

IV/5/6 Py 281/67 Böhm & Bullick KG, Dessau

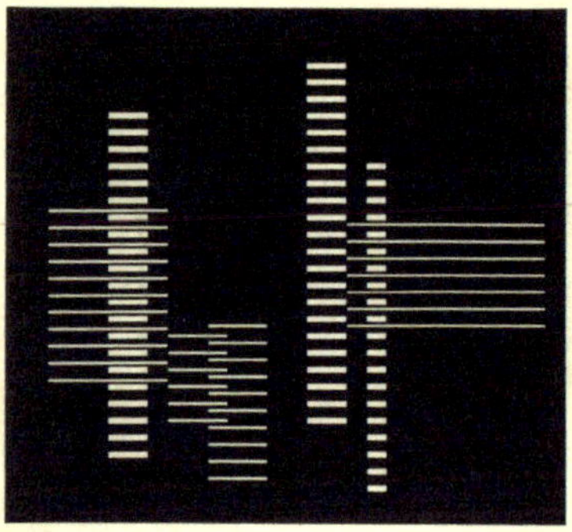

MODERNE FORMGESTALTUNG

DAS FORTSCHRITTLICHE ERBE DES BAUHAUSES

URKUNDLICHE GESCHICHTE DES BAUHAUSES

AUS DEN WERKSTÄTTEN DES BAUHAUSES

GEISTIGE UND BILDNERISCHE AUSWIRKUNGEN DES BAUHAUSES

AUSSTELLUNG IN DER STAATLICHEN GALERIE DESSAU

SCHLOSS GEORGIUM vom 1. April 1967 – 4. Juni 1967

ARBEITEN VON:

josef albers
theo balden
herbert bayer
umberto boccioni
marianne brandt
marcel breuer
hans joachim breustedt
giorgio de chirico
paul citroen
erich dieckmann
friedrich engemann
lyonel feininger
carl fieger
walter gropius
josef hartwig
johannes itten
alexej jawlensky
wassily kandinsky
ida kerkovius
paul klee
michael larionow
el lissitzky
gerhard marcks
adolf meyer
hannes meyer
ludwig mies van der rohe
laszlo moholy-nagy
lucia moholy-nagy
georg muche
konrad püschel
herbert reichel
hermann röseler
hajo rose
oskar schlemmer
joost schmidt
lothar schreyer
selman selmanagic
gebrüder thonet
vicoto vasarely
wilhelm wagenfeld
annemarie wimmer-lange
fritz winter

Hochschule für bildende Kunst Berlin-Weißensee – Hochschule für industrielle Formgestaltung Halle, Burg Giebichenstein – Webereien: Hellmut Hochbaum, Dessau

Leihgeber: Bauhaus Dessau
Hochschule für bildende Kunst Berlin-Weißensee
Hochschule für industrielle Formgestaltung Halle – Burg Giebichenstein
Institut und Museum für Geschichte der Stadt Dresden
Museum der bildenden Künste Leipzig

Fig. 13 Invitation (front and back) to the exhibition *Moderne Formgestaltung. Das fortschrittliche Erbe des Bauhauses*, Staatliche Galerie Schloß Georgium, Dessau, 1967. Graphic on cover: Josef Albers

of loans. Along with Bauhaus objects and artworks from private holdings in Dessau, many came directly from Bauhauslers. There were also loans from state museums and collections. In the catalogue and on a few photographs, probably taken by Hajo Rose, this can still be reconstructed today.

The catalogue is a unique document that makes it possible to discern many of the intentions and hopes associated with the exhibition. The title was a strategic choice: not the name "Bauhaus" stands in first place but the phrase "modern design," suggesting absolute topicality.[97] As we have already seen, industrial design was far less caught up in ideologically charged debates than, say, architecture or abstract art. The subtitle, in which the name Bauhaus then appears, emphasizes the type of modernity represented by the Bauhaus: it was "progressive." The Bauhaus as progressive heritage subsequently became the defining topos of the way the Bauhaus was received in the GDR.

In view of the animosity toward abstract art still prevalent in 1967, it seems all the more remarkable that the title page features a copy of a work by Josef Albers (from his time in Dessau in the 1920s), as had already also been the case for the 1963 publication by Pažitnov. The book opens to reveal a full-page woodcut by Lyonel Feininger (*Gelmeroda* from 1923). On the next page, the Bauhaus is tied to the GDR's official antifascist lineage: "For the Bauhauslers murdered by the fascists: / In memory of / Otti Berger, weaver / Lore Rothschild with her two children / Willi Jungmittag, photographer."

The preface is brief and matter-of-fact. From the outset, it makes clear that the exhibition had already been planned for the fortieth anniversary of the opening of the Dessau Bauhaus Building on December 4, 1966. The sole reason given for the delay is that the "collation of exhibition material" took considerably longer than expected. The key facilitators of the exhibition are then mentioned along with their contributions: Diether Schmidt provided useful tips on "collectors and earlier Bauhaus students"; Hajo Rose established contact with Marianne Brandt, lent materials of his own from his time at the Bauhaus, and helped design the exhibition; Wolfgang Paul "from Dessau City Council, civil engineering dept.," established contact with the Hochschule in Weimar and gave important advice on exhibition design. Finally, thanks are extended to the "director of the Dessau City Archive, Dr. Harksen, former member of Friends of the Bauhaus," and "Mr. Konrad Püschel, lecturer at the Hochschule für Architektur und Bauwesen in Weimar." Everyone else who supplied loans is thanked at the end. The preface is signed by the two women who directed the project: Julie Harksen and Ingrid Ehlert.

There is neither a word of welcome from a senior political dignitary nor an introduction. Following a concise table of contents, the catalogue proceeds to the exhibition layout. Visitors first entered a room with documents ranging from the 1919 Bauhaus manifesto to contemporary letters and articles emphasizing a specifically socialist internationalism: a letter from Czech architect Otokar Novy to Walter Gropius, a discussion of Lothar Lang's Bauhaus book by Halle-based art historian Wolfgang Hütt, an article by Herfried Behr

97 *Moderne Formgestaltung. Das fortschrittliche Erbe des Bauhauses*, Dessau 1967.

from the journal *Bildende Kunst* and an essay by Claude Schnaidt, lecturer at the Hochschule für Gestaltung in Ulm, translated for a Soviet periodical.

The exhibition interspersed chronologically ordered rooms with thematically arranged rooms on weaving and the visual arts, industrialization, and Bauhaus photography, followed by rooms documenting "the impact of the Bauhaus." This ranged from post-1933 works to late works by Hajo Rose, Marianne Brandt, Carl Fieger, Konrad Püschel, "Moholy-Nagy students," Johannes Itten (1888–1967), Paul Citroen, Paul Klee, Grete Reichardt (1907–1984), Karl Müller (1888–1972), and Wilhelm Wagenfeld. Of particular interest is the last room, which furnished a link to the present: "works by Selman Selmanagić and his students at the Hochschule für bildende und angewandte Kunst, Berlin-Weissensee," as well as works by Josef Albers and Hajo Rose. There is even a remarkable section devoted to "Bauhaus typography on record covers" (two covers of a Czechoslovakian label are illustrated in the catalogue).

This exhibition did more than provide a possible blueprint for future Bauhaus exhibitions. With over five hundred exhibits, it showed that it was possible to give a comprehensive survey of the Bauhaus by drawing solely on materials from Dessau and elsewhere in the GDR. The lengthier second part of the catalogue, which also acknowledges most of the lenders, sticks less strictly to the exhibition's structure and reads more like the catalogue of a future collection. In its mix of catalogue entries, biographies, shorter and longer texts on workshops and curricula, followed by a bibliography and timeline, it also offers a general introduction to the Bauhaus. The exhibition is noteworthy for the scope of its interest, which extends far beyond the classical museum genres: the objects on display range from visual artworks via furniture and architectural drawings to a loom and documents. A large number of loans, including first-rate paintings by Lyonel Feininger and works by Paul Klee, El Lissitzky, László Moholy-Nagy (1895–1946) and Fritz Winter, came from state museums—from the Staatliche Kunstsammlungen Dresden (Albertinum, Kupferstichkabinett (copperplate cabinet), Museum für Photographie), the Staatliche Galerie Moritzburg in Halle, the Museum der bildenden Künste in Leipzig, the Museum für Geschichte der Stadt Dresden and from Dessau's own gallery—more than thirty in all.

Private collections in the GDR were also represented: the Gerd Gruber collection (located in Plauen at the time), the Hans Harksen collection (Dessau), the Hans Hamisch collection (Dessau), the Rieseler collection (Dessau), Margarete Baitz's textile collection (Dessau), the collection of Frau Schmidt-Rom (Dessau), furniture belonging to Julie Harksen, objects from Hilde Freihammer's collection (Dessau), the estate of Carl Fieger (held by his widow in Dessau), works belonging to Bauhauslers Peter Keler, Marianne Brandt, Hajo Rose, Konrad Püschel, Selman Selmanagić, and Friedrich Engemann. Many objects can be identified that a decade later, mostly through the Galerie am Sachsenplatz, would go on to form the basis of today's Dessau Bauhaus collection. The following objects are clearly identifiable: Josef Albers' intaglio from 1956 (lent by Marianne Brandt), graphic art by László Moholy-Nagy (lent by Marianne Brandt), several photographs by Hajo Rose, works by Carl Fieger and Konrad Püschel, and a number of textiles by Grete Reichardt.

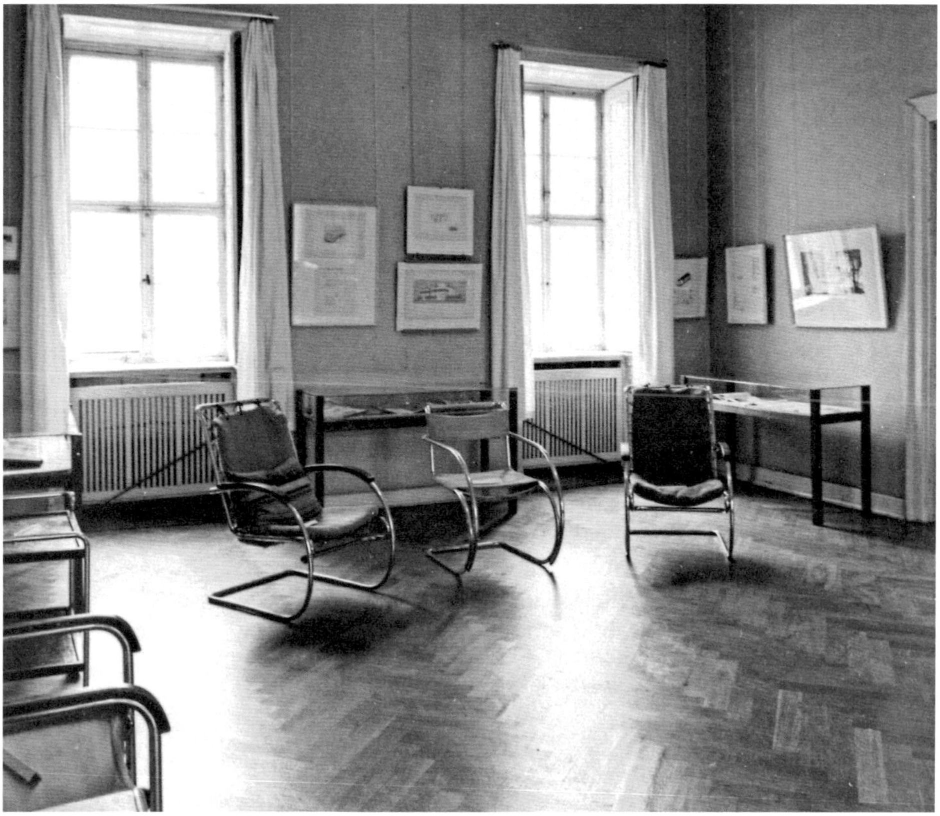

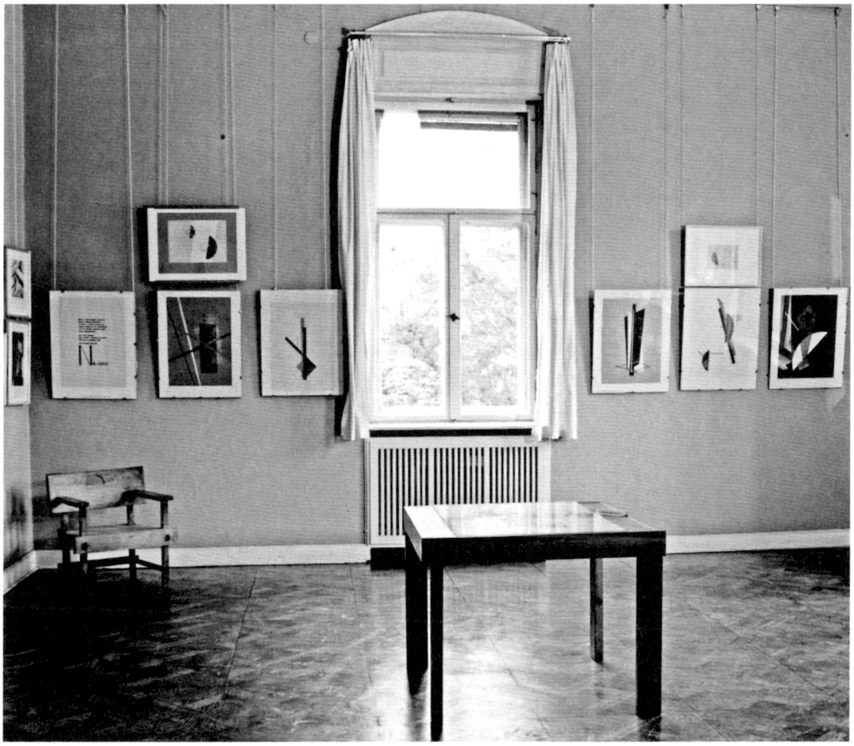

Fig. 14 Exhibition *Moderne Formgestaltung. Das fortschrittliche Erbe des Bauhauses*, Staatliche Galerie Schloß Georgium, Dessau, 1967: Room with tubular steel furniture (Ludwig Mies van der Rohe and others) and graphics and paintings (Lyonel Feininger et al., some works today at the Bauhaus Dessau Foundation)

Fig. 15 Exhibition *Moderne Formgestaltung. Das fortschrittliche Erbe des Bauhauses*, Staatliche Galerie Schloß Georgium, Dessau, 1967: Room with furniture by Marcel Breuer and lithographs by László Moholy-Nagy (some of them today at the Bauhaus Dessau Foundation)

Unfortunately, the exhibition project was given a lukewarm reception by the powers that be in Dessau and hence had no opportunity to make an impact beyond the region. There was grudging tolerance at best, rather than support. Helmut Erfurth recalls three topics that were to be avoided in Dessau in 1976: "no Junkers, no Bauhaus, and no criticism of the Party."[98] This adverse political climate was surely a factor behind the exhibition not opening until April 1967. Above all, it accounts for the distinct lack of interest towards the exhibition shown by both the provincial and national media. In the end, the mayor of Dessau and the SED district committee still viewed the Bauhaus with suspicion, not least because many of the most famous Bauhauslers were living and working in the United States at the time. In 1967, the political will to broker contact between Bauhaus circles and the Party was still missing. It would take another ten years for such contact to be established, and then mainly with the support of figures not living in Dessau. The "refreshingly brief"[99] opening of the 1967 exhibition in Dessau was thus devoid of all pomp and ceremony. It was followed by a privately sponsored standing buffet. Participants then made their way to a "club for the intelligentsia" located near the Bauhaus Building where they celebrated and debated until midnight while inspecting a parallel exhibition: Dessau writer, artist, and bookseller Christa Borchert[100] had supplied prints based on works by Bauhaus artists which were shown alongside works by local artists. This, too, was passed over in silence by the press.

The idea of building up a Bauhaus collection and exhibition was pursued further at the Staatliche Galerie Schloss Georgium, albeit to a very modest extent: for several years after 1969, visitors could enter a darkened ground-floor room containing Bauhaus-related objects and artworks from the gallery's holdings.

Fresh start in Weimar: The Bauhaus as socialist heritage (1970–1976)

The most instrumental figure in bringing about a sustained and widespread engagement with the Bauhaus turned out to be Bernd Grönwald. It is undoubtedly due primarily to Konrad Püschel's influence that his former student, a professor at the Hochschule für Architektur und Bauwesen, became enthusiastically committed to the cause of the Bauhaus from 1970 onwards. He soon demonstrated political skill in developing a strategy for bringing renewed attention to the Bauhaus in a way that went far beyond historical interest.[101] His aim was to foster appreciation of the intellectual as well as architectural legacy of the Bauhaus. From the outset, Grönwald had in mind a grand strategy for bringing together the different strands of Bauhaus reception. "Following internal

98 Helmut Erfurth in conversation with Wolfgang Thöner, Dessau, June 18, 2018.

99 Erfurth conversation. In a conversation with Wolfgang Thöner on October 19, 2018, Reinhard Melzer remarked that the exhibition had been an absolute insider tip. He heard about it in Leipzig and traveled to Dessau in 1967 to see the exhibition. This was also when he set eyes on the Bauhaus Building for the first time.

100 See Manfred Jendryschik, "Christa Borchert. Autorin, Zeichnerin und eine Dessauer Instanz," in: *Mitteldeutsche Zeitung*, February 4, 2013.

101 From 1973, Bernd Grönwald and his wife lived in the Haus Am Horn in Weimar, built in 1923 to a design by Georg Muche. On October 15, 1974, Georg Muche, guided by Grönwald and his wife, visited the Haus Am Horn and the Weimar Hochschule.

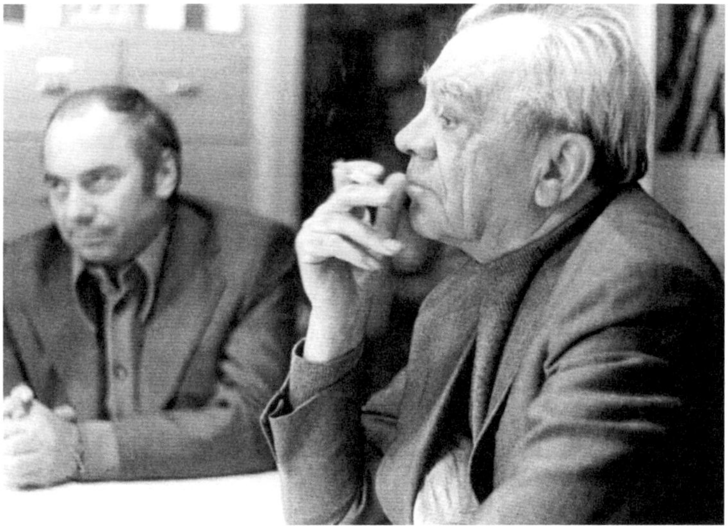

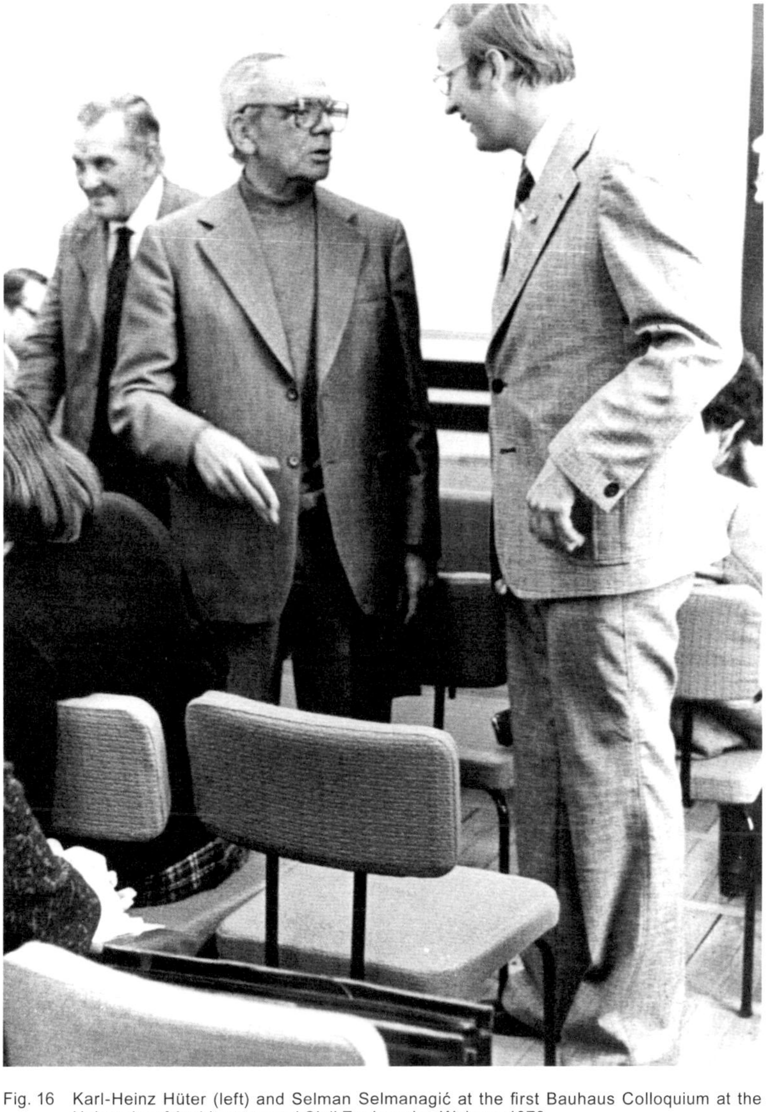

Fig. 16 Karl-Heinz Hüter (left) and Selman Selmanagić at the first Bauhaus Colloquium at the University of Architecture and Civil Engineering Weimar, 1976

Fig. 17 Richard Paulick, Selman Selmanagić, and Bernd Grönwald at the first Bauhaus Colloquium at the University of Architecture and Civil Engineering Weimar, 1976

discussions and debates, which cannot be reconstructed in detail, he received a 'Party instruction in regard to preserving the Bauhaus heritage.' On February 12, 1975, he sent a submission on the 'Bauhaus legacy' to the Scientific Division of the SED ZK (Central Committee) which was to have far-reaching consequences."[102] Grönwald's initiative was a success: "The Weimar Hochschule was entrusted with academic responsibility for Bauhaus studies in the GDR. Thereafter, discussions were held with numerous state institutions regarding future research into Bauhaus history, conservation of the material heritage, and preparations for the fiftieth anniversary of the Dessau Bauhaus Building, to be marked by an academic colloquium, an exhibition—*50 Years of Bauhaus Dessau*—and publications in the specialist press."[103]

In this context, Grönwald also saw to it that Karl-Heinz Hüter's Bauhaus book, which had existed in manuscript form since 1967, could finally be published. In late 1975, Christine Kutschke and Michael Siebenbrot, students at the Hochschule für Architektur und Bauwesen, completed a project that saw them produce documents for reconstructing the Bauhaus Building, especially the so-called "festive level" (Festebene). In their dissertations, they recommended a range of possible uses for the building. They "investigated turning one of the Masters' Houses into a Bauhaus museum and using the Bauhaus Building for the proposed relocation to Dessau of the Hochschule für industrielle Formgestaltung Halle, Burg Giebichenstein."[104]

Funding and logistics for the restoration of the Bauhaus Building were finalized at governmental level in 1975. Beforehand, a "Permanent Working Group for Bauhaus Studies in the GDR" was constituted in Weimar. Besides Konrad Püschel and Bernd Grönwald, the group included fellow teachers at the Hochschule für Architektur und Bauwesen in Weimar such as Christian Schädlich and Klaus-Jürgen Winkler. It rapidly built up a network comprising aforementioned Bauhauslers such as Lena Meyer-Bergner as well as Max Bill, Richard Paulick, and Georg Muche. The France-based architect Claude Schnaidt, former teacher at the HfG Ulm (Ulm School of Design) and author of the first monograph on Hannes Meyer, published in Switzerland in 1965,[105] was a unique figure in this circle. With Meyer-Bergner's assistance, Püschel and Grönwald laid out plans for a Hannes Meyer exhibition and received important information, documents, and photographs.[106] The exhibition was held in Weimar in 1976.

"On April 7, 1976, the Secretariat of the ZK of the SED passed a resolution regarding the 'preparation and observance of the fiftieth anniversary of the opening of the Bauhaus in Dessau.' With that, the Dessau Bauhaus was recognized politically as a 'humanistic and progressive cultural achievement,' the 'heritage of the German people,' and an integral part of the 'socialist national culture of the GDR.' With this resolution, the political verdict on Germany's most successful design school

102 Norbert Korrek and Christiane Wolf, *Das Internationale Bauhaus-Kolloquium in Weimar 1976–2016. Ein Beitrag zur Bauhaus-Rezeption*, Weimar 2016, 47.
103 Korrek and Wolf, 48.
104 Korrek and Wolf, 51.
105 See Claude Schnaidt, *Hannes Meyer. Projekte, Bauten und Schriften*, Teufen 1965.
106 See Konrad Püschel, letter to Lena Meyer-Bergner, February 27, 1976, Archive of the Bauhaus Dessau Foundation, Inv.-No. 18675.

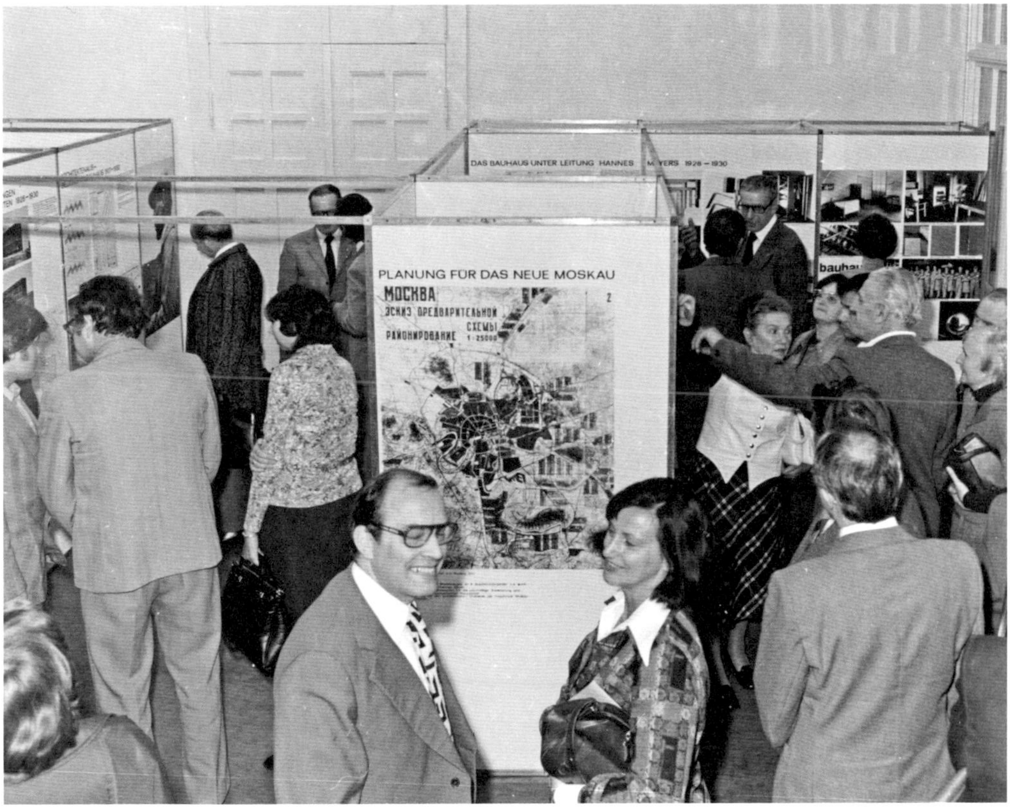

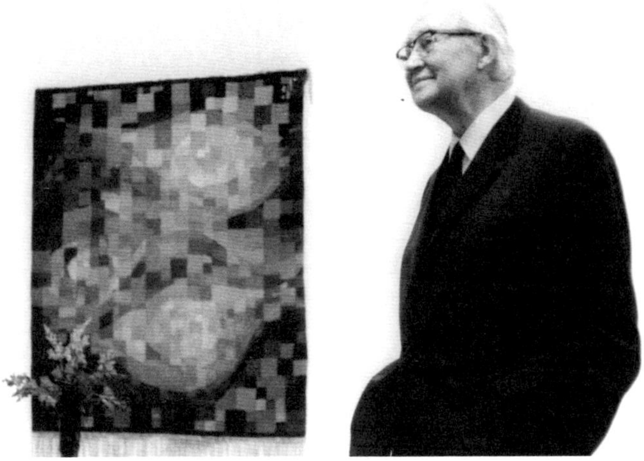

Fig. 18 Hannes Meyer exhibition at the University for Architecture and Civil Engineering Weimar, 1976

Fig. 19 Georg Muche at Haus Am Horn (Weimar) during the first Bauhaus Colloquium at the University for Architecture and Civil Engineering Weimar, 1976

delivered by Walter Ulbricht at the SED's Third Party Congress in 1950 in the context of the formalism debate ... was finally revoked."[107]

These diverse indications of a shift in the reception of the Bauhaus became apparent to a wider public from October 27 to 29, 1976, when the first International Bauhaus Colloquium took place in Weimar under the motto "Fifty Years of Bauhaus Dessau." The colloquium offered lectures and panel discussions in addition to the Hannes Meyer exhibition. Its full title spelled out the pronounced link to the Bauhaus's Dessau period and hence to Hannes Meyer, director of the school from 1927 to 1930: "The progressive ideas of the Bauhaus Dessau and its significance to the socialist development of town planning, architecture, and industrial design in the GDR." This is impressively documented in the accompanying publication: Edmund Collein, who in the early 1950s had been vice-president of the same Academy of Architecture that had launched a full-scale attack on his former teacher, now drew attention to Hannes Meyer's achievements and special relevance to the present. Konrad Püschel reported on his time with Hannes Meyer in the Soviet Union, and Claude Schnaidt wrote on the topicality of Hannes Meyer's ideas about teaching. Other contributors—notably Klaus-Jürgen Winkler, Karin Hirdina, and Christian Schädlich—likewise elaborated on Hannes Meyer's contemporary relevance.

Most of those involved in the Weimar colloquium—including Bauhauslers such as Konrad Püschel, Hubert Hoffmann, Max Bill, Edmund Collein, Richard Paulick, Grete Reichardt, Franz Ehrlich, and Hubert Hoffmann, almost all of whom had studied at the Bauhaus Dessau—reconvened a few weeks later, on December 4, 1976, to celebrate the opening of the restored Bauhaus Building. From now on, the Bauhaus was a revered part of the GDR's official culture, much as it was in West Germany following the 1968 Bauhaus exhibition in Stuttgart. The particularly high regard shown the second Bauhaus director, Hannes Meyer, continued until the end of the GDR.

Bauhaus studies in East Berlin (1976–1990)

1976 saw the beginning of a qualitatively new phase in the reception history of the Bauhaus, one that placed Hannes Meyer at the center of attention and investigated the Bauhaus more strongly than before in the light of present-day concerns. Two broad approaches characterized the nascent field of Bauhaus studies: one, based at the Hochschule in Weimar, tended to operate with the methods of biography and architectural history; the other, primarily associated with the Humboldt Universität in Berlin, was indebted mainly to cultural theory.

In Berlin, Bauhaus scholars Karin and Heinz Hirdina were instrumental in pioneering a new, positive relationship to the work of Hannes Meyer. In 1976, Karin Hirdina coined the phrase "Bauhaus functionalism."[108] Heinz Hirdina bore editorial responsibility for the Bauhaus special issues of the journal *form + zweck*, in which many former Bauhaus students also

107 Korrek and Wolf, 55.

108 See Karin Hirdina, "Zur Ästhetik des Bauhausfunktionalismus," in: *Wissenschaftliche Zeitschrift der Hochschule für Architektur und Bauwesen Weimar* 23, volume 5/6, 1976, 520–522.

gave their perspective on the school's teachings.[109] Harald Olbrich, likewise a professor at the Humboldt Universität in Berlin, laid the groundwork for a fresh understanding of art produced at the Bauhaus. More specifically, works by artists such as Paul Klee and Wassily Kandinsky were singled out for praise.[110]

To the Hirdinas, as to philosopher Lothar Kühne, the Bauhaus was not just an important historical reference point; it also provided a basis for current and future developments in architecture, design, art, and everyday culture. Hannes Meyer played a central role in all this, not least in bringing the theory of functionalism up to date. The art-centered aesthetic that had previously held sway in the GDR was thus enlarged into a discipline that judged the artistic qualities of ordinary objects less by their visual appeal than in terms of their practical, everyday functionality.[111]

At stake was a new, inclusive approach to space and design that emphasized social utility and made no attempt to disguise the human relations congealed in objects. Lothar Kühne advocated "the creation of new housing that combines the values of city life with those of nature for human use."[112] To Kühne, another key concept was "circumspection" (*Behutsamkeit*), especially with regard to the natural conditions of existence and social relations. From this perspective, he developed a critique of societal and, above all, material and architectural reality. His presented his ideas as almost unprecedented conceptual models.

One such precedent, however, was Hannes Meyer's ADGB Trade Union School building —the same building that had been pilloried by Walter Ulbricht and others in the formalism debate of 1951. Kühne abandoned his normally concise, austere diction to wax lyrical when he came to speak of Hannes Meyer's no less austere architecture: "Muted tones, no grand gestures, the school building set back from the street, nestled in the terrain and melting into the woods."[113]

109 See above all the special issues of *form + zweck* devoted to the Bauhaus: vol. 6, 1976 with contributions by Claude Schnaidt, Konrad Püschel and Selman Selmanagić, among others; vol. 3, 1979 with contributions by Lena Meyer-Bergner, Max Gebhardt and Roman Clemens, among others; vol. 2, 1983 with contributions by Bernd Grönwald and Claude Schnaidt, among others.

110 Harald Olbrich, "Maler am 'Bauhaus' – Probleme der Forschung und Rezeption," in: *Wissenschaftliche Zeitschrift der Hochschule für Architektur und Bauwesen Weimar* 26, vol. 4/5, 1979, 367–372.

111 See Authors' collective, *Ästhetik heute*, Berlin 1978.

112 Lothar Kühne, "Haus und Landschaft. Zu einem Umriss der kommunistischen Kultur des gesellschaftlichen Raums," in: Kühne, *Haus und Landschaft. Aufsätze*, Dresden 1985, 39.

113 Lothar Kühne, "Funktionalismus als zukunftsorientierte Gestaltungskonzeption," in: *form + zweck* 5, 1982, quoted in: Kühne, *Haus und Landschaft*, 185.

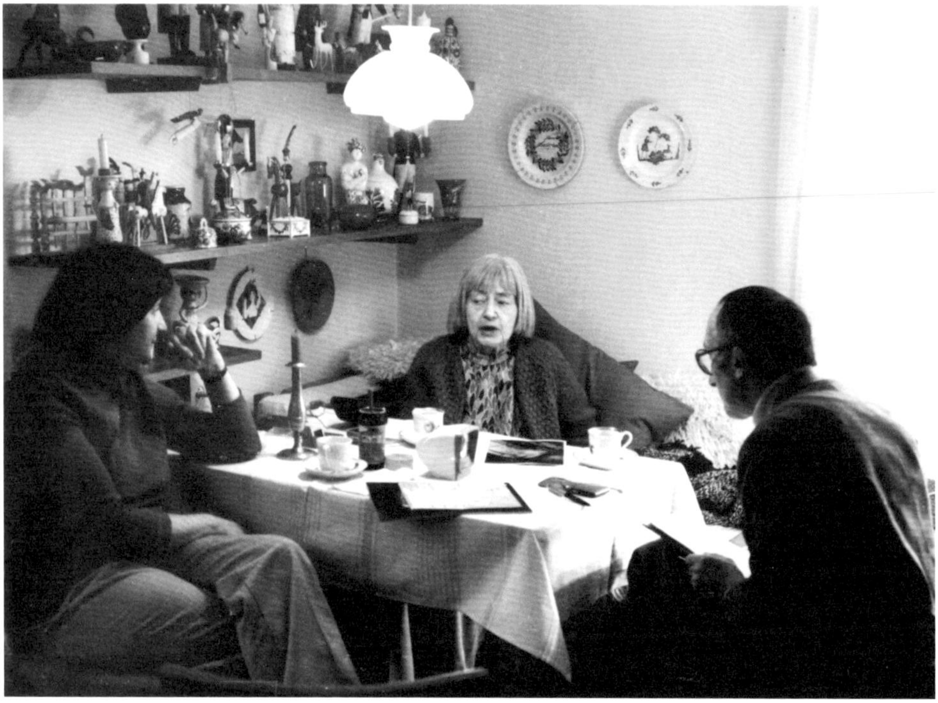

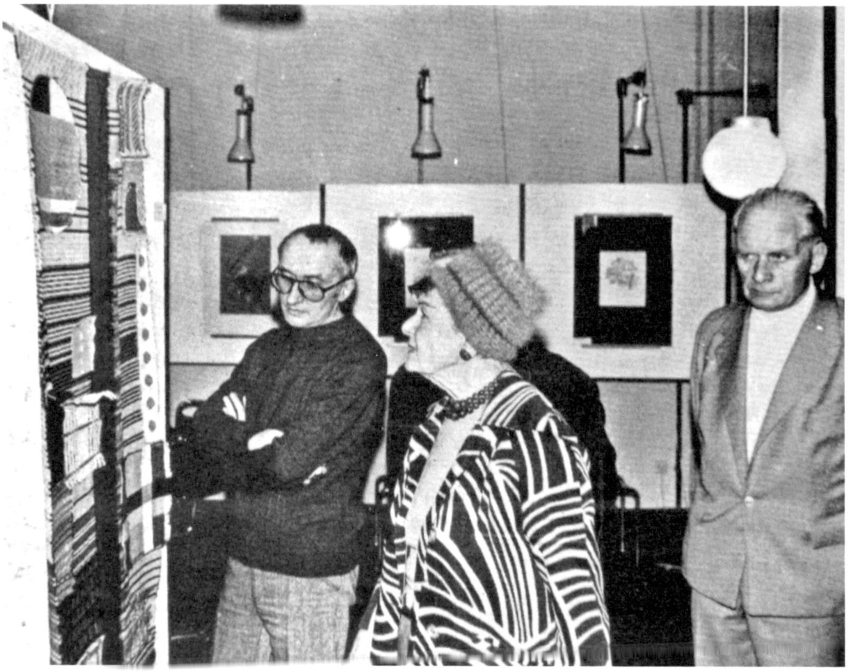

Fig. 20 Heinz Hirdina in conversation with Marianne Brandt (right) and her sister in the former Karl-Marx-Stadt (today Chemnitz) on January 21, 1979

Fig. 21 Heinz Hirdina, Ise Gropius, and Hajo Rose at the Bauhaus exhibition in the Bauhaus Building, Dessau, 1979

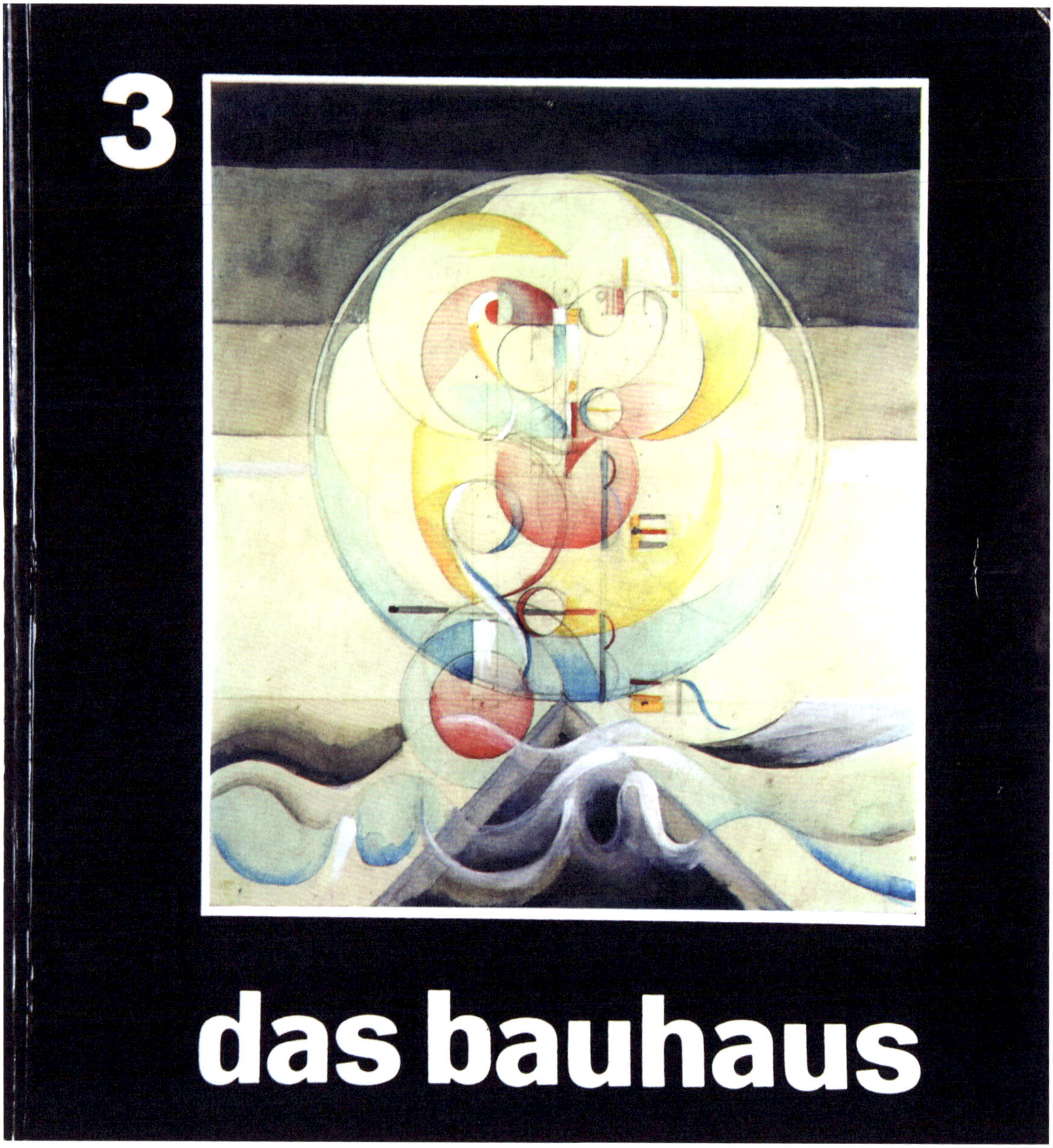

Fig. 22 Cover of catalogue no. 3 of the Galerie am Sachsenplatz Leipzig (first Bauhaus catalogue), 1976, cover: Gyula Pap, *Licht-Liebe-Leben*, 1922, watercolor (today in the collection of the Bauhaus Dessau Foundation)

3 The Bauhaus Collection, 1976–1990: People and networks

The Galerie am Sachsenplatz in Leipzig and its Bauhaus-related activities (1975–1983)

On March 11, 1973, the Galerie am Sachsenplatz opened as a sales cooperative at Katharinenstrasse 21 in Leipzig. On March 1, 1975, responsibility for the gallery was transferred from Leipzig City Council to the Staatlicher Kunsthandel, a government agency for exporting cultural goods in order to acquire foreign currency for the GDR. Hans-Peter Schulz and his wife Gisela ran the gallery from the beginning.[114] The two art-lovers put together a highly ambitious exhibition program unrivaled by any other gallery in the GDR. Through their impressive sales figures, they also became a lucrative source of revenue for the Staatlicher Kunsthandel.[115] In the ten years after they opened for business, the Schulzes sold 1,100 paintings, 3,000 watercolors, pastels and drawings, 15,000 prints, and more than 300 works of sculpture. Besides private collectors from at home and abroad, East German museums and West German art dealers were among the gallery's customers.[116] Every two years, the gallery put on "Leipzig Fine Art Auctions" featuring twentieth-century painting, graphic art, and sculpture. These auctions were some of the Staatlicher Kunsthandel's most important cultural events.[117] On the basis of their high turnover, Gisela and Hans-Peter Schulz were able to publish three or four handsomely produced exhibition catalogues each year.[118] Above all, the Galerie am Sachsenplatz proved very successful at presenting and marketing contemporary artists from the GDR.

The "Sachsenplatz" devoted an extraordinary series of exhibitions to the Bauhaus. In the period from 1976 to 1991, the gallery showcased works by teachers and students as well as different classes and formats at the Bauhaus Weimar and in Dessau. All of these

114 Hans-Peter Schulz, trained furrier and later insulator in the VEB combine Piping and Insulation Leipzig, was a passionate art collector. From the mid-1960s, he joined his wife in organizing exhibitions of contemporary art in his free time while also collecting art himself. One of the couple's friends was the Leipzig painter Bernhard Heisig, who recognized Schultz's talent and arranged for him to run a stall on behalf of the East German Ministry of Culture at the seventh GDR Art Exhibition in Dresden from October 5, 1972 to March 25, 1973. The considerable financial success of this stall prompted the Leipzig City Council and the Kunst der Zeit (Contemporary Art) cooperative to open the Galerie am Sachsenplatz and appoint Hans-Peter Schulz as director. See the letter dated March 15, 1973 from the chairman of the Kunst der Zeit cooperative, Kießling, to the city councilor for culture, Dr. Rudolf Gehrken, in: Stadtarchiv Leipzig, Stadtverordnetenversammlung und Rat der Stadt Leipzig, StVuR No. 21696, p. 102.

115 Because the Galerie am Sachsenplatz always exceeded its annual allocated target for the Staatlicher Kunsthandel, Hans-Peter Schulz was not impeded or restricted in his work. According to a note from March 30, 1977 filed in the cadre/education department of the Culture Ministry, Schulz was classified as "unsuitable for his function." However, the director of the Staatlicher Kunsthandel, Horst Weiß, took a different view. See BArch, DR 1/5689, Bl. 130. On the one hand, the gallery was an important element of the Staatlicher Kunsthandel's network of galleries for contemporary art. On the other, through its sales and the resulting inflow of foreign currency, the "Sachsenplatz" also met the target set for the Kunsthandel für die Kunst und Antiquitäten GmbH (the equivalent state agency for art and antiquities). See BArch, DL 210/1890, Bll. 564ff.

116 The Staatliche Kunstsammlungen Dresden acquired works from the Galerie am Sachsenplatz for its copperplate cabinet, sculpture collection and Neue Meister (New Masters) art gallery. In addition, the following museums made successful bids at the Leipzig Fine Art Auctions for works from the eighteenth to twentieth centuries: Nationalgalerie Berlin, Museum für bildende Künste Leipzig, Lindenau-Museum Altenburg, Galerie für Junge Kunst Frankfurt/Oder, Staatliche Galerie Moritzburg and Kunstsammlungen in Karl-Marx-Stadt (Chemnitz).

presentations were accompanied by extensively researched catalogues. A poster likewise appeared for each exhibition. Graphic designer and design teacher Frank Neubauer was commissioned to create the high-quality print material.[119] Through the exhibitions, Gisela and Hans-Peter Schulz succeeded in bringing almost 800 exhibits with a net purchase price of 600,000 marks into the collection of the Wissenschaftlich-Kulturelles Zentrum (WKZ) Bauhaus Dessau.[120]

This achievement would not have been possible without the commitment of the protagonists at the Galerie am Sachsenplatz. Yet it also required a prior change in political climate. In 1976, efforts to reconstruct the Bauhaus Building in Dessau played an important role. These efforts were a consequence of the program formulated at the Ninth SED Party Congress. Emphasis was placed on preserving and maintaining cultural heritage.[121] These points, along with the first International Bauhaus Colloquium, held in Weimar from October 27 to 29, were reported and discussed in numerous articles in the journal *Bildende Kunst*.[122]

Gisela and Hans-Peter Schulz thus developed a professional interest in the Bauhaus at precisely the right moment. In 1974 they were already considering an exhibition series dedicated to the Bauhaus, and they were pleased when the Dessau City Council, which had learned of the gallerists' efforts, made contact with them.[123] At this point in time, only two important exhibition projects had previously been devoted to the Bauhaus, one in Weimar and the other in Dessau.[124]

The first exhibition at the Galerie am Sachsenplatz officially took place from September 25 to October 27, 1976 under the title "The Bauhaus 1919–1933." The materials on display were not intended to provide anything like a conceptual overview of Bauhaus history.

117 The gallery's statistics reveal that it generated revenue of 440,000 marks at the first "Leipzig Fine Art Auction" in 1977 and 1.2 million marks at the sixth auction in 1989, for example. The auctions were held at the Alte Börse in Leipzig. See the statistics file in the archive of the Galerie am Sachsenplatz.

118 See Hans-Peter Schulz, in: Galerie am Sachsenplatz (ed.), *Ausstellung 98 – 99 – 100*, Leipzig 1982, 10.

119 Frank Neubauer, born in 1941, operated in Leipzig from 1975 to 1989 together with Jutta Damm-Fiedler and Jochen Fiedler under the name Gruppe PLUS.

120 See the accounts and sales receipts in the archive of the Bauhaus Dessau Foundation.

121 See Chapter 3 as well as the special publication of Erich Honecker's demands at the Ninth SED Party Congress in subitem 3: "Die Entwicklung der sozialistischen Kultur und Kunst," in: *Leipziger Volkszeitung*, May 19, 1976.

122 See among others Adalbert Behr, "Vernunft und Harmonie. Gedanken vor dem 50. Jahrestag der Einweihung des Bauhauses in Dessau," in: *Bildende Kunst* 5, Berlin 1976, 214–218; Adalbert Behr, "Vor vielfältigen Aufgaben. Wissenschaftliches Kolloquium zum progressiven Erbe des Bauhauses in Weimar," in: *Bildende Kunst* 1, Berlin 1977, 45–47; Karin Hirdina, "Zum ästhetischen Programm des Bauhauses," in: *Bildende Kunst* 4, Berlin 1977, 163–166.

123 See Hans-Peter Schulz's foreword in: Galerie am Sachsenplatz (ed.), *Das Bauhaus 1919–1933*, Leipzig 1976, 5.

124 See the exhibitions "Modern Design: The Progressive Heritage of the Bauhaus" in the Staatlichen Galerie Schloss Georgium in Dessau (1967) as well as "bauhaus weimar: Works from the wood, ceramics, metal, and textile workshops in the Weimar period of the Bauhaus, 1919–1925" in the Kunstsammlungen zu Weimar (1969). The latter was held to mark the "fiftieth anniversary of the founding of the Weimar Bauhaus" and aimed "to expand the permanent Bauhaus department into a special exhibition," according to the director of the Kunstsammlungen zu Weimar, Gerhard Pommeranz-Liedtke, in the preface to the accompanying catalogue: Kunstsammlungen Weimar (ed.), *bauhaus weimar. Arbeiten der Werkstätten für Holz, Keramik, Metall und Textilien der Weimarer Periode des Bauhauses 1919–1925*, Weimar 1969, 4.

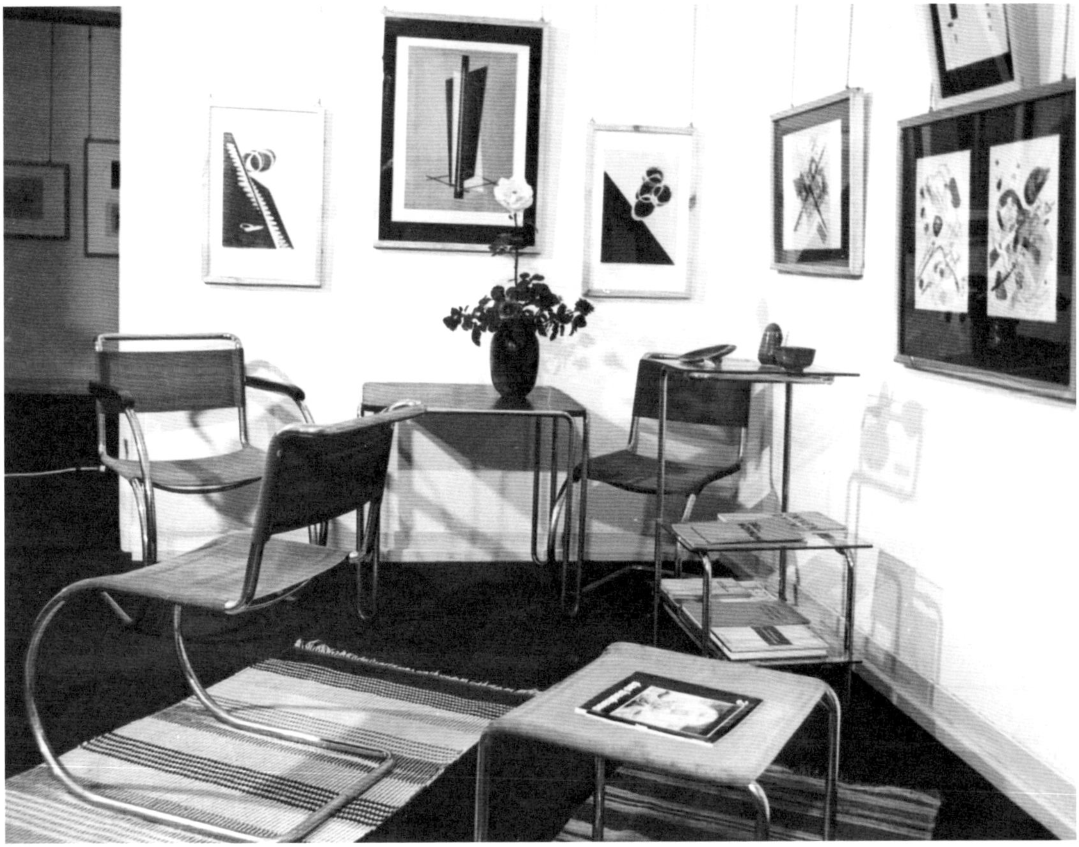

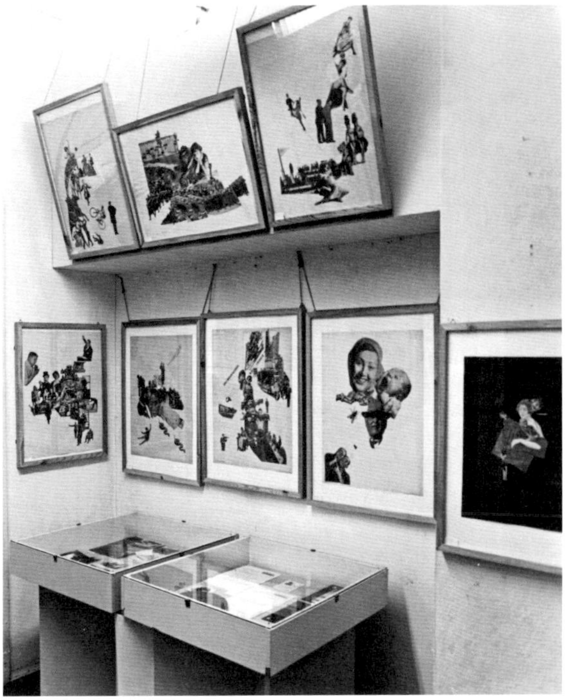

Fig. 23 First Bauhaus exhibition of the Galerie am Sachsenplatz Leipzig, 1976: room with works by László Moholy-Nagy, Wassily Kandinsky, Marianne Brandt, Ludwig Mies van der Rohe, and others (some of them today at the Bauhaus Dessau Foundation)

Fig. 24 First Bauhaus exhibition of the Galerie am Sachsenplatz Leipzig, 1976: room with works by Marianne Brandt (most of them today at the Bauhaus Dessau Foundation)

The selection was clearly and consciously determined by chance finds and discoveries. From the beginning, commercial considerations were at the forefront of Gisela and Hans-Peter Schulz's minds. The task of presenting "the Bauhaus in all its breadth" was better left to museums.[125]

The first exhibition showed works of painting, graphic arts, sculpture, drawings, workshop pieces, Bauhaus publications and documents, as well as photographs of former students and teachers. These discoveries only came about through the Schulzes' personal engagement.

The exhibition drew some 8,907 visitors—record attendance figures for the Galerie am Sachsenplatz—and was extended until November 9, 1976 due to public interest. "It is greatly to be welcomed that the city of Dessau has acquired the material in this exhibition in its entirety, as the basis for a long-awaited Dessau Bauhaus collection," remarked Rainer Behrends in the *Leipziger Volkszeitung*.[126] By unanimous decision of the Dessau City Council, 148 of the 200 works were bought for the sum of 145,000 marks. The city of Dessau also contributed to the costs of the exhibition catalogue.[127] Among the items purchased were works by Marianne Brandt, Franz Ehrlich, Lyonel Feininger, Paul Klee, László Moholy-Nagy, Reinhold Rossig, and Otto Lindig. With the support of the GDR Cultural Fund, additional works were acquired for the Bauhaus Dessau collection by right of advance purchase from the Galerie am Sachsenplatz or from the private holdings of Gisela and Hans-Peter Schulz. The couple had set themselves the goal of supplying the WKZ Bauhaus Dessau collection with a thousand items.[128]

The "bauhaus 2" exhibition held a year later, from October 29 to December 4, 1977, presented watercolors, documents, designs, photographs, photomontages, ceramics, paintings, metal works, montages, sculptures, typography, works from the preliminary course, tapestries, and drawings by Marianne Brandt, Christian Dell (1893–1973), Franz Ehrlich, Marguerite Friedlaender (1896–1985), Max Krehan (1875–1925), Otto Lindig, Carl Marx, Grete (Margaretha) Reichardt, Reinhold Rossig, Reinhold Weidensee (1880–unknown), and Frans Wildenhain (1905–1980). Works by Brandt, Ehrlich, Marx, Reichardt, Rossig, and Wildenhain formed the core of the exhibition. Hans-Peter Schulz also made works from the Dornburg ceramics workshop a focus of the presentation. Thanks to Max Krehan's daughter, the gallery was able to include an early (1922) work by the artist in the exhibition. She also made available several important individual pieces, including a brass bowl and brass ashtray by Dell, an

125 See Hans-Peter Schulz's foreword in: *Das Bauhaus 1919–1933*, 6.

126 Rainer Behrends, "Ein Vorentwurf für eine künftige Gesellschaft. Zur Ausstellung 'Das Bauhaus' in der Leipziger Galerie am Sachsenplatz," in: *Leipziger Volkszeitung*, October 9/10, 1976.

127 See the letter dated February 10, 1976 from Plug, the acting director of the Culture Department of the Dessau City Council, to the director of the Galerie am Sachsenplatz, Hans-Peter Schulz: "We wish to inform you on behalf of the Mayor of Dessau that we are very keen to acquire all the exhibits of your Bauhaus exhibition. ... At the same time, I wish to inform you that the Dessau City Council would like to be involved in publishing the exhibition catalogue" (Archiv Bauhaus Dessau Foundation).

128 Quote from Hans-Peter Schulz: "Our goal is to supply the Dessau Bauhaus collection with 1000 exhibits," in: Galerie am Sachsenplatz (ed.), *bauhaus 2*, Leipzig 1977, 82.

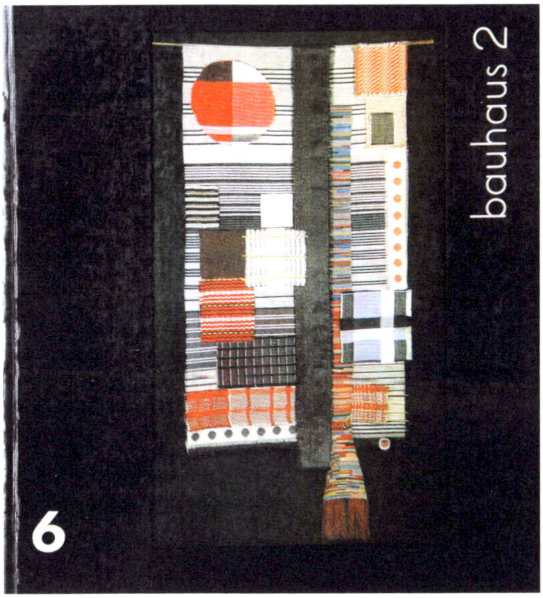

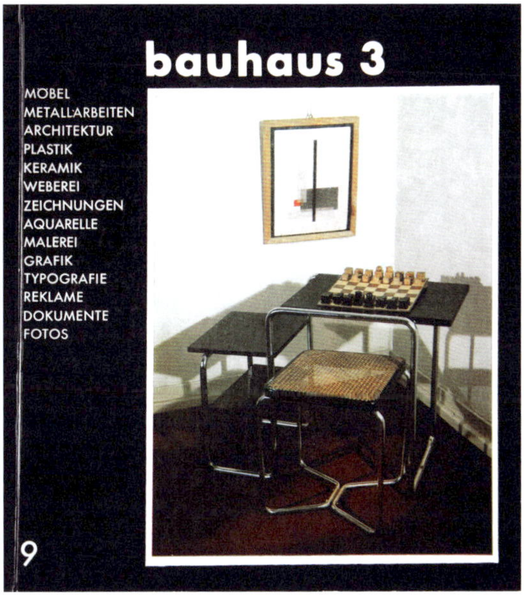

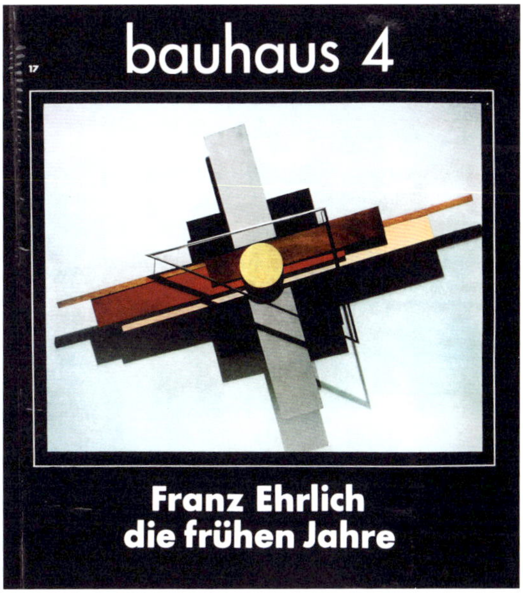

Fig. 25 Cover of the catalogue *bauhaus 2* of the Galerie am Sachsenplatz, 1977, cover: Grete Reichardt, *Gretel fabrics*, around 1931, textile work (today in the collection of the Bauhaus Foundation Dessau)

Fig. 26 Cover of the catalogue *bauhaus 3* of the Galerie am Sachsenplatz, 1978, cover photo: works by Marcel Breuer, László Moholy-Nagy, and others

Fig. 27 Cover of the catalogue *bauhaus 4. Franz Ehrlich, die frühen Jahre* of the Galerie am Sachsenplatz Leipzig, 1980

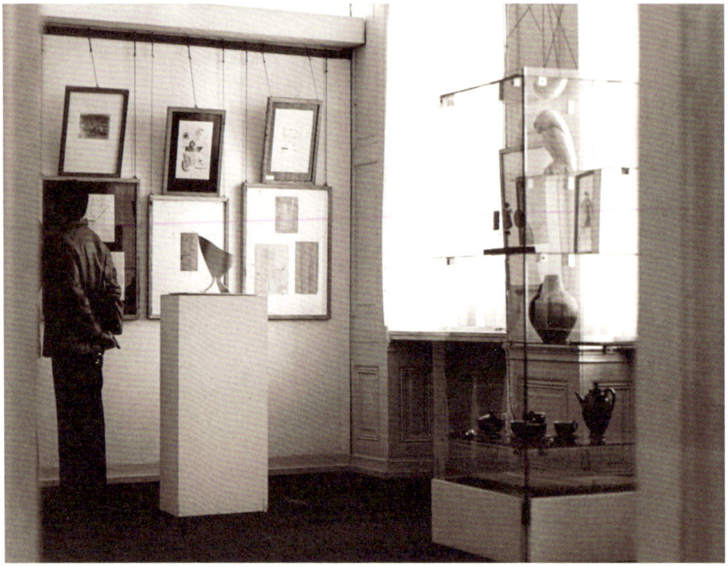

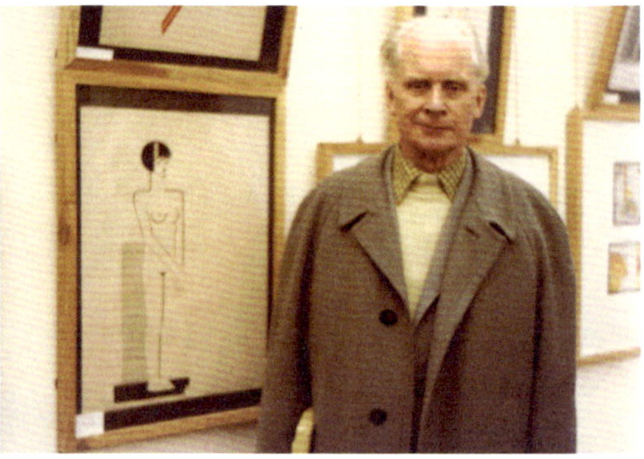

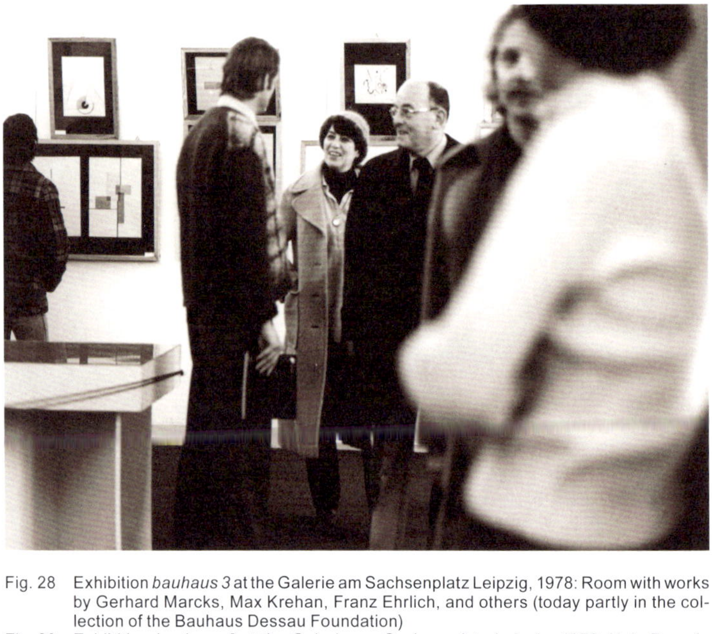

Fig. 28 Exhibition *bauhaus 3* at the Galerie am Sachsenplatz Leipzig, 1978: Room with works by Gerhard Marcks, Max Krehan, Franz Ehrlich, and others (today partly in the collection of the Bauhaus Dessau Foundation)

Fig. 29 Exhibition *bauhaus 3* at the Galerie am Sachsenplatz Leipzig, 1978: Hajo Rose in exhibition in front of his painting *Typoakt*, 1928

Fig. 30 Hans-Peter Schulz with the Leipzig artists Ursula Mattheuer-Neustädt and Wolfgang Mattheuer at the exhibition *bauhaus 3* at the Galerie am Sachsenplatz Leipzig, 1978: Room with works by Franz Ehrlich from his time in the penitentiary around 1937 (sheets from prison, today partly in the collection of the Bauhaus Dessau Foundation)

ashtray and stoneware vase by Friedlaender, and a wooden bread plate by Weidensee.[129]

"Works by Marianne Brandt (born in Chemnitz in 1893), who took over as director of the metal workshop following László Moholy-Nagy's departure in 1928, stand at the center of 'bauhaus 2.' ... Shown for the first time in Leipzig are works by seventy-year-old East Berlin architect Franz Ehrlich, painter Carl Marx (born 1911, currently residing in Dessau), and ASSO member Reinhold Rossig (East Berlin). Bauhaus weaver Grete Reichardt supplied ... two hand-woven carpets. ... Of particular interest are the photographs and documents unearthed by Gisela and Hans-Peter Schulz over the course of their detective work into the Bauhaus,"[130] wrote Camilla Blechen, who discussed and praised the exhibition in the *Frankfurter Allgemeine Zeitung* on November 26, 1977.

The exhibition catalogue featured 200 numbered exhibits, most of them photographically reproduced in black and white. Gisela and Hans-Peter Schulz further enriched the catalogue by publishing brief artist biographies and describing their first encounters with Grete (Margaretha) Reichardt and Marianne Brandt. The latter allowed them to print a letter she had received from László Moholy-Nagy in February 1935.[131] Carl Marx, Kurt Schmidt (1901–1991), and Franz Ehrlich also contributed to the publication.[132]

The first two Bauhaus presentations in the Galerie am Sachsenplatz were accompanied by so-called "Bauhaus evenings." On three different evenings in the context of "The Bauhaus 1919–1933," illustrated lectures were offered by Diether Schmidt on "Paul Klee and the Artists at the Bauhaus," by Rainer Behrends on "The Bauhaus, 1919–1933: Method – Evolution – Achievement – Impact (Attempt at a Critical Appreciation)," and by Annegret Janda on "The Weimar Bauhaus." Public interest in these events was so great that Hans-Peter Schulz decided beforehand to hold them in the large cinema auditorium of Leipzig-Information am Sachsenplatz.[133] All three evenings attracted an audience of over three hundred guests.

Timed to coincide with "bauhaus 2," the Bauhaus evenings were continued on November 18, 1977 with a lecture by Rainer Behrends in the Leipzig-Information cinema. On November 11, 1977, Hans-Peter Schulz convened an extra discussion evening in the exhibition rooms at short notice. Sixty-four people attended. The advertised lecture by Dieter Schmidt took a remarkable turn when the photographer Hajo (Hans-Joachim) Rose volunteered his personal reminiscences of his time at the Bauhaus and the course taken by Josef Albers.[134] The official "Second Bauhaus Evening" was advertised as a "roundtable conversation with Bauhauslers": Grete Reichardt, Carl Marx,

129 See Hans-Peter Schulz's foreword to the catalogue as well as the list of works in the exhibition catalogue, ibid., 6 and 54.

130 Camilla Blechen, "Das Bauhaus zum zweiten," in: *Frankfurter Allgemeine Zeitung*, November 26, 1977.

131 See *bauhaus 2*, 13.

132 See *bauhaus 2*, 7, 10–11 and 14–15.

133 The Leipzig-Information was in the northern part of the Sachsenplatz. In the period between 1969 and 2002, this officially referred to the area between Reichsstrasse and Katherinenstrasse in the Leipzig city center. See Gina Klank et al. (eds.), *Lexikon Leipziger Straßennamen*, Leipzig 1995, 185. Today, the Museum der bildenden Künste (Museum of fine arts) and the Stadtgeschichtliches Museum Leipzig (Leipzig city history museum) are located at the center of the square.

134 The conversation can be found as a recording in the Galerie am Sachsenplatz archive.

and Franz Ehrlich shared their memories in the Leipzig-Information auditorium.

The "roundtable conversations with Bauhauslers" format was revived for the "bauhaus 3" exhibition. At this third presentation, from November 18 to December 23, 1978, the protagonists from the "Sachsenplatz" displayed works by fifty former Bauhaus artists and presented paintings, graphic art, watercolors, drawings, sculpture, metal works, furniture, architecture, typography, documents, and photos. More than 4,000 visitors attended the exhibition, which again was accompanied by a catalogue. This featured 240 exhibits and contained, along with a foreword by Hans-Peter Schulz, specially written essays by Roman Clemens (1910–1992), Georg Muche, Max Gebhardt (1906–1990), Gerhard Marcks, Kurt Schmidt, Gyula Pap (1899–1993), Hajo Rose, Walter Puff, and Hermann Werner Kubsch (1911–1983). For "bauhaus 3," Gisela and Hans-Peter Schulz resorted to loans: specifically, photographs and tubular steel furniture by Mart Stam. December 1, 1978 saw Grete Reichardt, Max Gebhardt, Wolfgang Rössger (1909–1987), and Kurt Schmidt take part in the "second roundtable conversation with Bauhauslers" in the large cinema auditorium of Leipzig-Information. The conversation was moderated by art historian Diether Schmidt.

For "bauhaus 4: Franz Ehrlich, the Early Years," which ran from November 22 to December 21, 1980 and was specifically devoted to architect Franz Ehrlich, works from the years 1928 to 1939 were shown. There were 163 exhibits, including sketches, drawings, and calculations. Between 1978 and 1980, the sculptures and montages on display were produced especially for the exhibition on the basis of extant documents or cardboard models. One work from 1928, *Materialrelief* (in brass, copper, iron, and polyacrylic on canvas in wood), appeared in 1981 in a run of thirteen copies as P21 in the series "Gallery Editions of the Galerie am Sachsenplatz."[135]

The exhibition attracted interest from far beyond the region, drawing more than 2,400 visitors; East German state television broadcaster DFF covered it in a segment of its arts show on December 18, 1980.[136] The format of evening lectures held in tandem with the exhibition was reprised for "bauhaus 4." When art historian Rainer Behrends suddenly canceled his scheduled lecture, a public conversation between Hans-Peter Schulz and Franz Ehrlich was held in its stead on December 5, 1980. A tape recording of the conversation, stored in the archive, conveys a vivid impression of the atmosphere at the Bauhaus and the Bauhaus festivals.[137] The second part of the evening featured a lecture by art historian Andreas Hüneke on "Oskar Schlemmer and the Theater."

The exhibition "bauhaus 5," which ran from November 21 to December 20, 1981, mainly thematized "Dr. Rabe's house in Zwenkau" near Leipzig, but it also displayed gifts from artists that the Galerie am Sachsenhaus then forwarded to the WKZ Bauhaus Dessau as well as recent acquisitions, including works by Theo Balden (1904–1995), Friedl Dicker

135 Along with *Materialrelief*, the work *Räumliches aus Flächen* (1931, brass on a wooden base) is announced in the exhibition catalogue as an edition. It was only realized for the exhibition, however.

136 See the statistics file in the Galerie am Sachsenplatz archive.

137 The conversation was recorded on tape and can be found today in the Galerie am Sachsenplatz archive.

(1898–1944), Wassily Kandinsky, Benita Koch-Otte (1892–1972), Walter Köppe (1906–1973), Gerhard Marcks, and Fritz Winter. The catalogue showcased 102 items; all 1,100 copies were out of stock by the end of the exhibition. Along with a lengthy contribution by Arnd Schultheiss, written with the help of Rabe's daughter, it contained an article by Andreas Hüneke on "Oskar Schlemmer and the Bauhaus Stage" as well as texts by Roman Clemens, Werner Drewes (1899–1985), Jean Leppien (1910–1991), and Walter Puff recounting their impressions of their time at the Bauhaus. On January 22, 1982, a gallery discussion took place in the rooms of the gallery. Arnd Schultheiss introduced Dr. Rabe's house in Zwenkau, showed slides and was supported by remarks made by Frau Schwarzer, whose father had commissioned and lived in the building.

"bauhaus 6" was split into two parts, one held from November 5 to 20 and the other from November 26 to December 23, 1986. The first was specifically dedicated to works by Irena Blühová (1904–1991) and Albert Hennig (1907–1998) as well as Czechoslovakian photographers from the years 1900 to 1940, including Alfons Mucha, František Drtikol, Drahomír Josef Růžčka, Jan Lauschmann, Irena Blühová, Josef Kubin, Karol Aufricht, Oldřich Straka, Sergej Protopopov, Ilia J. Marko, Eugen Wiškovský, Jaromír Funke, Jaroslav Rössler, Jindřich Štyrský, and Tibor Honty. The second part displayed the gallery's recent acquisitions of works by Rudolf Baschant (1897–1955), Willi Baumeister (1889–1955), Herbert Bayer (1900–1985), László Moholy-Nagy, Johannes Berthold (1898–1987), Marianne Brandt, Franz Ehrlich, Albert Hennig, Hubert Hoffmann, Otto Hofmann (1907–1996), Gerhard Marcks, Walter Puff, Hajo Rose, Kurt Schmidt, Georg Teltscher (1904–1983), and Frans Wildenhain, as well as a portfolio published by the gallery itself, *Bauhaus Photography*. Released on May 18, 1983 to mark the hundredth anniversary of Walter Gropius's birth, the portfolio appeared in the series of gallery editions as portfolio M10 in a limited run of forty copies for purchase and ten artists' copies not intended for sale. It consisted of a box containing an introduction as well as thirteen card-mounted silver gelatin prints, each signed, numbered and dated by the artists. In the portfolio there were two prints each by Irene Blühová, Marianne Brandt, Lotte Gerson-Collein (1905–1995), Albert Hennig, Gyula Pap, and Hajo Rose. A work by Edmund Collein was also included.

These two Bauhaus exhibitions—for a long time the last put on by the gallery—came in for criticism from the press. Peter Guth wrote in the *Sächsisches Tageblatt:* "An overview of the works makes the problem obvious. Only a tiny fraction of the exhibits come from the Bauhaus period, that is, the years between 1919 and 1933." He went on to write: "bauhaus 6 is an utterly unsensational exhibition."[138] He also saw the single year that Irena Blühová (1931–1932) and Albert Hennig (1932–1933) spent studying at the Bauhaus as "hardly adequate" to find "the best social Bauhaus demands" reflected in their works.[139] While Guth's criticism was overblown with respect to the list of works presented, there was some justification to it.

138 See Peter Guth, "Bauhaus 6 – des Weiteren. Zum 2. Teil der Ausstellung in der Sachsenplatzgalerie," in: *Sächsisches Tageblatt,* December 10/11, 1983.

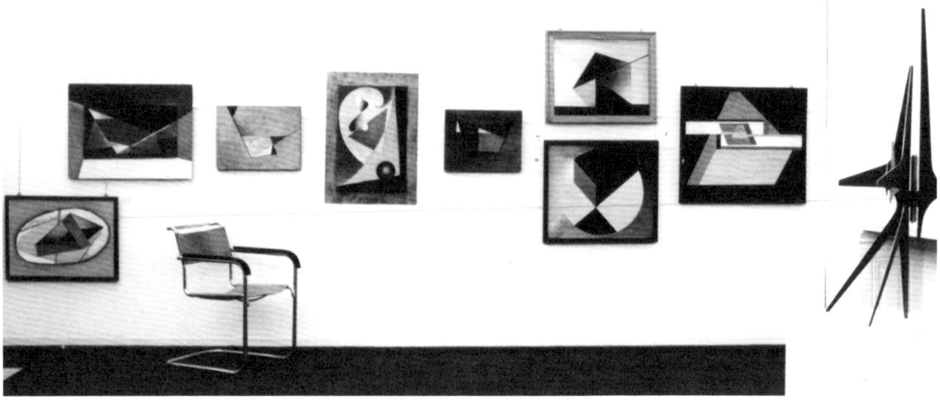

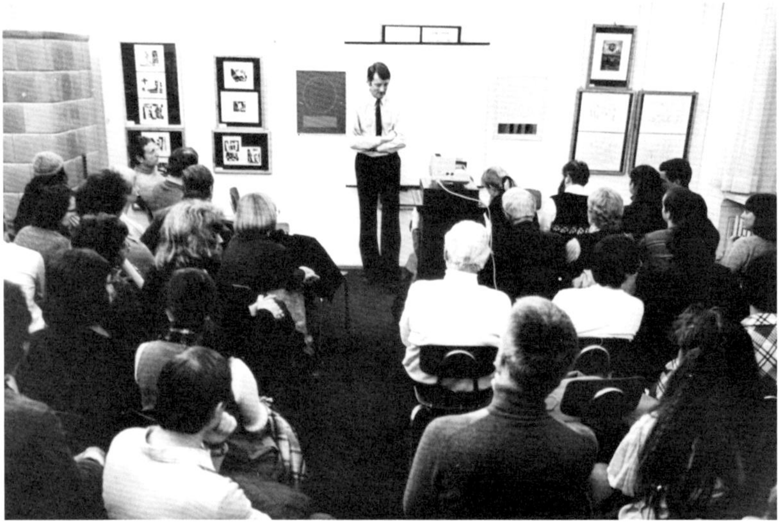

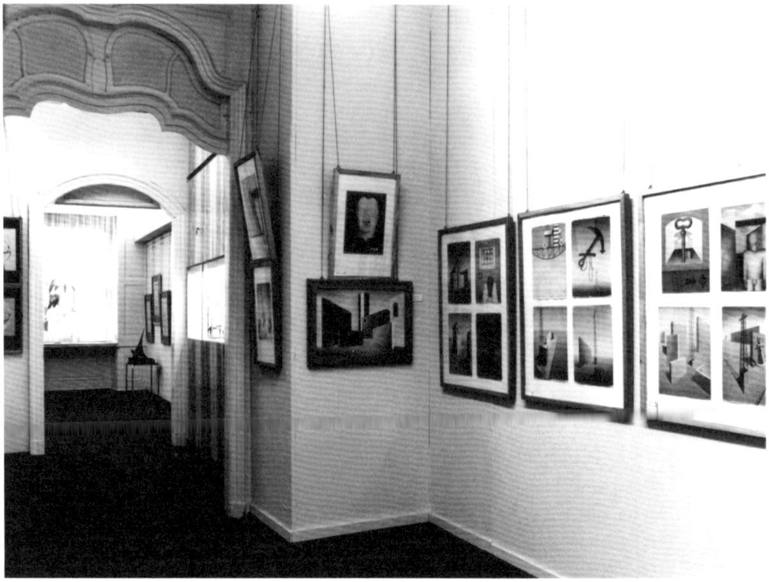

Fig. 31 Exhibition *bauhaus 4. Franz Ehrlich, the early years* at the Galerie am Sachsenplatz Leipzig, 1980. Room with works by Franz Ehrlich from his time in prison around 1937 (sheets from prison, today partly in the collection of the Bauhaus Dessau Foundation)

Fig. 32 Gallery discussion with Hans-Peter Schulz during the exhibition *bauhaus 5*. House Dr. Rabe, 1983

Fig. 33 Exhibition *bauhaus 4. Franz Ehrlich, the early years* at the Galerie am Sachsenplatz Leipzig, 1980: Room with works by Franz Ehrlich from the Bauhaus period (today partly in the collection of the Bauhaus Dessau Foundation)

In order to draw attention to the gallery's interest in Bauhaus-related works, Hans-Peter Schulz regularly published appeals in his catalogues: "The Galerie am Sachsenplatz has long exerted itself on behalf of the Bauhaus. ... If we are to continue putting on interesting and varied exhibitions of the Bauhaus legacy, we ask all readers of this catalogue and friends of the gallery to help us discover new pieces." And again: "We are looking for painting, graphic art, sculpture, photography, photograms, typography, letters to the Bauhaus, correspondence or written documents of any kind, invitations to Bauhaus festivals, theater or dance performances, and lectures as well as programs, manifestos, charters, and much more."[140] Gisela and Hans-Peter Schulz went to unparalleled lengths to promote the cause of the Bauhaus, but their activities would have been futile without their personal contacts with Bauhaus artists and tips from friends and collectors.[141]

In this regard, they were particularly helped by their extensive network and their plan to channel the artworks they collected to the Bauhaus in Dessau. Leipzig-based photographer and collector Hajo Rose, a friend of the gallery, first arranged contact with Marianne Brandt. She then facilitated relations with Grete Reichardt, who in turn put the gallery in touch with Kurt Schmidt and Franz Ehrlich. Hans-Peter Schulz had known Max Bill and Tut Schlemmer (Helena Tutein, 1889–1987) since he had initiated an exchange of letters in 1964. Other meetings with artists came about by chance. Thus, Hans-Peter Schulz met Carl Marx in 1972 at the Seventh GDR Art Exhibition in Dresden and Jean (Kurt) Leppien in 1979 at the first International Bauhaus Colloquium in Weimar. The friendship he forged with Leppien allowed Schulz to play a part in curating the exhibition "Résistance – Deportation 1933–1945," held in 1980 in the Musée de l'Ordre de la Libération. On this occasion, he personally got to know Tut Schlemmer and returned to Leipzig laden with donations (already mentioned in connection with "bauhaus 5") from Moses Bahelfer (1908–1995), Werner Drewes (1899–1985), Jean Leppien,

139 See Peter Guth, "'Bauhaus 6' am Sachsenplatz. Irena Blühová, Albert Hennig und tschechoslowakische Fotografien," in: *Sächsisches Tageblatt*, November 16, 1983.

140 Both quotes are found in Galerie am Sachsenplatz (ed.), *bauhaus 4. Franz Ehrlich – die frühen Jahre*, Leipzig 1980, 60.

141 The Galerie Henning in Halle (Saale) will be characterized here to describe one example of provenance in more detail. From May 1947 until a few months before his suicide in June 1962, businessman Eduard Henning (1908–1962) organized an extensive exhibition and catalogue program in Halle. The exhibitions were changed each month and were largely devoted to modern and contemporary art. Henning exhibited artists such as Karl Hofer, Max Pechstein and Karl Schmidt-Rottluff, but he also collected Bauhaus artists such as Wassily Kandinsky, Johannes Itten and Albert Hennig. However, Eduard Henning's artistic program and his numerous international contacts made him suspicious in the eyes of the SED. From 1957, his gallery received nothing but brickbats from the GDR press. Following the death of her husband, Henning's wife applied to continue running the gallery but was refused permission. Letters from artists remain in the family's possession to this day. The collection also contains portfolio editions, artist posters, watercolors and oil paintings. Gisela and Hans-Peter Schulz were in close contact with Eduard Henning's heirs, regularly trading and exchanging art works. They always placed great value on discretion. Many collectors appreciated this quality in the Schulzes. On the history of the Galerie Henning, see Christin Müller-Wenzel, "Kunst oder Dekadenz – Die Galerie Henning in Halle (Saale)," in: Stiftung Mitteldeutscher Kulturrat (ed.), *Mitteldeutsches Jahrbuch für Kultur und Geschichte* 18, Bonn 2011, 102–110.

Albert Mentzel (1909–1994), and Jean Weinfeld (1905–1992).[142]

All these activities did nothing to alter the fact that it was becoming increasingly difficult to track down works and objects in private collections. Eight years later, the seventh and last exhibition, "bauhaus 7: new acquisitions since 1984," was held from May 25 to June 22, 1991. The exhibition presented over 200 pieces and drew more than 1,000 visitors to the "Sachsenplatz." Portfolio M16, *Bauhaus Photography 2*, was released to coincide with the exhibition. With forty copies available for purchase and ten not for sale, it featured a total of seventeen photographs by Bauhaus artists from Czechoslovakia, Switzerland, Hungary, and Germany, including two prints each by Irena Blühová, Marianne Brandt, Edmund Collein, Franz Ehrlich, Ladislav Foltyn (1906–2002), Lotte Gerson-Collein, Gyula Pap, and Xanti Schawinsky (1904–1979), along with a work by Albert Hennig.

Through their commitment to the Bauhaus at the Galerie am Sachsenplatz and their ever-increasing interest and expertise, Gisela and Hans-Peter Schulz played a vital role in building up today's Bauhaus Dessau collection.

The Wissenschaftlich-Kulturelles Zentrum (WKZ) Bauhaus Dessau (1976–1986)

A number of different factors had to come together for the Wissenschaftlich-Kulturelles Zentrum Dessau to be founded. It required, firstly, Grönwald's idea for a new institution combined with his political tenacity, not least in securing institutional finance. Only in this way could a repetition of what happened in 1967 be avoided, when a big exhibition failed to have any lasting effect. It needed, secondly, the beginnings of a collection provided through the work of the Galerie am Sachsenplatz, and thirdly, the restoration of the iconic building that housed the institution and collection. Bernd Grönwald's strategy went beyond merely researching the Bauhaus: he aimed to establish an institution that would provoke and inspire design work from the perspective of present-day concerns. Having initially derived its authority from the newfound prestige of the Bauhaus, the institution's scope thus eventually widened to take in pressing issues of urban development in the GDR, in particular.[143]

Until 1986, the Wissenschaftlich-Kulturelles Zentrum (WKZ) Bauhaus was administered by the city of Dessau, and until 1983, its internal affairs were managed almost exclusively by the Hochschule für Architektur und Bauwesen Weimar. Increasingly, the WKZ Bauhaus Dessau lent the Bauhaus visibility and continuity through exhibitions, lectures,

142 See Hans-Peter Schulz's foreword in: Galerie am Sachsenplatz (ed.), *bauhaus 5*, Leipzig 1981, 5.

143 Harald Kegler, "Die Bauhaus-Kolloquien in Weimar (und Dessau) – Wiederholung als Chance," in: Christoph Bernhard, Thomas Flierl, and Max Welch Guerra (eds.), *Städtebau-Debatten in der DDR*, Berlin 2012, 163–176.

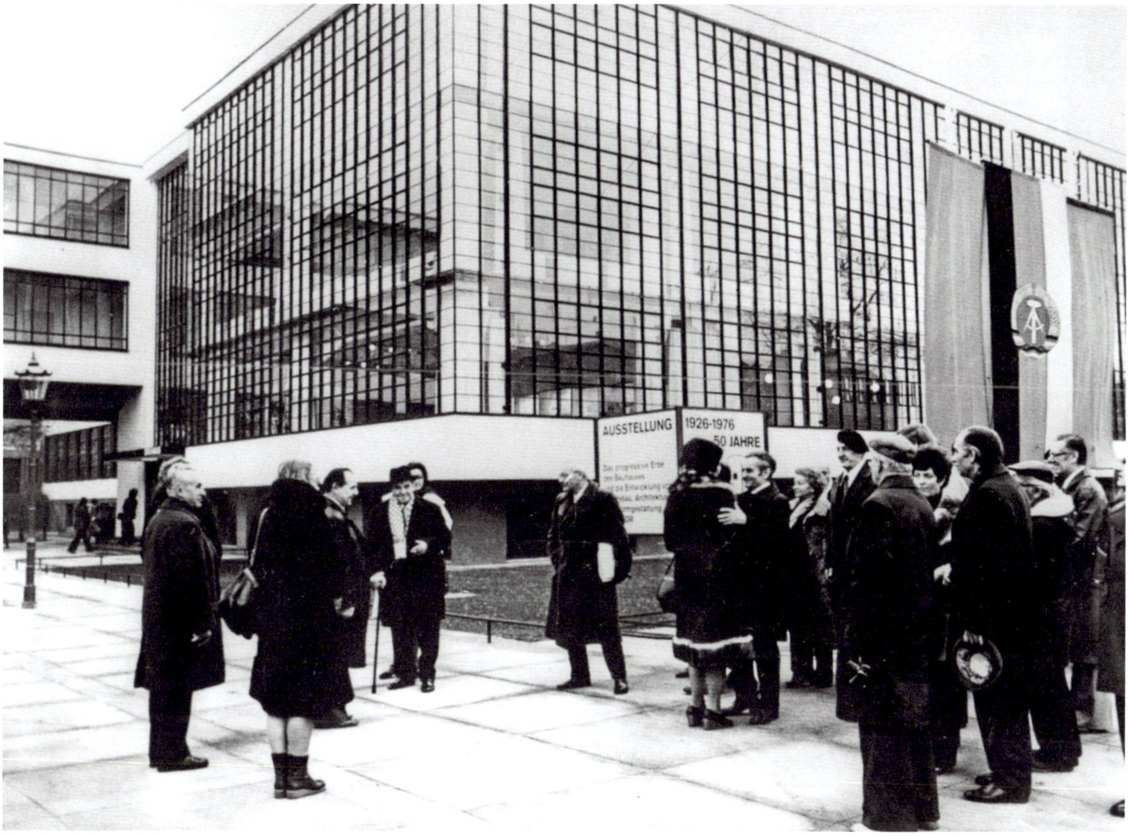

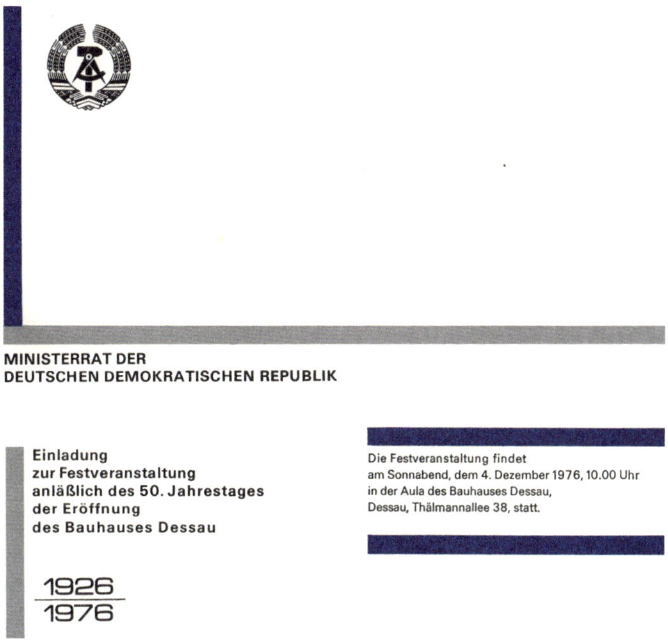

MINISTERRAT DER
DEUTSCHEN DEMOKRATISCHEN REPUBLIK

**Einladung
zur Festveranstaltung
anläßlich des 50. Jahrestages
der Eröffnung
des Bauhauses Dessau**

1926
1976

Die Festveranstaltung findet
am Sonnabend, dem 4. Dezember 1976, 10.00 Uhr
in der Aula des Bauhauses Dessau,
Dessau, Thälmannallee 38, statt.

Fig. 34 Bauhauslers and guests in front of the Bauhaus Building on the day of the ceremony commemorating *50 years of Bauhaus Dessau*, December 4, 1976

Fig. 35 Invitation to the ceremony on December 4, 1976

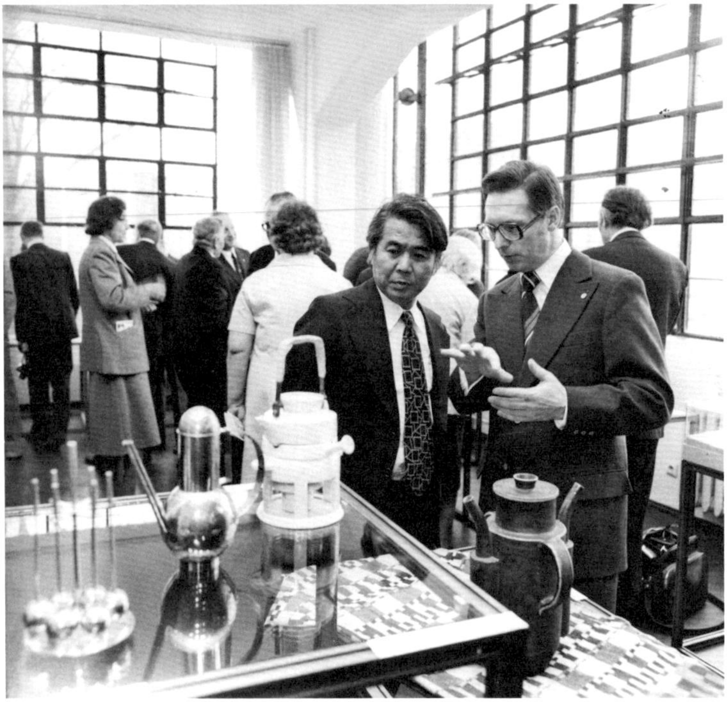

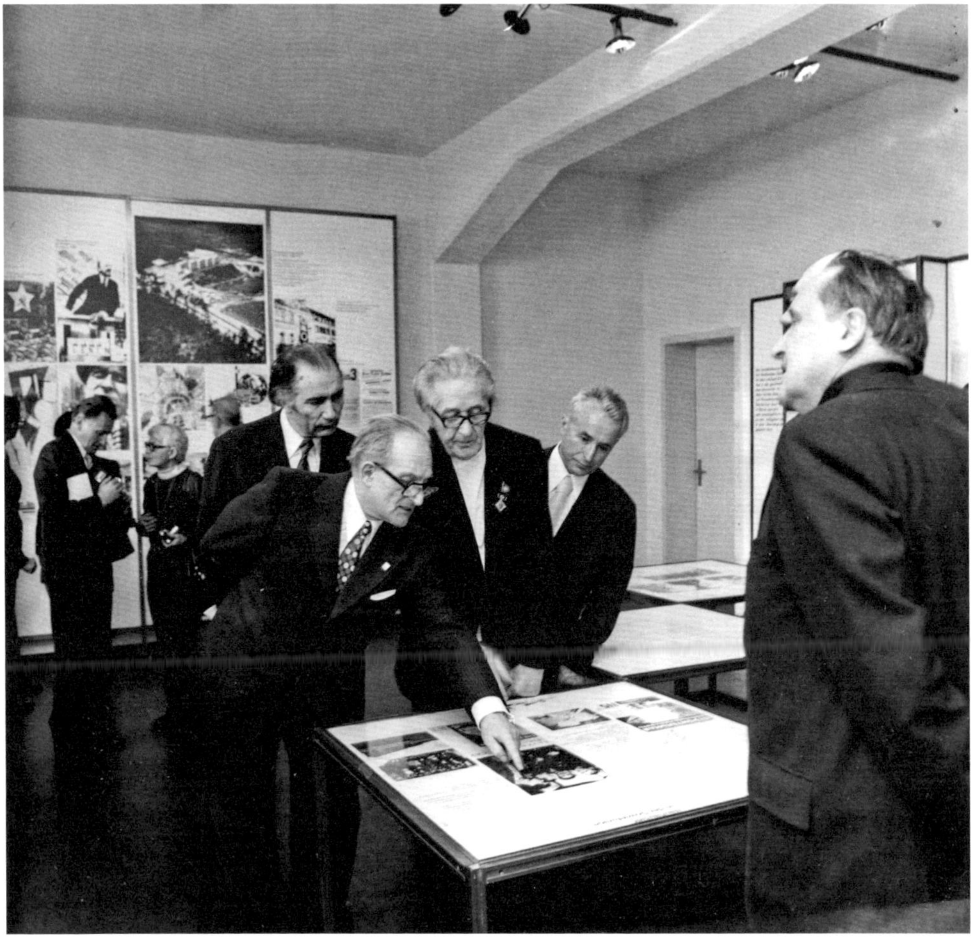

Fig. 36 Kenji Ekuan and Martin Kelm in the Bauhaus exhibition at the workshop wing of the Bauhaus Building on December 4, 1976
Fig. 37 Bauhaus exhibition in the workshop wing of the Bauhaus Building on December 4, 1976

stage events, and a growing collection.[144] Until 1986, its director was the Dessau teacher and historian Georg Opitz (1921–1987): "Georg Opitz was employed as a researcher in the architecture department of the Hochschule für Architektur und Bauwesen Weimar, where he had his academic home in a working group for Bauhaus studies.... His actual workplace, however, was in the Bauhaus Building in Dessau."[145] His colleagues there included Manuela Falkenberg, who oversaw day-to-day organization, along with Werner Fröhlich, who mainly worked as a tour guide, and museologist and historian Günter Ziegler. The latter began making an inventory of the ever-expanding collection.

The WKZ Bauhaus Dessau was naturally involved in the Weimar Bauhaus colloquia. With four more colloquia held by 1989, increasingly close links were forged between the "Bauhaus community," consisting of former Bauhaus students and Bauhaus researchers, and groups interested in topics of acute contemporary relevance. What is striking, at least in retrospect, is that the focus was overwhelmingly on urban planning and architecture. Collection and exhibition work, and especially the field of current critical art, photography, and stage work cultivated from 1983 (or 1985) by newly appointed staff at the WKZ Bauhaus Dessau, were of secondary concern.[146]

The WKZ Bauhaus Dessau opened in December 1976 with a small permanent Bauhaus exhibition curated by Klaus-Jürgen Winkler in Weimar. In its early years, it displayed only a few original exhibits and more closely resembled an information center. Situated in the so-called north area of the Bauhaus Building, the exhibition paid as much attention to the life and work of Hannes Meyer as to those of Walter Gropius and Ludwig Mies van der Rohe; it was later supplemented by a brochure on the Bauhaus written by Christian Schädlich.[147] Along with the small permanent exhibition covering just 60 m² of floor space, special exhibitions were shown from 1978 in the equally cramped adjacent room, but these were conceptually and artistically unconvincing.

Hein Köster, subsequently director of the GDR design collection in Berlin, visited the 1979 exhibition, "Workshop Works," and wrote in the weekly *Sonntag*: "It takes courage to mount an exhibition at the Bauhaus, to be measured, so to speak, against the yardstick of those who once worked here."[148] After describing the various objects amassed in the three years since the collection was started, he concluded: "How does all this hold up in the gleaming Gropius building? Georg Opitz, the WKZ's director, sees 'Workshop Works' as a way of making objects in the growing Bauhaus collection accessible to the public. Granted. But an exhibition that presents things only in loose thematic groups and otherwise arranges them purely aesthetically lags behind the host building's utilization of space. Pictures hanging above the living room cabinet carry a whiff of cozy domesticity, toys and

144 The first information exhibition on the Bauhaus was planned by Klaus-Jürgen Winkler in coordination with Bernd Grönwald.

145 Bernd Grönwald, "Georg Opitz 1921–1987," in: *form + zweck* 5, 1987, 2.

146 See Wolfgang Thöner, "Bewahren und Aktualisieren. Bauhaus-Institutionalisierungen in Dessau von 1945 bis 1994," in: *bauhaus global*, Berlin 2010.

147 See Christian Schädlich, *bauhaus 1919–1933*, Broschüre des Wissenschaftlich-Kulturellen Zentrums Bauhaus Dessau, Dessau 1983.

148 This and subsequent quotations are taken from Hein Köster, "Werkstattarbeiten," in: *Sonntag* 10, 1979.

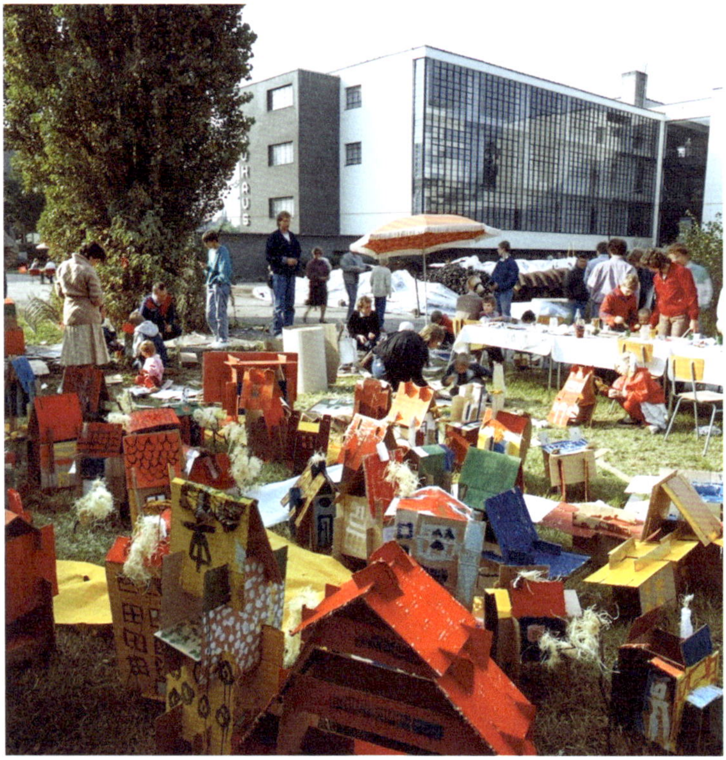

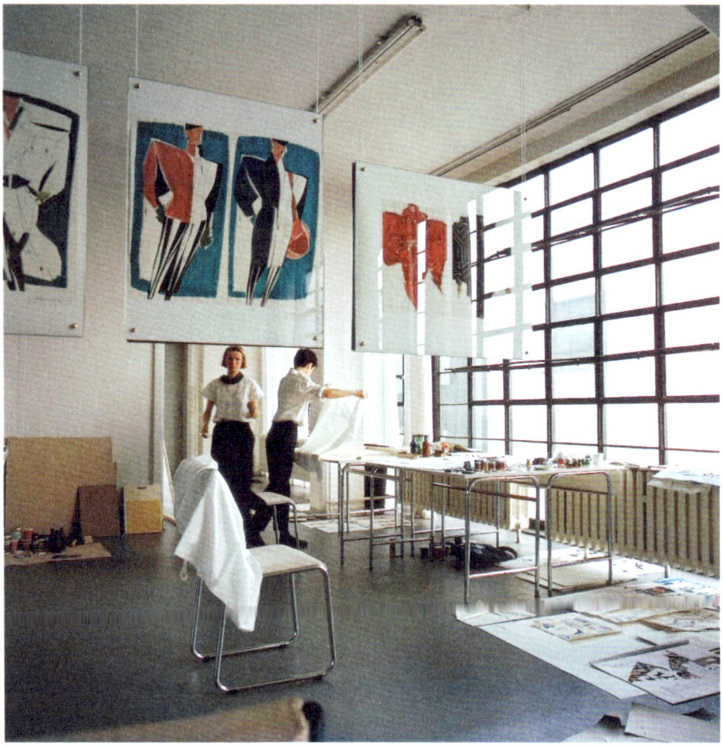

Fig. 38 Bauhaus meeting place, Bauhaus Dessau, 1987
Fig. 39 Fashion seminar at the Bauhaus Dessau, 1987

preliminary course works in the bookcase become mere bric-a-brac." Köster also offered a recommendation: "Today, it is surely preferable to develop and realize utilization concepts that put us in a more productive relationship to the mutability of industrial products and environmental situations."

Letters written by Georg Opitz to Franz Ehrlich indicate that as the collection grew, serious consideration was given at the WKZ (and no doubt in Weimar as well) to creating a much bigger, more informative, and more comprehensive presentation. On January 29, 1979, Franz Ehrlich wrote to Georg Opitz that he welcomed his plan to set up a large permanent exhibition on the Bauhaus. At the same time, he put to him his own version of a more Bauhaus-specific usage of the stage in the Bauhaus Building, perhaps in collaboration with the Musikhochschule Leipzig. Ehrlich wrote: "A group of interested young actors and musicians could surely be won over. And I'd be happy to offer advice on staging and set design. That way, I think our youngsters' hunger for a revival of the revolutionary Twenties could be satisfied. If it should come to a permanent exhibition, consideration should also be given to reconstructing scenes and figurines from the historical Bauhaus stage."

On February 5, 1979, Opitz replied that he intended "to transform the 'Workshop Works' exhibition into a permanent exhibition," since "guests from at home and abroad want to see more than just the house as architecture." Opitz referred to the previously mentioned space next to the small permanent exhibition in which other original exhibits were already on display. The goal was to reconfigure these two spaces: "In 1976, this exhibition (The Progressive Heritage of the Bauhaus and the Development of Town Planning, Architecture, and Design in the GDR) was opened. It has now fulfilled its purpose."[149] It was not until December 1986 that the former carpentry workshop was repurposed to house the first big permanent exhibition of the WKZ Bauhaus Dessau. Franz Ehrlich replied on February 21, 1979 that he would not just integrate replicas of Bauhaus figurines into a future permanent exhibition but envisaged, above all, "an exhibition on instruction methods with striking results."[150]

149 Georg Opitz, letter to Franz Ehrlich, February 5, 1979, Bauhaus Dessau Foundation.
150 Franz Ehrlich, letter to Georg Opitz, February 21, 1979, Bauhaus Dessau Foundation.

The collection at the Bauhaus Dessau (1986–1990)

In the mid-1980s, research activities at the WKZ in Dessau got underway with the appointment of the first young scholars there. These researchers came from the two preexisting centers of Bauhaus studies in the GDR: Lutz Schöbe and Wolfgang Thöner had studied at the Humboldt Universität, while Michael Siebenbrodt and Folke Dietzsch hailed from Weimar.[151] Along with personal exhibitions on two still-living Bauhauslers, Selman Selmanagić (a former student of Hannes Meyer) and Carl Marx, they curated the biggest-ever Bauhaus exhibition in the GDR to date, drawing on objects from the Dessau Bauhaus collection to give Hannes Meyer equal stature to Gropius and Mies. They also initiated a series of exhibitions and art events that enabled the institution to reprise its old role as a laboratory for critical multimedia art.[152]

Until the end of the GDR, the Hochschule academics grouped around the now-retired Konrad Püschel and Bernd Grönwald, who became vice-president of the Bauakademie in 1986, were to remain the key decision-makers on all matters concerning both the WKZ Bauhaus Dessau and the Bauhaus Dessau, reestablished in 1987 under director Rolf Kuhn. Of the numerous authors published in the context of the Bauhaus colloquia, Klaus-Jürgen Winkler deserves special mention as a representative of the Weimar school of Bauhaus studies.[153]

Besides the WKZ, the Bauhaus Building soon accommodated an institute of further education affiliated with the Hochschule für Architektur und Bauwesen Weimar and, from 1983, a similar experimental and educational center run by the East German Amt für industrielle Formgestaltung (AiF, Bureau of Industrial Design). In 1980, Bernd Grönwald had already articulated his ideas for the future use of a new Bauhaus Dessau. These were then taken up by the Ministers for Building, Higher Education and Vocational Training and Culture, as well as the director of the AiF (directly subordinate to the GDR ministerial council) and the chair of the Halle District Council. The Ministry for Higher Education and Vocational Training was charged with reestablishing the Bauhaus Dessau as a design center.

In early 1987, Rolf Kuhn was appointed director of the newly formed Bauhaus Dessau, which was now split into the areas of architecture, town planning, Bauhaus collection, product design, and environmental design. A board made up of representatives of the Ministry for Culture, the Building Ministry, and the AiF assumed oversight of the new institution.

151 Lutz Schöbe had written his honors thesis on Franz Ehrlich, Michael Siebenbrodt was involved with the reconstruction of the Bauhaus Building (among other things), and Folke Dietzsch researched students at the Bauhaus, while Wolfgang Thöner had mostly dealt with Bauhaus pedagogy.

152 See Wolfgang Thöner, "Staatsdoktrin und Regimekritik. Die Bauhausrezeption in der DDR 1963–1990," in: Philipp Oswalt (ed.), *Bauhaus Streit*, Ostfildern 2009, 232–248.

153 In 1976, he took over from Konrad Püschel the project of bringing out a selection of Hannes Meyer's writings, working in close collaboration with Lena Meyer-Bergner. Klaus-Jürgen Winkler wrote the introduction and worked on a number of the texts. Edited by Lena Meyer-Bergner, the book appeared in 1980 under the title *Building and Society* (Verlag der Kunst, Dresden). In 1977, Lena Meyer-Bergner also paid a visit to the Bauhaus in Dessau as a guest of the Püschels.

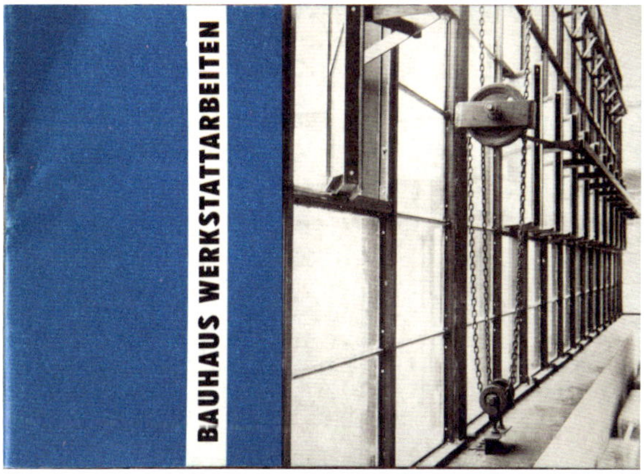

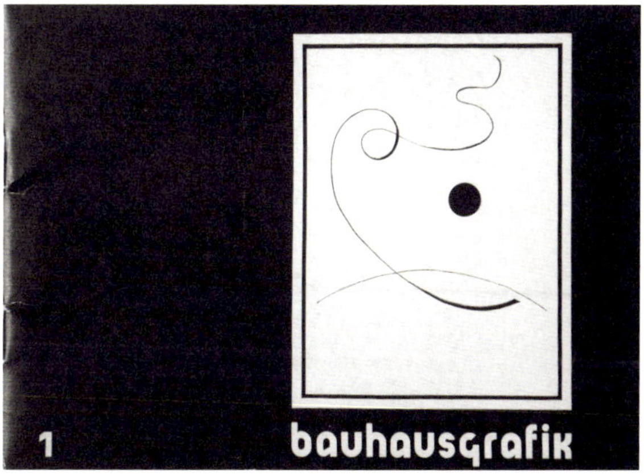

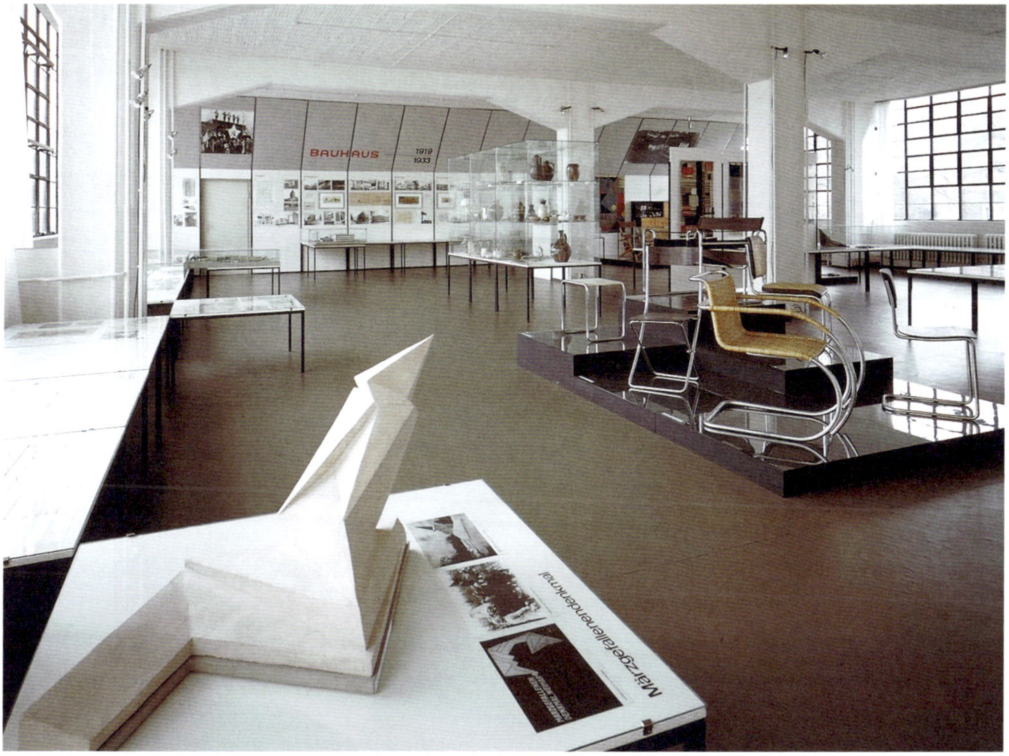

Fig. 40 Catalogue of the exhibition *workshop works* at the WKZ Bauhaus Dessau, 1979
Fig. 41 Catalogue of the exhibition *bauhausgrafik* at the WKZ Bauhaus Dessau, 1978: Cover using the graphic *Kontraste* by Marinanne Brandt, 1923
Fig. 42 Permanent exhibition in the Bauhaus Building, December 1986 to spring 1988

Taking his cue from Grönwald, Rolf Kuhn led the Bauhaus Dessau from 1987 as an interdisciplinary institute that sought to provide stimulus for inner-city developments, in particular.[154] Until 1989, the Bauhaus Dessau under Rolf Kuhn's leadership had evolved entirely along the lines proposed by Grönwald. It was in the process of "carving out a niche as an experimental institute for urban development at a time of significant change for industrial society. ... With that, the Bauhaus in Dessau assumed the role of the experimental 'wing' of the institution in Weimar, which taught and researched in the field of architecture and town planning."[155]

The Bauhaus Dessau was unique in providing opportunities for professional exchange—not just at Bauhaus symposia—with a select group of foreign researchers, architects, designers, and town planners, including some from Western Europe and West Germany. There were workshops, lectures, and seminars at which Hannes Meyer was sometimes discussed or referred to. From 1982 to 1986, for example, the Bauhaus Dessau hosted the Hannes Meyer design seminars, organized by the Hochschule für Architektur und Bauwesen. The results of the 1986 seminar were assessed by a number of Hannes Meyer's former students at the Bauhaus Dessau, notably Selman Selmanagić and Waldemar Alder (1906–1999).

The cultural-political highlight of these years was undoubtedly the West Berlin Bauhaus-Archiv's "Experiment Bauhaus" exhibition, held in the late summer of 1988. This show was one outcome of the cultural agreement between East and West Germany reached in 1986. Despite finding some common ground in their assessment of the Bauhaus, the speakers at the exhibition opening revealed telling differences in their evaluation of the institution's contemporary relevance. In the speech he delivered at the opening in Dessau, Eberhard Diepgen, mayor of West Berlin, emphasized the "self-imposed freedom of teaching and education" at the Bauhaus, while Karl Schmiechen, GDR State Secretary for Urban Development, Housing, and Public Works, saw the GDR's housing policy confirmed in the "scientific basis for the construction of social housing developed at the Bauhaus."[156]

From 1976 to 1990 it was the policy of the Bauhaus Dessau, as the central and only such institution in the GDR—the preexisting Bauhaus collections and archives of the Kunstsammlungen zu Weimar and the Weimar

154 Rolf Kuhn, "Hannes Meyer und wir," in: *Hannes Meyer. Beiträge zum 100. Geburtstag 1989. 5. Internationales Bauhaus-Kolloquium in Weimar*, Schriften der Hochschule für Architektur und Bauwesen Weimar, vol. 86, Weimar 1990.

155 Harald Kegler, "Die Bauhaus-Kolloquien in Weimar (und Dessau)" (= n. 143).

156 Eberhard Diepgen, "Rede zur Eröffnung der Ausstellung 'Experiment Bauhaus' am 6.8.1988 in Dessau," quoted in: Martin Bober, *Von der Idee zum Mythos. Die Rezeption des Bauhaus in beiden deutschen Teilen Deutschlands in Zeiten des Neuanfangs (1945 und 1989)*, dissertation Kassel 2006, 154; Karl Schmiechen, "Rede zur Eröffnung der Ausstellung 'Experiment Bauhaus' am 6.8.1988 in Dessau," ibid. 152. On the exhibition, see also Peter Hahn, in: *form + zweck* 2, 1989, 33–35. Like all projects and events put on by the Bauhaus Dessau, the opening of the exhibition was surveilled by operatives of the Stasi, the East German Ministry for State Security. See Peter Boeger and Elise Catrain (eds.), *Stasi in Sachsen-Anhalt. Die DDR-Geheimpolizei in den Bezirken Halle und Magdeburg,* Broschüre der Bundesbeauftragten für die Unterlagen des Staatssicherheitsdienstes der ehemaligen Deutschen Demokratischen Republik, Berlin 2016, 123–126.

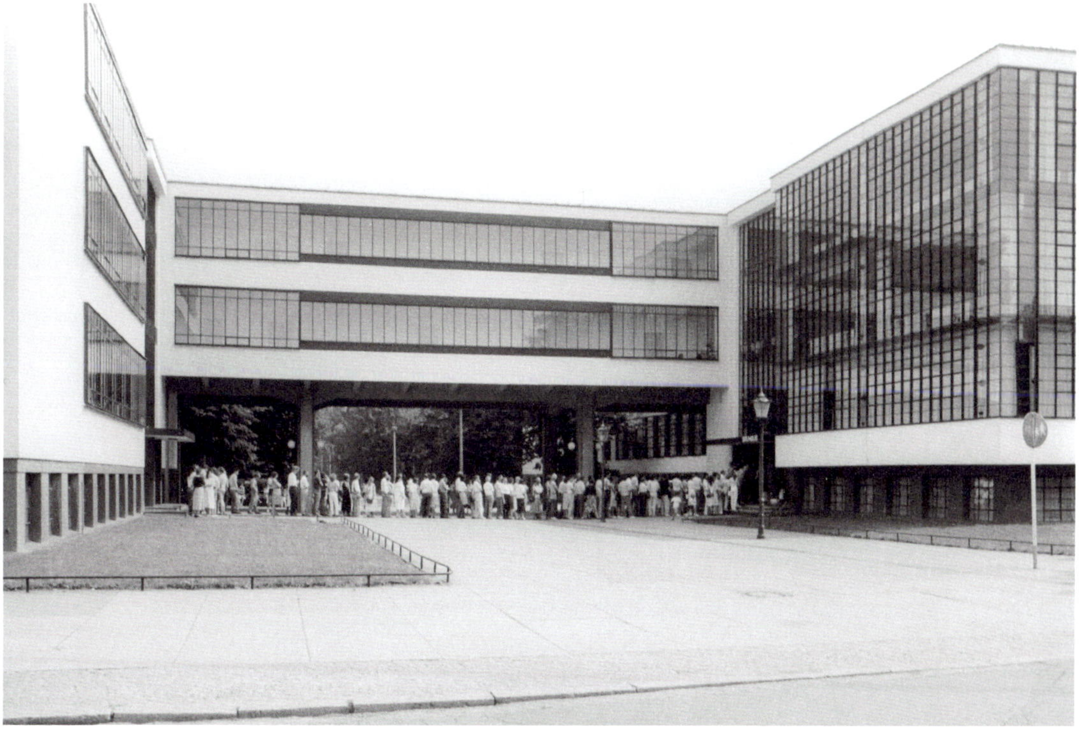

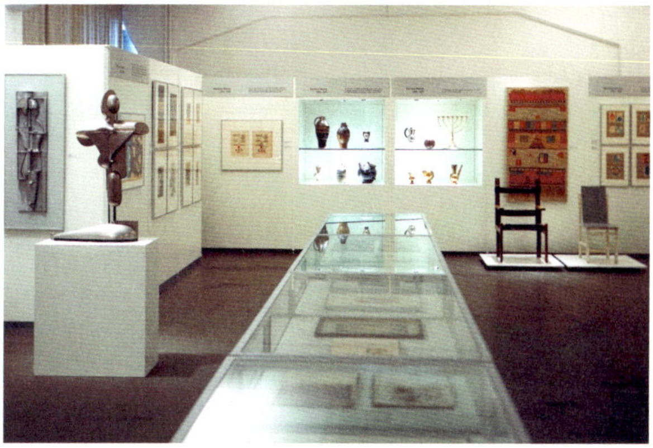

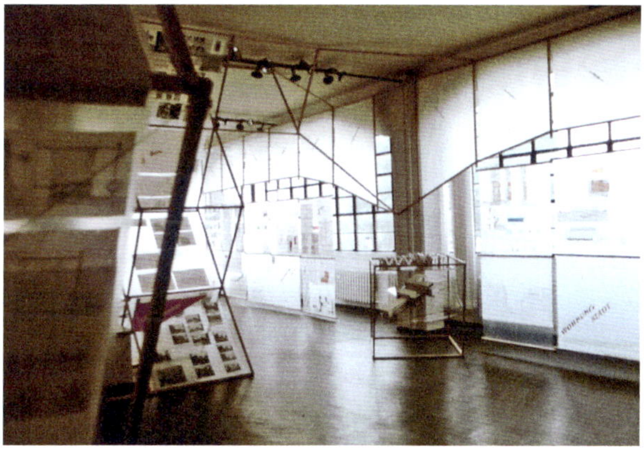

Fig. 43 Queue of visitors to the exhibition *Experiment Bauhaus*, 1988
Fig. 44 Exhibition *Experiment Bauhaus* at the Bauhaus Archive Berlin, Summer 1988
Fig. 45 Exhibition of the results of work at the Bauhaus Dessau, 1988

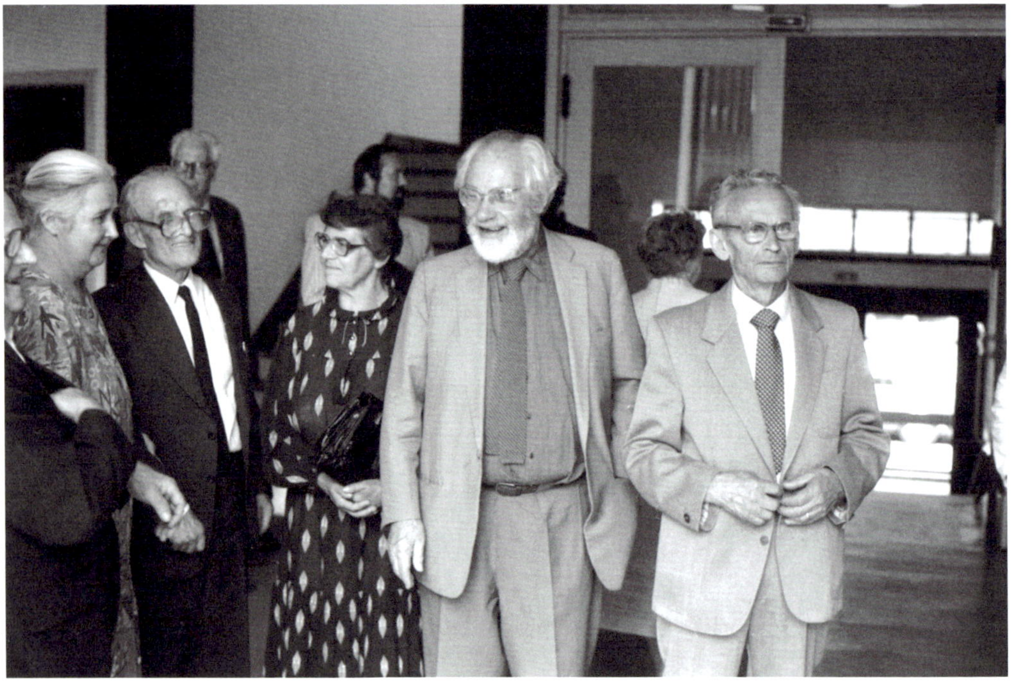

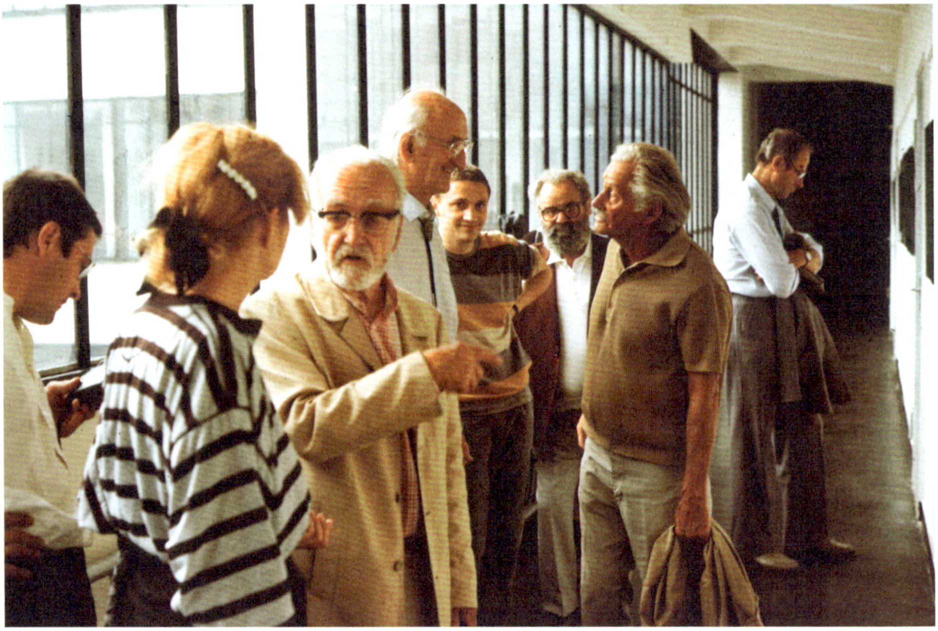

Fig. 46 Lilo Aniceto-Meyer (2nd from left), Philipp Tolziner (3rd from left), Max Bill (5th from left), and Konrad Püschel (6th from left) in the Bauhaus Building, July 1, 1989

Fig. 47 The Bauhauslers Hubert Hoffmann (3rd from left), Carl Bauer (4th from left), and Carl Marx (7th from left) in the Bauhaus Building, July 1, 1989

Hochschule would not be expanded until 1995—to collect literally any and every artistic and cultural artefact related to the Bauhaus and the subsequent activities of Bauhauslers (former teachers and students). A small annual purchasing budget, combined with bequests, allowed the collection to acquire enough original objects to provide an (initially modest) overview of the institution's history.

With the new start in 1986, however, Bernd Grönwald and researchers from the GDR Bauakademie formulated another goal that went well beyond consolidating a Bauhaus collection. In 1989, in a brief report in the journal *form + zweck* on a seminar "held at the Bauhaus Dessau under the auspices of the GDR Bauakademie," Grönwald announced: "In late November 1988, researchers in the field of architectural history gathered at the Bauhaus Dessau ... to begin a collaborative research project on the history of architecture and urban development in the GDR in preparation for the fortieth anniversary of the GDR. Theses outlining the development of town planning and architecture since the victory over Hitler fascism will be elaborated by October 1989. A long-term research project, leading to the publication of a book on GDR architectural history and the systematic buildup of the architecture collections at the Bauhaus Dessau will also be commenced."[157] This was accompanied by plans for an architecture and design museum in the former employment office, the Gropius-designed Arbeitsamt. These plans were taken no further, nor was consideration given to the archival and exhibition spaces, staffing, and finance such a collection would have required. They were made obsolete by the events of autumn 1989 at the latest.

Needless to say, the Bauhaus Dessau was not unaffected by the tremendous changes in state and society that occurred from November 1989. Following attempts by an association to take over the Bauhaus Dessau, it was financed solely by the Federal Republic of Germany in 1990 and then co-financed by Saxony-Anhalt after its creation as a federal state. From 1994 the Bauhaus Dessau was jointly administered by the federal government, the state of Saxony-Anhalt, and the city of Dessau as the Bauhaus Dessau Foundation.

157 Bernd Grönwald, "Projekt zur DDR-Architekturgeschichte," in: *form + zweck* 1, 1989, 2.

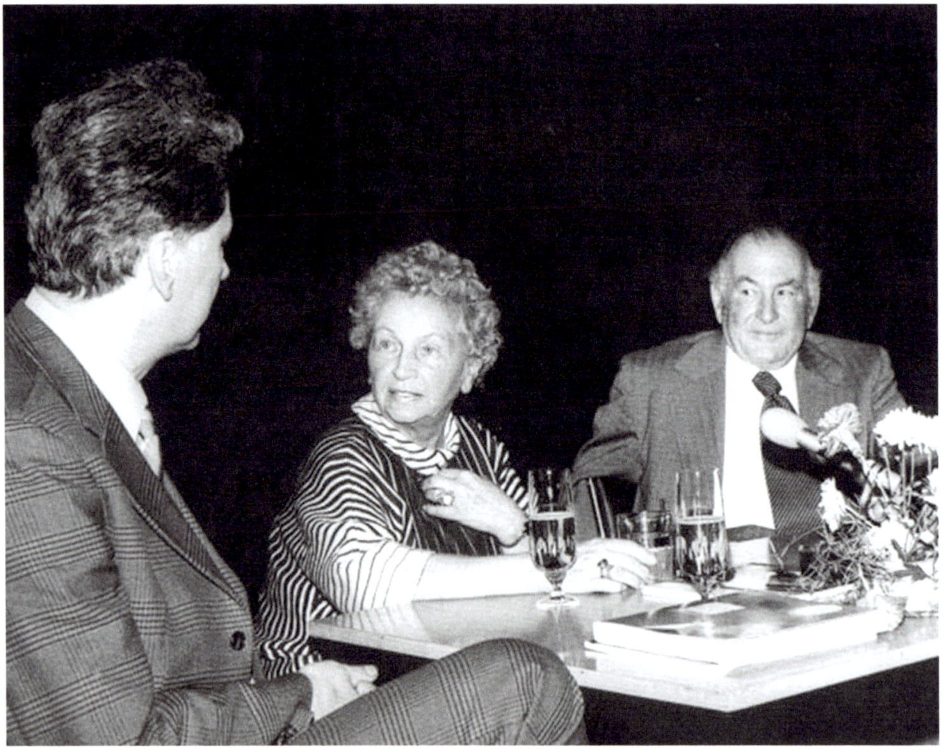

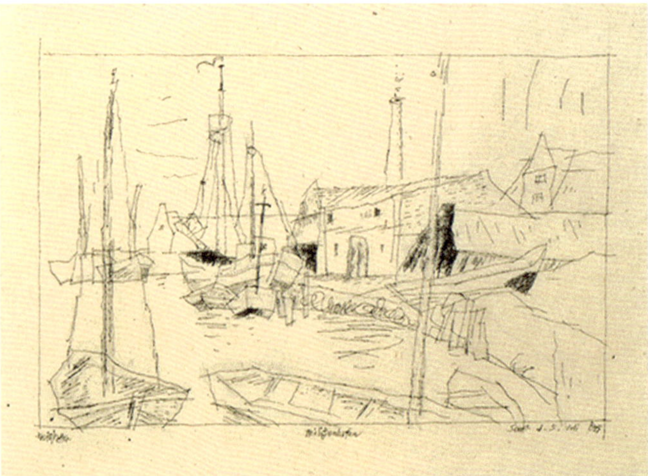

Fig. 48 Hans-Peter Schulz in conversation with Grete Reichardt and Franz Honest during the first Bauhaus exhibition at Galerie am Sachsenplatz Leipzig, 1976

Fig. 49 Lyonel Feininger, *Heiligenhafen*, 1919, pen drawing over traces of a chalk sketch on beige handmade paper, 28.6 × 37.8 cm

4 Consolidating the Collection, 1976–1990

First acquisitions: The Bauhaus exhibitions at the Galerie am Sachsenplatz

The first exhibition held at the Galerie am Sachsenplatz in Leipzig, "The Bauhaus 1919–1933" (1976), presented two hundred exhibits, including paintings, graphic arts, sculpture, designs, workshop works, publications, and documents from the Bauhaus Weimar, Bauhaus Dessau, and Bauhaus Berlin, as well as photographs of former students and teachers.[158] The Dessau City Council learned of Gisela and Hans-Peter Schulz's activities and approached the gallerists in December 1974. It was agreed that the collection would be acquired "almost in its entirety" as the basis of "a future Bauhaus collection in Dessau."[159] The city of Dessau thus enabled the Schulzes to work on a larger scale and in a more targeted fashion than hitherto, since they could now win active support for their initiative from initially skeptical Bauhaus artists and private collectors.

For the Culture Department of the Dessau City Council, important discoveries in the exhibition included a pen and ink drawing by Lyonel Feininger, *Heiligenhafen* (1925), as well as five woodcuts by the same artist, *Alte Brigantine* from 1947, *Hafen* from 1950, *Leuchtturm* from 1951, *Gelmeroda* from 1953, and *Straße im Schnee* from 1957, some of which existed only in editions of two to three copies or a few manual prints.[160]

The city of Dessau, represented by the mayor, acquired the pen and ink drawing for 25,000 marks and the woodcuts for 7,500 marks apiece, with the exception of *Hafen*, which it purchased for 8,500 marks.[161] All these works went towards the WKZ Bauhaus Dessau's growing collection. To Councilor for Cultural Affairs Rüdiger Döhring, it was "in the public interest to preserve ... as a whole the exhibits brought together in the exhibition."[162]

The first exhibition also presented a 1923 color lithograph by László Moholy-Nagy, *Komposition*, featuring a dedication "to Frau Marianne Brandt" in the lower heft-hand corner.[163] Particularly worth mentioning, in retrospect, are *Ausgrabung* (oil on canvas, 1924) by Hungarian artist Gyula Pap, the student works of Hajo Rose and Reinhold Rossig, and four photocollages by Marianne Brandt, *Pariser Impressionen* from 1926, *Mit allen zehn Fingern* from 1927, as well as *Kontraste* and *Die Turner* from 1928.[164] Today, Brandt's collages are considered important evidence for the widespread adoption of the constructive photomontage technique pioneered by Moholy-Nagy, who had shrugged aside the influence of Dadaism to open up a whole new field of commercial graphic design.

Three paintings by Hajo Rose also ended up in the WKZ collection: *Figur auf der Straße*

158 On the activities of the Galerie am Sachsenplatz, see chapter 3.

159 See Hans-Peter Schulz's foreword in: Galerie am Sachsenplatz (ed.), *Das Bauhaus 1919–1933*, Leipzig 1976, 5.

160 See *Das Bauhaus 1919–1933*, 30–31 as well as the illustrations on pp. 33 and 38.

161 See the Galerie am Sachsenplatz's invoice no. 48/76 from November 1, 1976, in Archive of the Bauhaus Dessau Foundation.

162 See the text by the Councilor for Cultural Affairs, Rüdiger Döhring, from July 1976, in: *Das Bauhaus 1919–1933*, 9.

163 See *Das Bauhaus 1919–1933*, 34 as well as the illustration on p. 45.

164 For Marianne Brandt's photocollages, see Galerie am Sachsenplatz (ed.), *Das Bauhaus 1919–1933*, Leipzig 1976, 30 and 39 (illustration). The Dessau City Council acquired the collages for a total of 2,900 marks; see the Galerie am Sachsenplatz's invoice no. 48/76.

from 1929, *Angler mit Katze* from 1930, and *Farb- und Formenkomposition* from 1931/32. Reinhold Rossig's watercolor *Architektur-Studie* from 1925, along with two of his preliminary course works from 1929 and *Bedrohung* (pen in colored ink, chalk and watercolor, 1930) were bought for the collection.[165]

Other drawcards for the exhibition "The Bauhaus 1919–1933" were works from the workshops of Marianne Brandt, Hinrich Bredendieck (1904–1995), Marcel Breuer (1902–1981), Otto Lindig and Ludwig Mies van der Rohe. Thus, several specimens of the tubular steel furniture of Breuer and Mies, characterized by its austere functionality and aesthetic beauty, made their way to Dessau: a table with a black wooden tabletop and two stools with red cloth covers from 1928 as well as four chairs from 1929/1930, including two with black wooden armrests and red linen covers.[166] Hinnerk Scheper's woodcuts *Stadtkirche St. Peter und Paul zu Weimar* and *Gasse in Altweimar*, both from 1920, should not be forgotten, nor should Gerhard Marcks' woodcuts *Grabengel* from 1928, *Schnitter, Die Krauthexe*, and *Frauen mit Kiepen* from 1923 and *Frauenkopf* from 1934/35. In addition, seven of the fourteen *Bauhaus books* were purchased, as were numerous publications of the Bauhaus Weimar and the Bauhaus Dessau such as *Der Sturm, Die Form. Zeitschrift für gestaltete Arbeit, Fotothek*, and *ReD* 5.

All these works are listed and some also depicted in the exhibition catalogue, which appeared in an edition of 1,600 copies. The works not presented in the Galerie am Sachsenplatz for lack of space are likewise listed in the publication. It additionally contains a foreword by gallerist Hans-Peter Schulz as well as articles by art historian Diether Schmidt.[167] There are also contributions from Bauhaus students Hajo Rose and Kurt Schmidt in the catalogue, along with excerpts from letters written by Gunta Stadler-Stölzl (1897–1987), Kurt Schmidt, Hin Bredendieck, Max Olderock (1895–1972), and Hannes Meyer.

188 of the works exhibited only a year later in the "bauhaus 2" exhibition at the Galerie am Sachsenplatz ended up in the WKZ collection.[168] This selection included two watercolors by Franz Ehrlich, *Relief* and *Rotes Zentrum* from 1930, several collages by Marianne Brandt, for example *... und sie lacht* from 1928, as well as more than twenty works by Carl Marx, such as the watercolors *§218* and *Kurfürstendamm* from 1932. Studies and tasks from courses taught by Joost Schmidt, such as "Studie aus dem Vorkurs Schmidt" or "aufgabe – inserat mit rand," both from 1932, were also purchased. The biggest collection of works from the "bauhaus 2" exhibition was bought by the Dessau City Council from Grete Reichardt, including two carpet designs from 1928 as well as a highly ornate textile collage, *Gretel-Stoffe*, dating from around 1931.[169]

165 Galerie am Sachsenplatz, invoice no. 48/76.
166 See Galerie am Sachsenplatz (ed.), *Das Bauhaus 1919–1933*, Leipzig 1976, 49 as well as p. 7 for the illustrations. See the Galerie am Sachsenplatz's invoice no. 48/76.
167 In 1966, Diether Schmidt (1930–2012) brought out one of the first pioneering books on the Bauhaus in the GDR. See Diether Schmidt, *Bauhaus. Weimar 1919 bis 1925, Dessau 1925 bis 1932, Berlin 1932 bis 1933*, Dresden 1966.
168 See the Galerie am Sachsenplatz's invoice no. 61/77 from December 3, 1977, Archive of the Bauhaus Dessau Foundation.
169 See the Galerie am Sachsenplatz's invoice no. 36/78 from June 10, 1978, Archive of the Bauhaus Dessau Foundation.

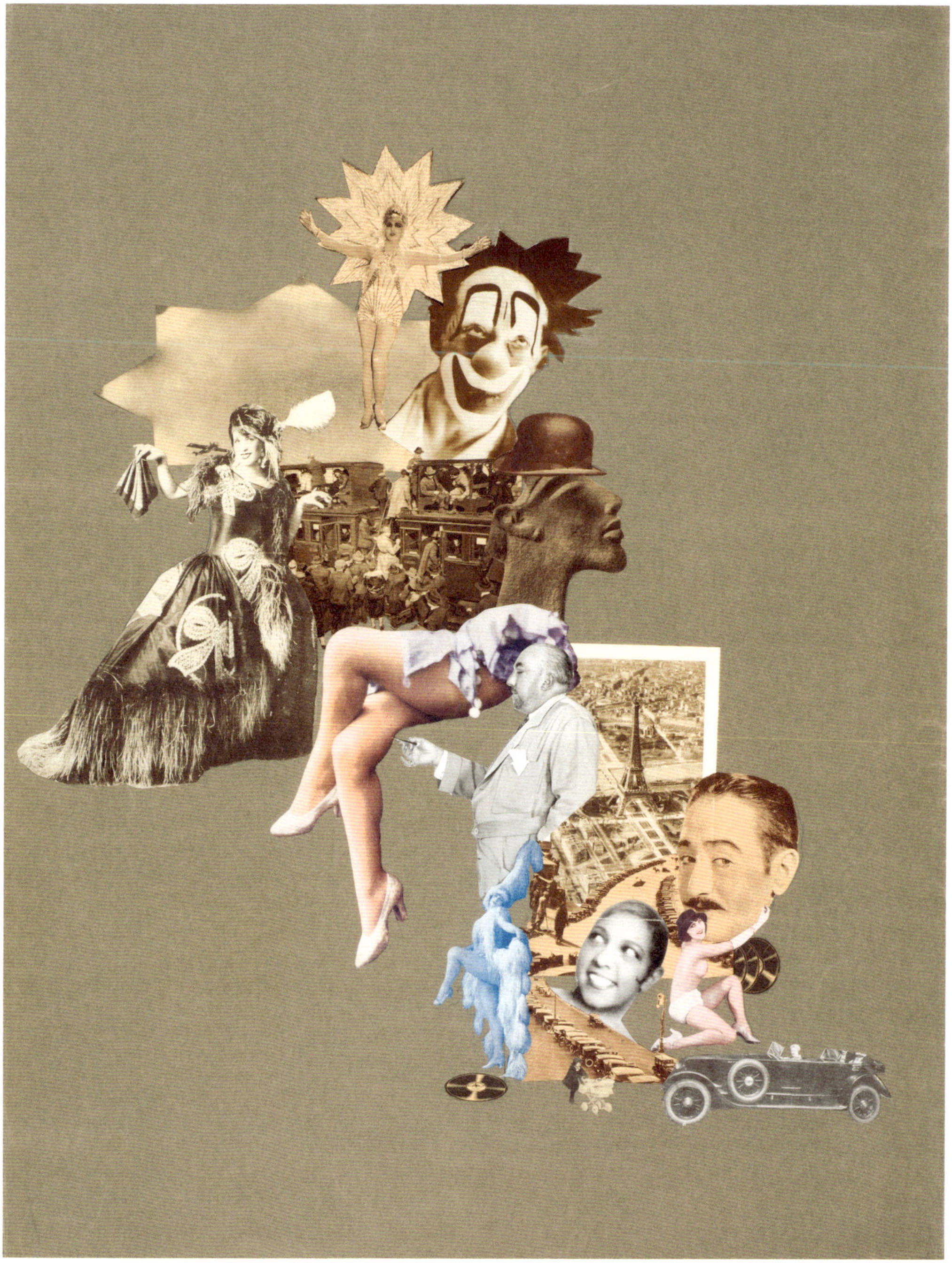

Fig. 50 Marianne Brandt, *Pariser Impressionen*, 1926, collage

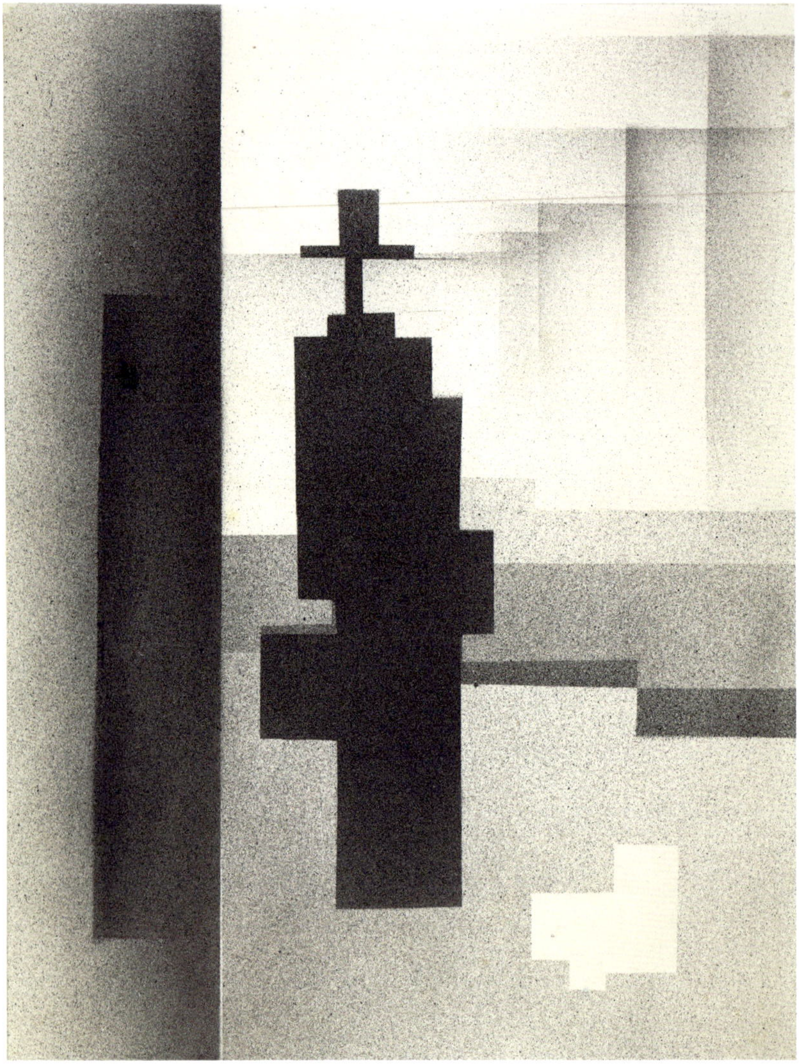

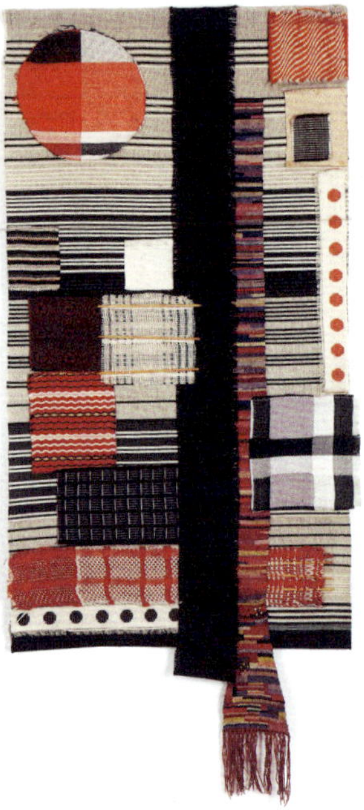

Fig. 51 Hajo Rose, *figure on the street*, 1929/30, ink on cardboard
Fig. 52 Grete Reichardt, *Gretel fabrics*, around 1931, textile collage

By the end of the "bauhaus 3" exhibition (1978), Gisela and Hans-Peter Schulz could point with some pride to 554 exhibits they had directed to the WKZ collection since 1976.[170] In particular, Lyonel Feininger's watercolor *Dreimaster*, dated December 24, 1936, was bought for 14,000 marks[171] and László Moholy-Nagy's watercolor *Kleine Komposition* from 1923 for 17,000 marks.[172] The 1923 prototype of a desk lamp by Wilhelm Wagenfeld also caught the interest of the WKZ Bauhaus Dessau's director, Georg Opitz, who likewise acquired it for the collection.

In the course of the fourth exhibition, "bauhaus 4: Franz Ehrlich, The Early Years" (1980), the gallery again granted the WKZ "unqualified first purchase rights" to the items on show. This is how twenty-five paintings and drawings by Franz Ehrlich ended up in the Dessau collection, including the oil painting *Landschaft* from 1927, the montage *Diagonale über Kurven* from 1930 and the drawings *Komposition mit Rechtecken II* and *Geometrische Spannungen*, both from 1930.[173]

With "bauhaus 5" (1981), on "Dr. Rabe's house in Zwenkau" near Leipzig, the Galerie am Sachsenplatz not only sold works from the exhibition; it also accepted donations from artists which were then added to the WKZ's collection, including works by Moses Bahelfer, Werner Drewes, Jean and Suzanne Leppien (1907–1982), Albert Mentzel, and Jean Weinfeld. But the Dessau City Council also made new acquisitions, such as a rare early lithograph by Walter Peterhans (1897–1960), *Das Paar* from 1920, a watercolor over pencil by Benita Koch-Otte, *Komplementär rot und wenig grün*, a lithograph from 1922 by Friedl Dicker, *Stephan W. gewidmet*, and works by Gyula Pap, Theo Balden, Erich Mende (1905–1948), Walter Puff, Walter Köppe, and Lothar Schreyer (1886–1966).[174]

Immediately after the second part of the "bauhaus 6" exhibition (1983) came to a close, seventeen photographs by Irena Blühová from the period 1930–1936 as well as twenty-six photographs by Albert Hennig from the years 1928–1932 were sent on to the WKZ. The Dessau City Council additionally purchased, among other things, an etching by Rudolf Baschant, *Nebelimpressionen* from 1931, a lithograph by Willi Baumeister, *Statische Figur* from 1922, as well as fourteen

170 Along with works by Grete Reichardt, August Agatz, Johannes Berthold, Walter Köppe and Hermann Werner Kubsch documenting the various preliminary course at the Bauhaus, works by Johannes Driesch, Josef Hartwig, Johannes Itten, Wassily Kandinsky, Wilhelm Löber, Else Moegelin, Walter Puff and Lothar Schreyer were also acquired from the "bauhaus 3" exhibition by the Dessau City Council for a total of around 150,000 marks. See invoices of the Galerie am Sachsenplatz no. 82/78 from December 4, 1978, no. 99/78 from December 18, 1978, no. 27/79 from April 17, 1979, no. 76/79 from November 3, 1979 and 84/79 from December 1, 1979, in the Archive of the Bauhaus Dessau Foundation.

171 See invoice no. 76/79 from November 3, 1979, in the Archive of the Bauhaus Dessau Foundation.

172 See invoice no. 27/79 from April 17, 1979, in the Archive of the Bauhaus Dessau Foundation.

173 See invoices 6180-1310-1212 from December 12, 1980 and 1884-1310-1505 from May 15, 1981 itemizing acquisitions from the Galerie am Sachsenplatz, Archive of the Bauhaus Dessau Foundation.

174 See Lutz Schöbe, "Bauhaus Dessau Foundation. Geschichte und Profil der Sammlung," in: Fachausstellungen Heckmann GmbH (ed.), *Herrenhausen '96. 28. Kunst- und Antiquitäten-Messe Hannover-Herrenhausen 20.–28. April 1996,* Hannover 1996, 15–22, here p. 18. See also the Galerie am Sachsenplatz's invoice no. 4281-1310-0812 from December 8, 1981, Archive of the Bauhaus Dessau Foundation.

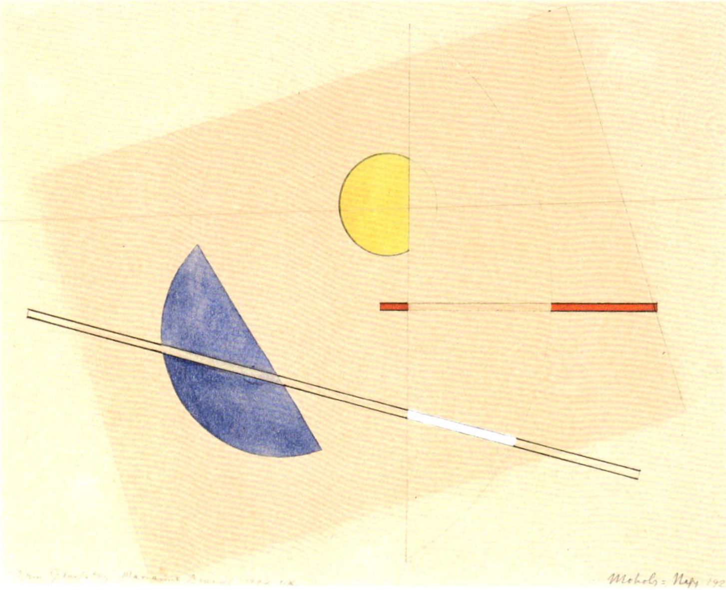

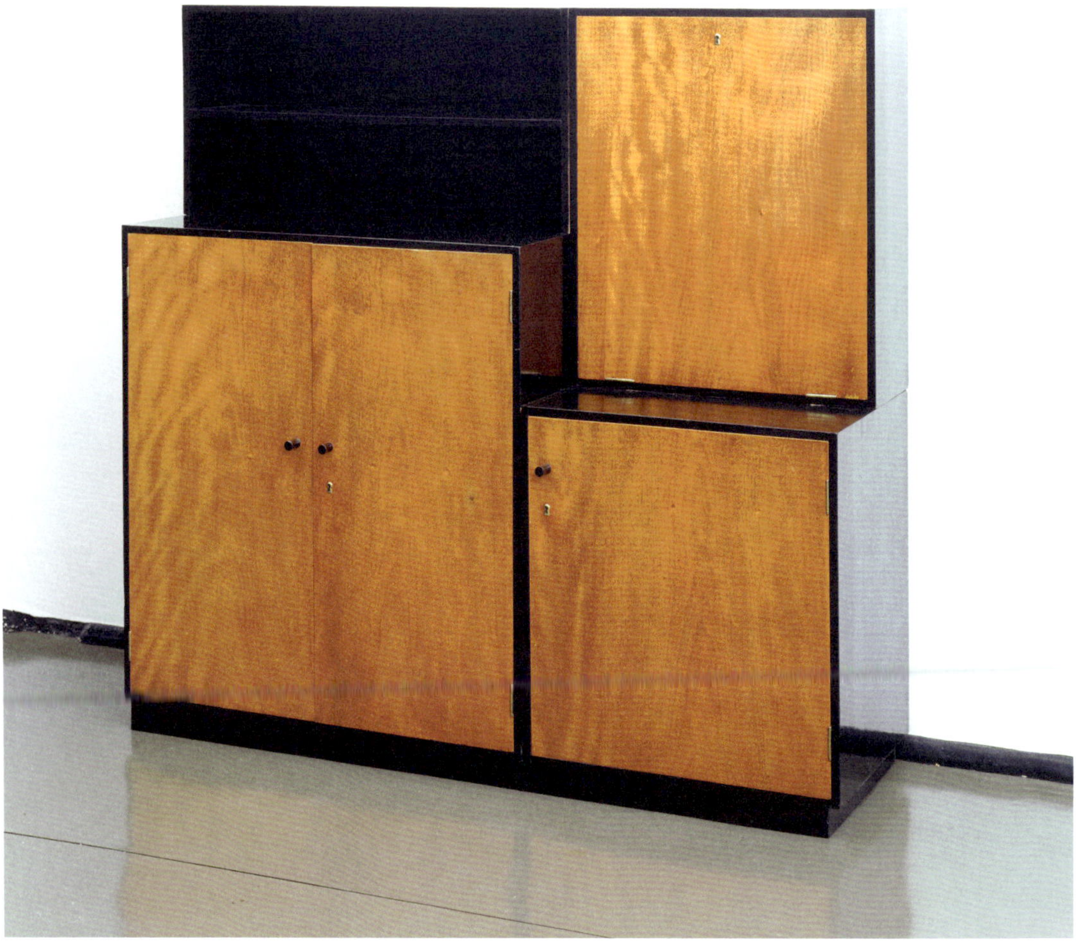

Fig. 53 László Moholy-Nagy, *Kleine Komposition*, 1923, watercolor (with dedication to Marianne Brandt)
Fig. 54 Marcel Breuer (design), carpentry workshop of the Bauhaus Dessau (production), living room cupboard (Bauhaus sample furniture for the settlement in Dessau-Törten), 1926, pine, birch, shellac

woodcuts and lithographs by Otto Hoffmann, for a total sum of 9,970 marks.[175]

For the remainder of the 1980s, no further Bauhaus-related sales exhibitions were mounted by the Galerie am Sachsenplatz. However, the gallery continued to collect works and pass them on to the WKZ Bauhaus Dessau. Worth mentioning are various photographs, drawings by Walter Puff, drawings and woodcuts by Gerhard Marcks, ten lithographs by Otto Hoffmann, the portfolio *Bauhaus Photography* (published as Edition M10 of the Galerie am Sachsenplatz), as well as a teapot, two cups, and a vase by Frans Wildenhain.[176] Other acquisitions included a Rietfeldt chair, the bronze *Bildnis Elisabeth Ehrlich* by Franz Ehrlich from 1927/28, *Bauhaus books* numbers 9 and 11, five lamp designs in light metal by Marianne Brandt from around 1950, diverse items of pottery (both functional and decorative) by Otto Lindig and Frans Wildenhain, and ten paintings by Carl Marx.[177] The last two purchases, made in 1987, were two limewood sculptures by Johannes Berthold, *Ruhende Mutter* from 1958 and *Lebensspirale* from 1952/56.[178]

Further acquisitions from the GDR state art agency

In the 1970s, the GDR state art agency (see 3.1) opened other galleries which—although by no means comparable to the Galerie am Sachsenplatz—likewise offered works by Bauhaus artists.[179] Thus the WKZ Bauhaus Dessau acquired three graphic works by Kurt Schmidt (deed of sale from June 28, 1978) as well as works by Peter Keler and Albert Henning (deed of sale from December 13, 1978) from the Galerie am Hansering in Halle. The gallery of the state art agency organized the so-called Berlin Art Auction. At the sixth Berlin Art Auction in 1986, a drawing by Gerhard Marcks from 1919, the year the Bauhaus was founded, was bought (deed of sale from May 5, 1986) and at the eighth Berlin Art Auction in 1988, the WKZ bid successfully for graphic works from the early Bauhaus period of Lyonel Feininger, Paul Klee, and Gerhard Marcks (deed of sale from April 25, 1988). Additional woodcuts by Gerhard Marcks were acquired from the Galerie Oben in Karl-Marx-Stadt (deed of sale from April 27, 1987).[180]

175 See the Galerie am Sachsenplatz's invoice no. 4383-1310-0212 from December 2, 1983, Archive of the Bauhaus Dessau Foundation.

176 See the Galerie am Sachsenplatz's invoice no. 1784-1310-1005 from May 10, 1984, Archive of the Bauhaus Dessau Foundation.

177 See the Galerie am Sachsenplatz's invoices no. 4385-1310-2310 from October 23, 1985, no. 3886-1310-0412 from December 4, 1986 and no. 1987-1310-0807 from July 8, 1987, Archive of the Bauhaus Dessau Foundation.

178 See the Galerie am Sachsenplatz's invoice no. 2987-1310-1112 from December 11, 1987, Archive of the Bauhaus Dessau Foundation.

179 The GDR Staatliche Kunsthandel (state art agency) initially established three galleries for contemporary art. By 1989 the number had grown to forty. See Hartmut Pätzke, "Von 'Auftragskunst' bis 'Zentrum für Kunstausstellungen'. Lexikon zur Kunst und Kunstpolitik in der DDR," in: Eugen Blume and Roland März (eds.), *Kunst in der DDR. Eine Retrospektive der Nationalgalerie*, Berlin 2003, 327ff.

180 The Galerie Oben had been founded in 1973 in Karl-Marx-Stadt (today's Chemnitz) as a sales cooperative of the GDR Association of Visual Artists. It primarily represented the avant-garde artists' group Clara Mosch.

Private purchases and bequests

The most important privately owned pieces in Dessau, most of which had already been shown at the 1967 exhibition in Dessau, entered the Dessau Bauhaus collection via the Galerie am Sachsenplatz. Between 1977 and 1990, the WKZ or the Bauhaus Dessau acquired artworks—mainly furniture—from seven private individuals. Many of these pieces, including those belonging to Dessau artist Heinz Szillat (1977) and dance partners Herr and Frau Kammrath (1987), had been in everyday use for decades.[181] The first such purchase was of furniture designed by Marcel Breuer for the Dessau-Törten housing estate and made in the carpentry workshop in 1927: the deed of sale with Annemarie Michaelis is dated May 17, 1977. Two stools were bought from Ilse Horn in the same year. From Herr Spielmeyer, the Bauhaus Dessau purchased forty-nine original glass negatives with photographs by Erich Consemüller (1902–1957) and T. Lux Feininger (1910–2011), among others (deed of sale from December 9, 1986).

Private individuals also soon directly approached the WKZ with offers to sell or donate their possessions. The first offer of donation (photographs and magazines from the Bauhaus period) came from Dresden in November 1976 via the Dessau City Council. It was brought to the attention of "the architectural custodians of the Bauhaus Dessau, Prof. Selmanagić and Prof. Püschel." The donor had evidently seen media reports of the upcoming celebrations to mark the fiftieth anniversary of the Bauhaus Dessau. Steel-tube chairs, magazines, and other documents were acquired from a private individual in 1981, while the same person sold the WKZ documents from the estate of Frau Elisabeth Hofer, the former domestic helper of the third Bauhaus director, Ludwig Mies van der Rohe.

During the settlement of the Jena household of the former secretary of the Staatliche Bauhochschule (State Building Academy) in Weimar, an entire furniture ensemble by Erich Dieckmann (1896–1944) was acquired along with the relevant papers. In 1988 the nephew of Dessau historian Bernhard Hesse donated an etching by Wassily Kandinsky, given to members of Friends of the Bauhaus as a gift in 1932.

There were also donations and purchases directly from Bauhauslers Walter Köppe, Albert Hennig, Walter Puff, Hubert Hoffmann, Irena Blühova, Hermann Klumpp (1902–1987), Carl Marx, and Walter Allner (1909–2006). These were often made in connection with an exhibition in the Bauhaus Building, as was the case for the 1986 Carl Marx exhibition, the 1988 exhibition with works by Albert Henning, and the exhibition devoted to New York resident Walter Allner. All three men personally visited the exhibitions held in their honor.

181 Four steel-tube chairs and a table were bought from Heinz Szillat in 1977; the Kammraths sold a set of tubular steel stools, among other things, in 1987.

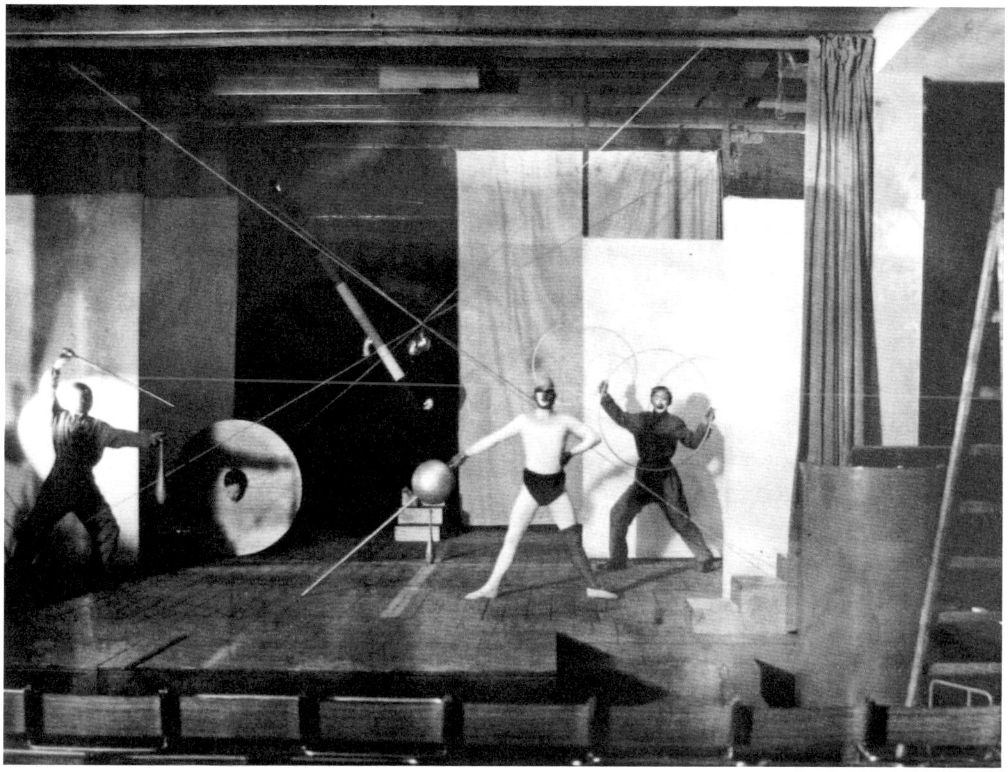

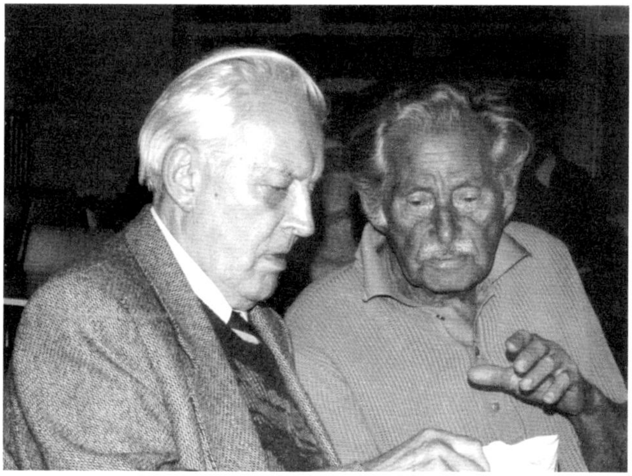

Fig. 55 Bauhaus dance *Equilibristik* (choreography: Oskar Schlemmer) on stage in the Bauhaus Building, modern print from the original glass negative. Photo: Erich Consemüller

Fig. 56 Albert Hennig and Carl Marx at the opening of the Albert Hennig exhibition in the Bauhaus Building, 1988

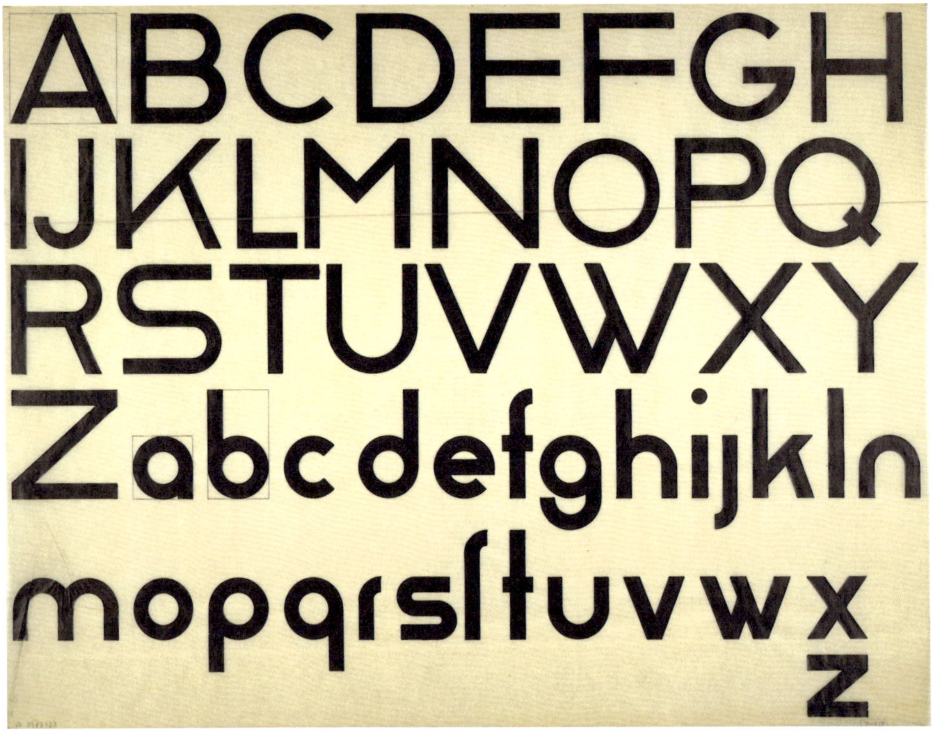

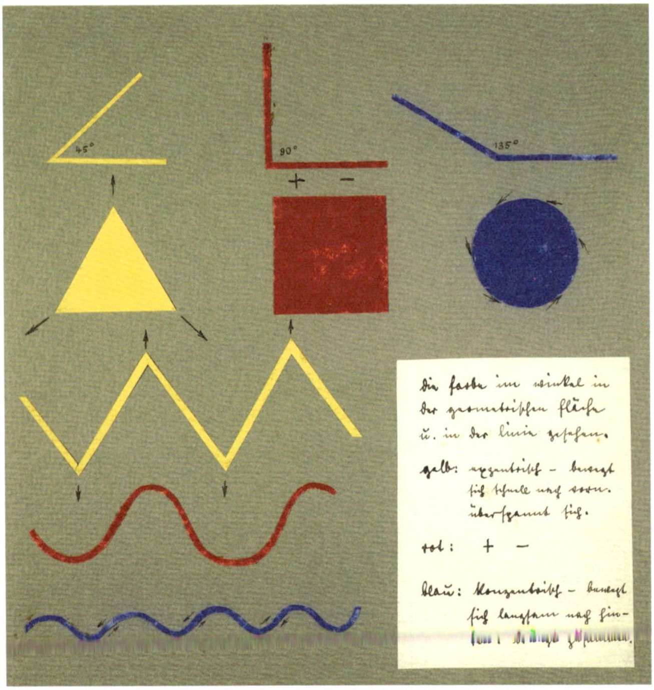

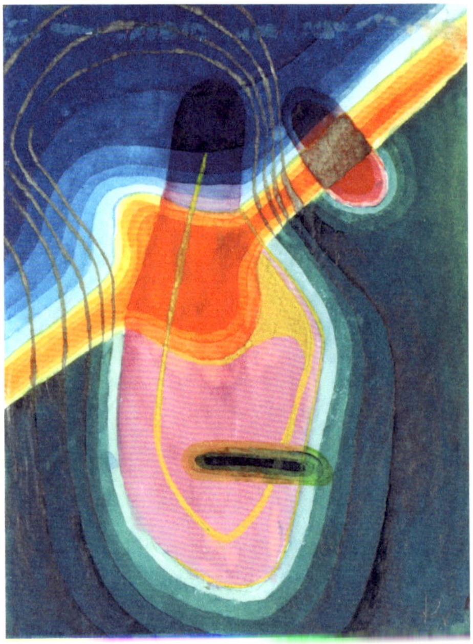

Fig. 57 Reinhold Rossig, draft of a grotesque typeface (exercise from the lessons with Joost Schmidt), 1929, pencil and ink on tracing paper

Fig. 58 Reinhold Rossig, *Die Farbe im Winkel, in der geometrischen Fläche und in der Linie gesehen* [The color in the angle, in the geometric surface and in line] (exercise from Wassily Kandinsky's lessons), 1929, tempera on paper, mounted on cardboard

Fig. 59 Erich Krause, *Untitled*, around 1930, watercolor and ink

The Erich Krause papers

The first coherent, more substantial addition to the collection from a Bauhausler's hand was the set of 300 preliminary course works, photographs, and artistic studies by Erich Krause (1909–1979). Dessau resident Frieda Bley discovered it in a bulging folder in the attic of her house in Fichtenbreite, where Erich Krause had apparently boarded while studying at the Bauhaus. She sold it to the WKZ Bauhaus Dessau. It bears unique testimony to the young man's special artistic and graphic gifts.

All that is known about Erich Krause, born in 1909, is that he studied at the Bauhaus between 1928 and 1930. After that he disappeared without a trace.

The Reinhold Rossig estate

Although the architect, civil engineer, and artist Reinhold Rossig (1903–1979) lived in the GDR, he barely played a role in the reception of the Bauhaus. It was not until 1976 that contact was made with the WKZ Bauhaus Dessau and the Hochschule für Architektur und Bauwesen in Weimar.

After finishing his apprenticeship, Reinhold Rossig started studying at the Königliche Kunstgewerbeschule (Royal School of Arts and Crafts) in Dresden before transferring to the local state building school and training to become a civil engineer. He studied at the Bauhaus in Dessau from 1929 to 1931, then returned to Dresden. In 1934 he was accused of making preparations for high treason, placed under arrest, and imprisoned at Bautzen. After his release in 1936, Rossig worked for a private architecture firm in Rostock and in 1938 continued this employment in Berlin. Following military service and wartime captivity, he returned to Germany in 1946. Until retiring in 1968, he worked for DEFA, the East German state-owned film studio, in Potsdam-Babelsberg and at the GDR Bauakademie in Berlin. He made paintings and drawings while still working as an architect.

After Rossig's death, his widow transferred her husband's estate in three stages. A first handover was made in 1979 to the Hochschule für Architektur und Bauwesen in Weimar; in November 1980 and Summer 1981, two further parts of the estate came to the WKZ. Finally, on September 24, 1981, a transfer agreement was reached with Waltraud Rossig. It stated: "The transfer of the artistic estate of Reinhold Rossig by Waltraud Rossig is occurring because the Hochschule für Architektur und Bauwesen Weimar, represented by department head Prof. Dr. Dr. Bernd Grönwald, and the Wissenschaftlich-Kulturelles Zentrum Bauhaus Dessau, represented by director Dr. Georg Opitz, have shown the keenest interest in the artistic oeuvre of Reinhold Rossig."

In the contract, the WKZ Bauhaus Dessau pledged to archive and catalogue the estate and make it accessible to the public. The means to do so were provided by the GDR Culture Fund. On November 19, 1981, Opitz declared that "in consultation with the Halle district Culture Department, the Hochschule für Architektur und Bauwesen Weimar (Faculty of Architecture), Frau Rossig/Berlin, Krautstrasse, the Culture Department of the Dessau City Council and the Wissenschaftlich-Kulturelles Zentrum Dessau (WKZ Bauhaus Dessau)," the allocated government funds had been used "to work on processing the Reinhold Rossig estate," that is, to pay for the three employees assigned the task. The employees in question were Folke Dietzsch (who worked at the WKZ from 1985), Heike Scheller, and Susanne Hofmann.

The estate contains more than 1,300 pages of drawings and graphic art, including architectural designs, as well as thirty-eight paintings and 307 documents.

The Franz Ehrlich estate

Like Reinhold Rossig, the architect, designer, and artist Franz Ehrlich (1907–1984) did not figure actively in the reception of the Bauhaus until after 1976, at first through the Galerie am Sachsenplatz and then also at the WKZ Bauhaus Dessau. The bequest of his estate resulted not least from the research undertaken by Lutz Schöbe for his honors thesis at the Humboldt-Universität Berlin. This is how on September 23, 1983, while Franz Ehrlich was still alive, the bulk of the artistic and architectural work he had produced to that point was transferred to the WKZ. On November 3, 1983, all his extant correspondence was handed over as well. Several pieces of furniture from his Berlin office went to the AiF design collection in Berlin. In the same month, the GDR Akademie der Wissenschaften (Academy of Sciences) also registered its interest in parts of Franz Ehrlich's estate. This prompted the Dessau City Council to host a meeting on January 17, 1984 aimed at sorting out the competing claims, albeit without yet arriving at a solution. On February 27, 1984, Bernd Grönwald stepped into the talks to resolve them in the WKZ's interest. In a letter from April 11, 1984 to Hannes Hörnig, director of the scientific division of the SED Central Committee, Grönwald offered to clear up the dispute, which was then evidently decided in the WKZ's favor. Additional individual art objects in private hands were donated to the WKZ. On June 26, 1985, arrangements were made with the widow for the last part of the estate to be bequeathed to the Dessau collection upon her death.

Franz Ehrlich came to the Bauhaus in Dessau in 1927 as a trained mechanical engineer. Following the obligatory preliminary course with László Moholy-Nagy and Josef Albers as well as classes with Paul Klee and Wassily Kandinsky, he attended Joost Schmidt's sculpture workshop where, among other things, he was involved in building architectural models for the Total Theater of Walter Gropius (1927/28). In 1930 Ehrlich attended the Bauhaus carpentry workshop. After Summer Semester 1930, he left the Bauhaus Dessau and worked initially as a furniture designer and commercial artist. Having completed his studies, Ehrlich founded Studio Z along with fellow Bauhaus graduates Fritz Winter and Heinz Loew.

As a member of the KPD (German Communist Party), banned since 1933, Ehrlich agitated against the Nazi regime from the underground. He was arrested in 1934 and thrown into prison, followed by a spell in Buchenwald concentration camp from 1937 to 1939. There he succeeded in drawing attention to his architectural abilities. This was how the SS came to commission designs for buildings from political prisoner Franz Ehrlich. Following his release from the camp, he continued working as an architect for the SS. In 1943 Ehrlich entered prison battalion 999 and ended up as a Yugoslav prisoner of war.

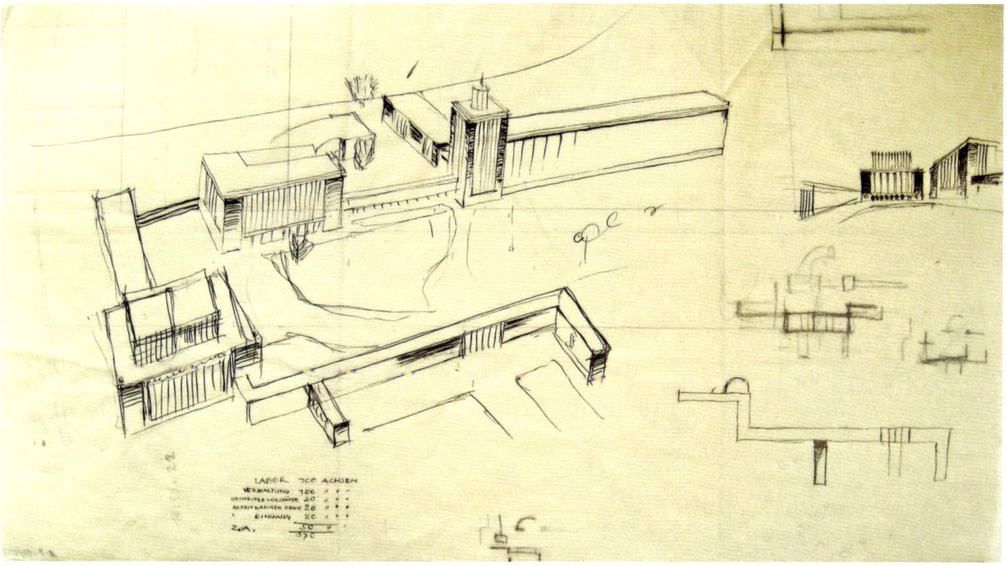

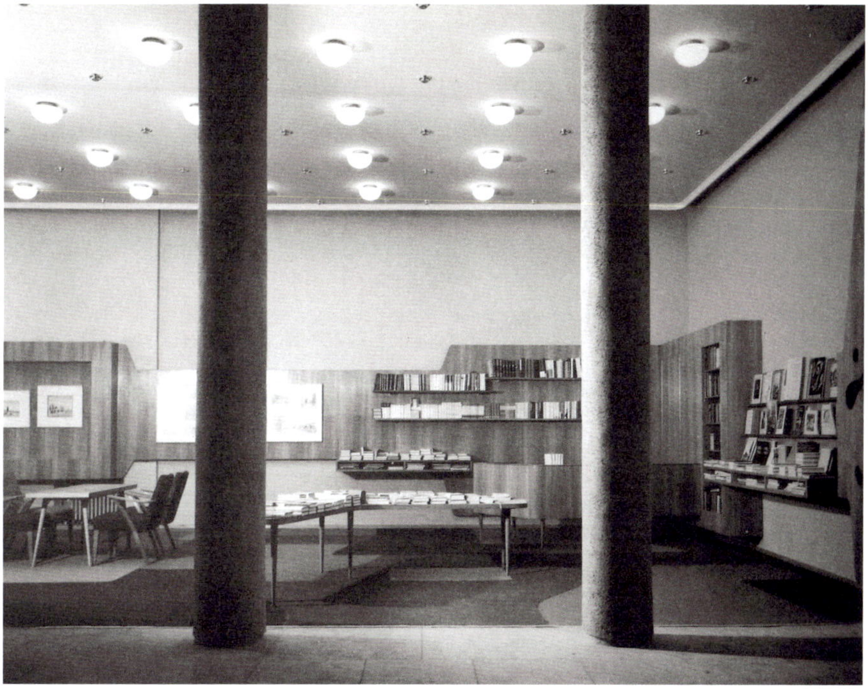

Fig. 60 Franz Ehrlich, preliminary design of the radio braodcast building complex Berlin-Nalepastraße, 1954, pencil and ink on tracing paper

Fig. 61 Franz Ehrlich, Library in the "Johannes R. Becher" Club of Creative Artists in Berlin, 1958

Following his return from captivity in 1946, Ehrlich worked as an architect and town planner in Dresden. He designed stands for "publicly owned Saxon enterprises" at postwar trade fairs in Leipzig and drew up plans for a university city in Leipzig. From 1950 to 1952, he was technical director at the industrial-design wing of the VVB (Vereinigung Volkseigener Betriebe, Association of Publicly Owned Enterprises) in Berlin. Alongside this, he worked on commission for the East German Foreign and Domestic Trade Ministry and as a furniture designer for VEB workshops in in Dresden-Hellerau. His most important project was designing and building the former radio center in Berlin's Nalepastrasse (1951–1956).

Of all the bequests made to the Stiftung Bauhaus collection, that of Franz Ehrlich is the largest. It contains 293 individual documents, more than 1,000 artistic works, 50 pieces of furniture, 2,650 photographs, more than 3,000 drawings, plans and other papers on architectural and design projects, and hundreds of newspaper and journal articles.

The Carl Fieger estate

Carl Fieger (1893–1960) was an architect and Bauhaus teacher. In 1925 he moved to Dessau as a thirty-year-old, working in Walter Gropius's office and teaching at the Bauhaus, which became the focus of his life after a period spent working for Peter Behrens and for Walter Gropius in Berlin and Weimar. It was in Dessau that he got to know his future wife, Dora, and built a house for them to live in once they had married. Apart from some gaps between 1930 and 1945, they lived there until his death in 1960 and his widow's death in 1966. It was here in Dessau that he carried out his most important projects: besides his house, the restaurant Kornhaus an der Elbe (1929/30). After the Nazis initially banned him from plying his trade, he found employment in the office of Werner March. From 1952 to 1953, Fieger worked at the Deutsche Bauakademie in East Berlin.

His estate comprises some 700 items, including architectural drawings, photographs, furniture, publications, and documents. He was a longstanding and close colleague to Walter Gropius, known above all for drawing the latter's architectural designs such as the Bauhaus Building, but he was also a reputable architect in his own right. Examples of his later work can also be found in his posthumous papers.

Although Dora Fieger had bequeathed her husband's estate to the Bauhaus Dessau, her will was unfortunately declared invalid, as it had been typed, not handwritten, and had not been certified by a notary. Negotiations over the purchase sum thus began with the heir, Wolfgang Sommer. The deed of transfer dates from December 13, 1988.

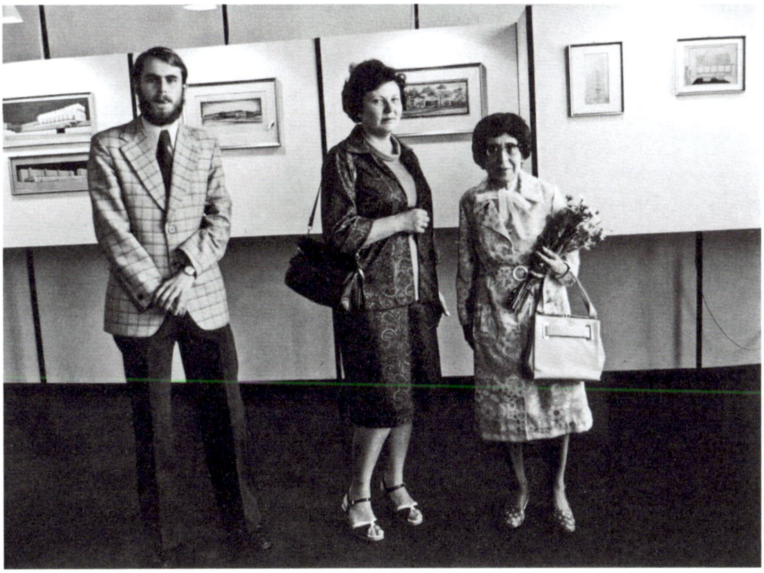

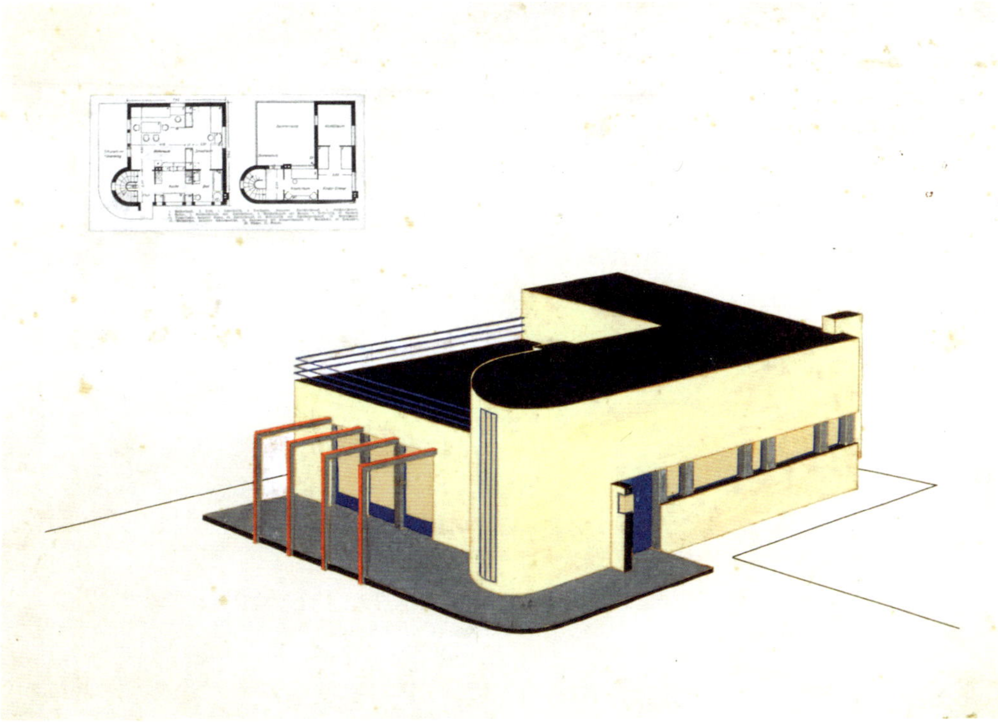

Fig. 62 Exhibition curator William Howarth, Dessau's Lord Mayor Thea Hauschild, and Dora Fieger at the Carl Fieger exhibition in the workshop wing of the Bauhaus Building, 1978

Fig. 63 Carl Fieger, *House Fieger*, 1926, tempera and ink over pencil on cardboard

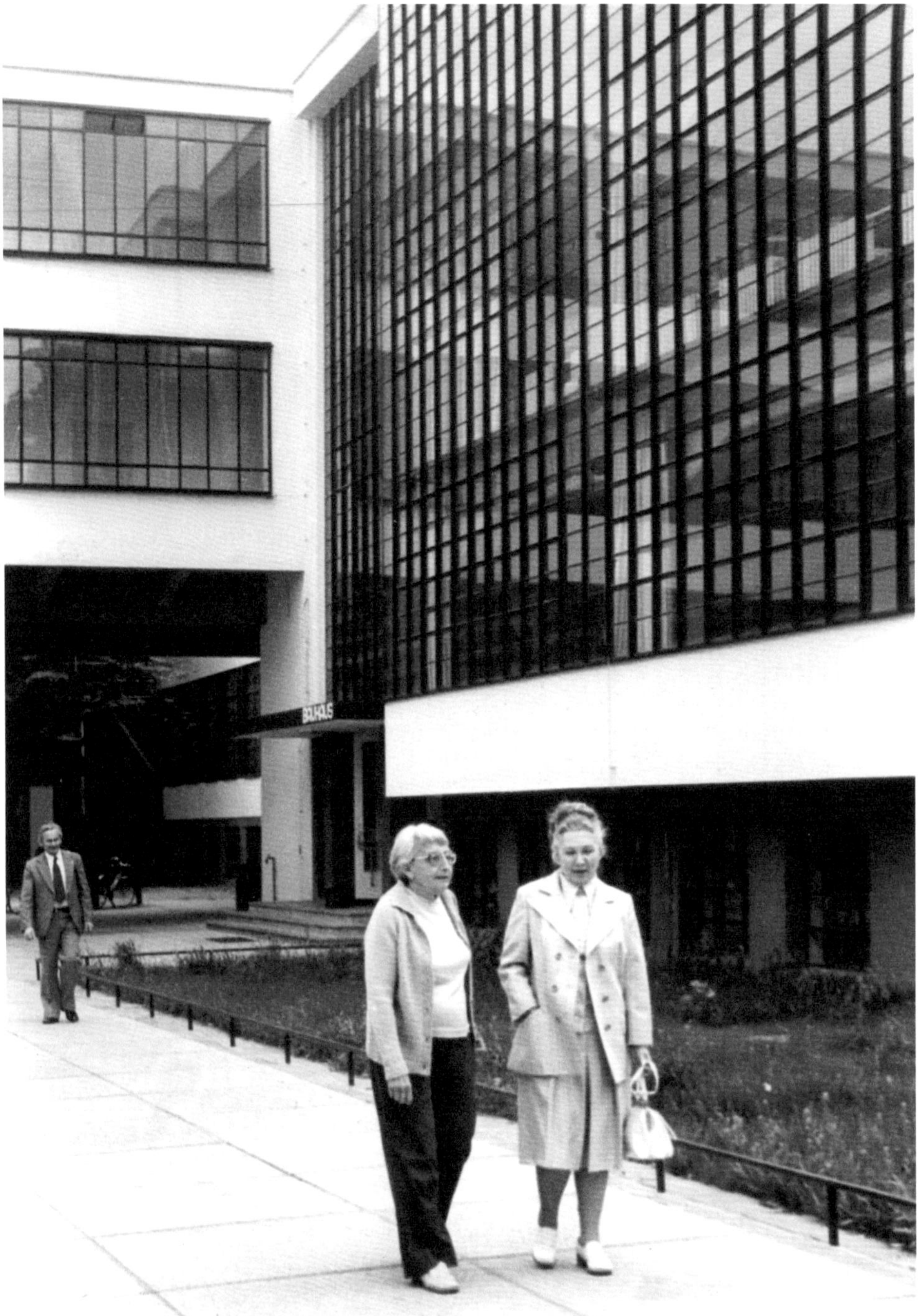

Fig. 64 Konrad Püschel (in the background), Lena Meyer-Bergner (front left), and Lilo Püschel in front of the Bauhaus Building, 1979

The Hannes Meyer partial estate

The process of acquiring Hannes Meyer's estate for the Dessau Bauhaus collection, which dragged on from 1981 to 1989, is particularly well suited to illustrating the ambitious strategy that lay behind the growth of the Dessau collection. It will therefore be examined here in some detail. As outlined above, Hannes Meyer (along with his creative legacy) had always been a more problematic figure in the GDR than the other two directors, largely due to the radically functionalist approach he adopted in most of his theoretical statements from the Bauhaus years. Hannes Meyer came under fire in the formalism debate for having denied architecture the status of an art form. Even in the mid-1960s, this was still the main reason why he was shunned in the GDR in favor of Gropius and Mies. In 1952, living in Switzerland and having long since distanced himself from his radical views, Hannes Meyer was pained by the attacks of his East German critics. He remarked with bemusement that he was "the only architect ... polemicized against over there" and professed outrage at the invective directed "against the bauhaus & my view of architecture in particular," as he wrote in a letter to a sympathetic ex-colleague.[182] In another letter to the same addressee, he wrote: "Bernau & my architecture are still stirring up a great deal of controversy. The Bauhaus is condemned, and my architecture and theory are seen as worse than those of Gropius."[183] A more nuanced approach to Hannes Meyer would have to wait until a reckoning with the Stalinist past. A number of former Bauhaus students working in the GDR also kept their distance from the second Bauhaus director, in contrast to their open admiration of Gropius or Mies.

By 1976, these assessments of Hannes Meyer had been turned on their head: with the comprehensive rehabilitation of the Bauhaus in recent articles on the topic, Hannes Meyer was now considered the most important Bauhaus director with the most to teach the present. As if history were playing a practical joke, the functionalist attitudes that had been distilled from his theoretical and practical work, having incurred such opprobrium twenty-five years earlier, were now largely what brought him back into favor. A new aspect came into play from 1980 onwards as several theorists discovered the "green" Hannes Meyer, the architect who urged caution in dealing with place and landscape. Hubert Hoffmann coined the term "green Bauhaus" in his final productive years.[184] Hubert Hoffmann had been forced to leave Dessau in 1947 and later resettled in Graz. From there he remained in friendly and supportive contact with the newly founded Bauhaus from 1976, but especially from 1986 and after 1990.

182 Hannes Meyer, letter to Kay B. Kulmala from April 24, 1952, Archive of the Bauhaus Dessau Foundation, Inv.-No. I 19157. Kay B. Adams (Kulmala after her marriage in 1951) worked with Hannes Meyer in Mexico from 1942 to 1947.

183 Hannes Meyer, letter to Kay B. Kulmala from January 31, 1952, Archive of the Bauhaus Dessau Foundation, Inv.-No. 19156. In the letter to Kulmala from December 20, 1952, Meyer reports that he had learned from Karola Bloch that the vice president of the Bauakademie, Edmund Collein, had publicly corrected previous statements about his views at a conference (Inv.-No. 19163). On January 8, 1953, Meyer wrote that he intended "to write to the Bauakademie in the near future": "A great purification is underway, as I have learned from various letters." (Inv.-No. 19165). He apparently never carried out this intention.

184 See Bauhaus Dessau Foundation (ed.), ... *das bauhaus zerstört* ..., Dessau 1996.

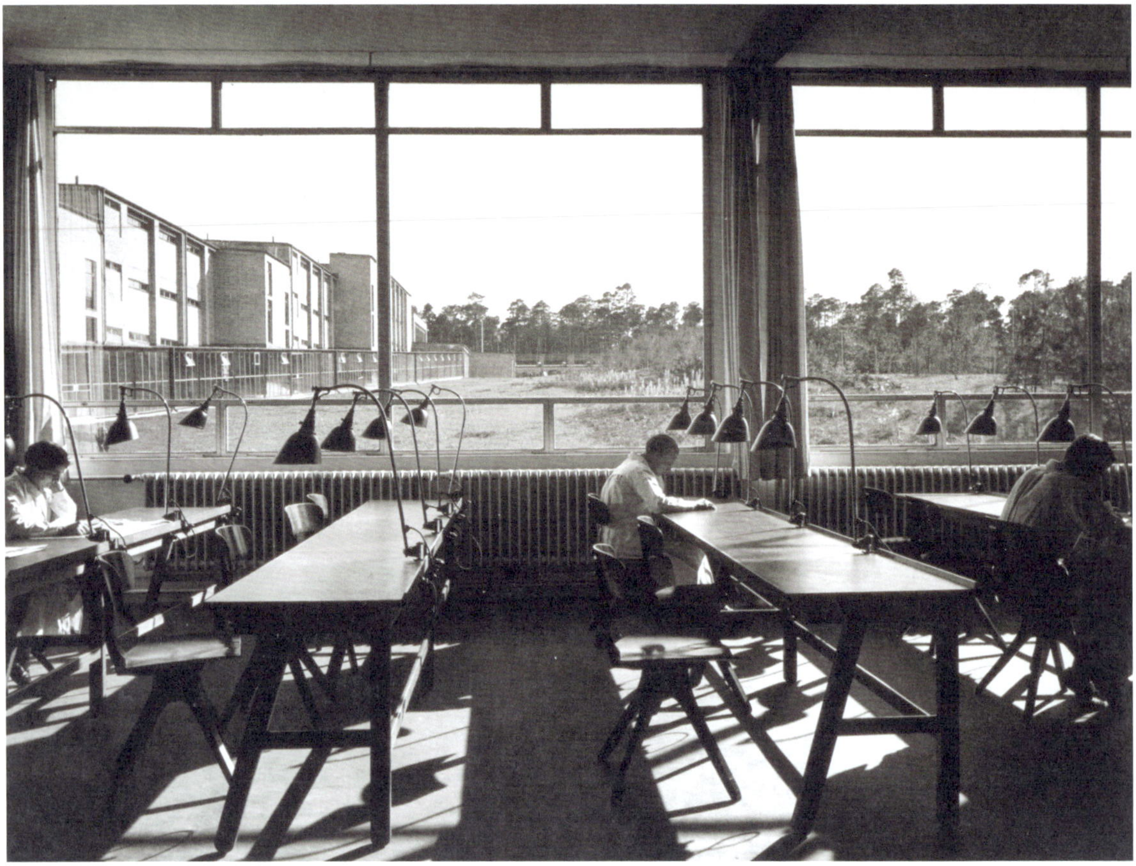

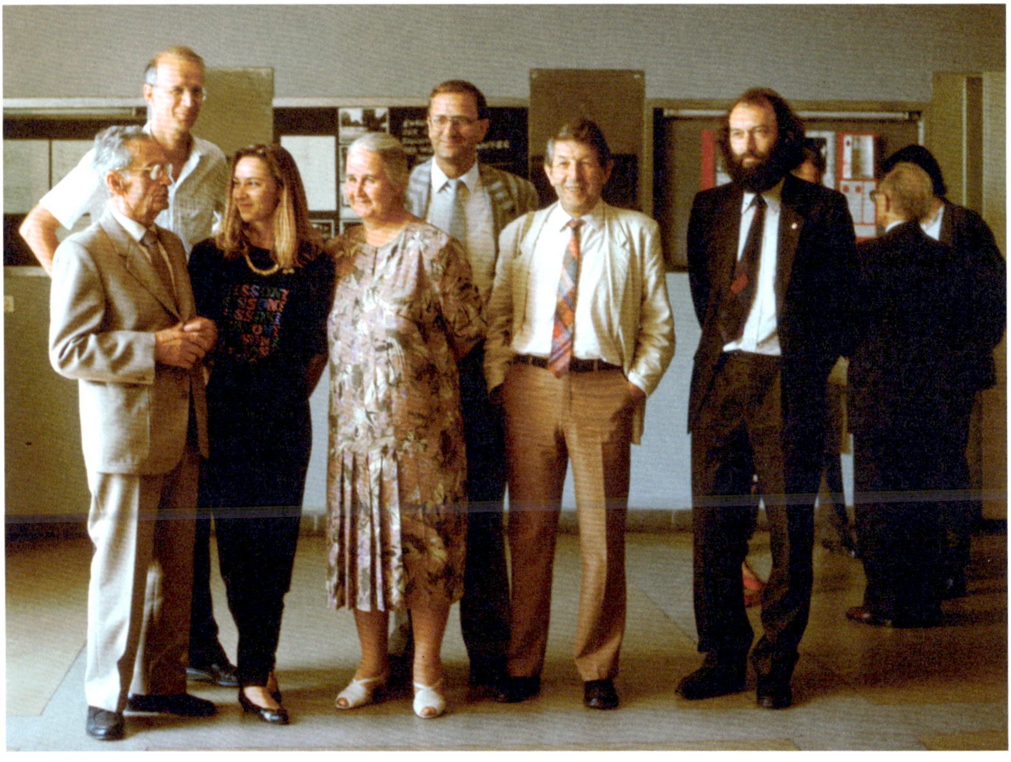

Fig. 65 Hannes Meyer and Hans Wittwer, Federal School of the ADGB in Bernau near Berlin, view from the library, 1930. Photo: Walter Peterhans

Fig. 66 Konrad Püschel (far left), Lilo Aniceto-Meyer (fourth from left), Bernd Grönwald (fifth from left), and Rolf Kuhn (seventh from left) in the Bauhaus Building, July 1, 1989

One of the Dessau collection's most important acquisitions was the part of Hannes Meyer's estate covering his time in Dessau, the Soviet Union, and Mexico. Even before 1976, Lena Meyer-Bergner had donated a selection of objects and documents to the Hochschule für Architektur und Bauwesen Weimar. After her death on January 23, 1981, there began a struggle for control of Hannes Meyer's estate that lasted until 1989, unbeknownst to the public and most workers at the Bauhaus Dessau until near the end. The key players in this struggle on the East German side were Konrad Püschel, Bernd Grönwald, and Klaus-Jürgen Winkler. Their excellent contacts with Claude Schnaidt were what made purchasing this estate possible in the first place. The fact that the GDR was prepared to provide the financial and other means (approval for official trips to Switzerland, etc.) needed to acquire the estate shows the strategic importance for research and for the Dessau collection that the strong-willed protagonists, particularly Grönwald, attributed to the work of the second Bauhaus director. In a letter to Claude Schnaidt from 1982, Grönwald wrote: "In my view, it is very important that we move quickly to secure the entire estate for the GDR, since we could then give significant weight internationally, for example, to the depositing of the Hannes Meyer estate in a refunctioned Bauhaus Dessau."[185] From the outset, Schnaidt was the central and most committed force in this process, which can only be related here in a very condensed form.

Initially, the ETH Zurich claimed for its own gta archive the part of the estate containing architectural plans, referring to an (unsigned) deed of sale with Lena Meyer-Bergner.[186] A little later, the heirs of Hannes Meyer's former partner, Hans Wittwer, asserted their rights to the projects drawn up by the two architects (St. Peter's School in Basel, 1926, Palace of Nations, 1926/27, and the ADGB Trade Union School building in Bernau, 1928–1930).[187] Lena Meyer-Bergner's son from before her marriage, now living in West Germany (Wolf Bergner), the two daughters from Hannes Meyer's first marriage living in Switzerland (Claudia Meyer and Livia Meyer-Klee), the son living in Mexico (Mario-Pierre Meyer), and the daughter of Hannes and Lena Meyer-Bergner living in Switzerland (Lilo Aniceto-Meyer) were long unable to reach agreement. The children from the first marriage favored Zurich as the destination for their father's estate, while Lena Meyer-Bergner and her children preferred Dessau.

Following their mother's death in autumn 1981, the latter were represented by Claude Schnaidt, Bernd Grönwald, and Konrad Püschel (acting, of course, on behalf of the relevant East German authorities), who were in turn represented by a Swiss attorney. Schnaidt had informed Grönwald and Püschel from the beginning that the estate should in his opinion "under no circumstances go to Zurich, but rather to Weimar."[188] All the points in

185 Bernd Grönwald, letter to Claude Schnaidt from June 25, 1982, Archiv des gta der ETH Zürich, Nachlass Claude Schnaidt, 187-2-53-3. I have Philipp Oswalt to thank for drawing my attention to this sheaf of posthumous papers and placing copies of the documents at my disposal.
186 Letter from the commissioned attorney's office to the Basel Estates Office from February 24, 1981, ibid.
187 Letter from the commissioned attorney's office to the Basel Estates Office from February 25, 1981, ibid.
188 Claude Schnaidt, letter to Bernd Grönwald and others, February 23, 1981, ibid.

dispute can be reconstructed from the voluminous documentation in Claude Schnaidt's posthumous papers at the ETH Zurich and from the invoices sent by the Swiss attorneys appointed by the GDR to acquire the portion of the estate labeled "abroad" for the Bauhaus Dessau.[189]

The longest delay occurred when Wolf Bergner, acting with the consent of some of the other heirs, took in trust all of the estate except the plans archive but then sold off parts of it without consulting anyone else, mainly to the newly established Deutsche Architektur Museum (DAM, German Architecture Museum) in Frankfurt am Main. This purchase by the DAM—it concerns almost exclusively the documents and photographs from Hannes Meyer's estate—was taken into consideration in the course of several legal processes and subsequent negotiations. On March 10, 1988 at the Basel Estates Office, Meyer's plans archive was split in precisely stipulated parts between Martin Kieren (ETH Zurich) on the one side and Rolf Kuhn (Bauhaus Dessau) and the attorney Stefan Hofer (Basel) on the other. The protocol, preserved in the archive of the Bauhaus Dessau Foundation, is signed by Werner Oechslin and Rolf Kuhn.[190] Both sides were guaranteed access and agreed to provide each other copies. The estate was then transferred from the East German embassy in Switzerland to Dessau via Austria and Czechoslovakia. Ever since, Dessau has housed the parts of the estate relating to the Bauhaus and to Meyer's time in the Soviet Union and in Mexico, while the Swiss part remains in Zurich.[191]

At a ceremony in Dessau on June 30, 1989, the chairman of the AiF, Martin Kelm, officially handed over the part of the estate earmarked for the Bauhaus Dessau, which had been archived over the previous months. The resulting exhibition in the Bauhaus Building was opened the next day by Bernd Grönwald in the presence of Bauhauslers such as Max Bill, Hubert Hoffmann, Philipp Tolziner (1906–1996), Konrad Püschel, and Carl Marx. It was the conclusion to the last Bauhaus colloquium in the GDR, dedicated to Hannes Meyer's hundredth birthday. On this July 1, 1989, the key figures involved in acquiring the estate finally met: Konrad Püschel, Claude Schnaidt, Bernd Grönwald, Lilo Aniceto-Meyer, and the two Swiss attorneys. An article on the Hannes Meyer estate in Dessau appeared in the journal *form + zweck*.[192]

In 1989, the processing of the parts of Hannes Meyer's estate located in East and West Germany and Switzerland led to what, to this day, remains the largest-ever exhibition on the second Bauhaus director. Scholarly articles were contributed by authors from both East and West.[193] Klaus-Jürgen Winkler's book *The Architect Hannes Meyer: His Work and Views* appeared in the GDR,[194] while

189 Solicitor's office Stein, Hofer, Schmid, Legal dispute concerning the Hannes Meyer's plans archive, fee note, efforts from 1982 to 1989, June 23, 1989, Basel; Archive of the Bauhaus Dessau Foundation.

190 Protocol concerning the handover of parts of the estate of Hannes Meyer on March 10, 1988 in the Basel Estates Office, ibid.

191 Lena Meyer-Bergner's estate was unaffected by the negotiations. It was offered and sold to the Bauhaus Dessau by Wolf Bergner in 1992.

192 Luise Schier, Nachlaß Hannes Meyer, in: *form + zweck* 4, 1989, 30–31.

193 Bauhaus-Archiv Berlin and Deutsches Architekturmuseum Frankfurt am Main (eds.), *Hannes Meyer. Architekt Urbanist Lehrer*, Berlin (West) 1989.

194 Klaus-Jürgen Winkler, *Der Architekt Hannes Meyer. Anschauungen und Werk*, Berlin 1989.

contributions from the section of the 1989 Bauhaus colloquium devoted to Hannes Meyer were compiled and published shortly after reunification. The exhibition "Hannes Meyer: Architect, Urbanist, Teacher," jointly organized by the German Architecture Museum Frankfurt am Main, the Bauhaus-Archiv Berlin and the ETH Zurich, was held from 1989 to 1990 in Frankfurt am Main, West Berlin and Zurich. The Bauhaus Dessau was one of the lenders. The fall of the Wall in November 1989 made possible an unexpected and unplanned fourth station: workers at the Bauhaus Dessau were delighted when they could present this exhibition in the Bauhaus Building in Dessau in June 1990, just before the GDR ceased to exist.[195]

The Konrad Püschel estate

Relations between the WKZ Bauhaus Dessau and the Bauhaus Dessau had been very close ever since the WKZ had been set up in 1976. Konrad Püschel had therefore decided early on not just to transfer his estate to the archive, but to organize it himself and provide relevant information. The estate was purchased in this condition in 1988 and 1989. A large part of the sum was contributed by the AiF.

Konrad Püschel learned the trade of a carpenter before enrolling at the Bauhaus Dessau in Winter Semester 1926/27. He was involved in projects such as the ADGB Trade Union School building in Bernau and the competition for the Berlin-Haselhorst estate as well as the houses with balcony access in the Dessau-Törten estate. In 1931 he moved to the USSR at Hannes Meyer's invitation, where he designed schools and technical training centers and worked as a town planner. In 1937 Püschel returned to Germany and resumed working as an architect. After wartime service and captivity, he returned to Germany once again in 1947. His subsequent career has already been outlined (see 2.3).

The estate consists of 800 pieces of correspondence, 400 graphic works, 140 architectural drawings, and hundreds more photographs, objects, and documents.

The Marianne Brandt collection

Marianne Brandt (1893–1983) was one of the most important Bauhaus and modern designers of the 1920s. Her artistic education began in 1921 in Weimar at a private art school. She then continued her studies at the Hochschule für Bildende Kunst in Weimar. In 1922 she embarked on a study trip with stays in Paris and the south of France. She arrived at the Staatliches Bauhaus in Weimar in 1923 before continuing her training at the Bauhaus in Dessau. In 1926 she designed the first light fittings for the Bauhaus Building in Dessau. The following year she directed experiments in lighting technique in the metal workshop. She left the Bauhaus at the end of 1929 and worked in Walter Gropius's architectural office. From 1930 to 1932 she led the design department at the metalware factory Ruppelwerk GmbH in Gotha. In 1933 she moved to Chemnitz and lived there in seclusion until 1945. From 1949 to 1954 she lectured at the Hochschule der Bildenden Künste in Dresden and

195 The exhibition ran from June 26 to August 26, 1990 in the Bauhaus Building in Dessau.

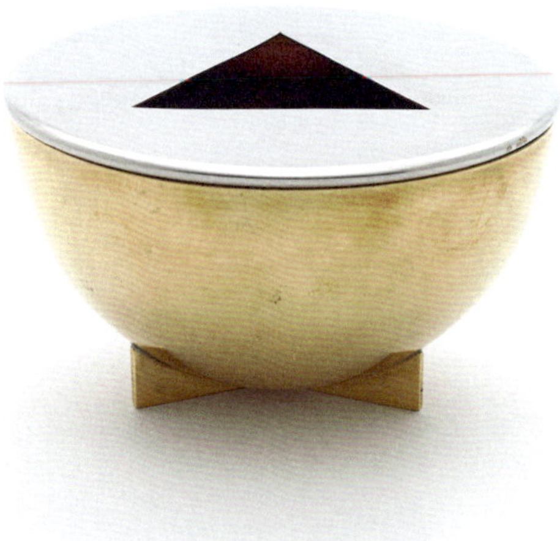

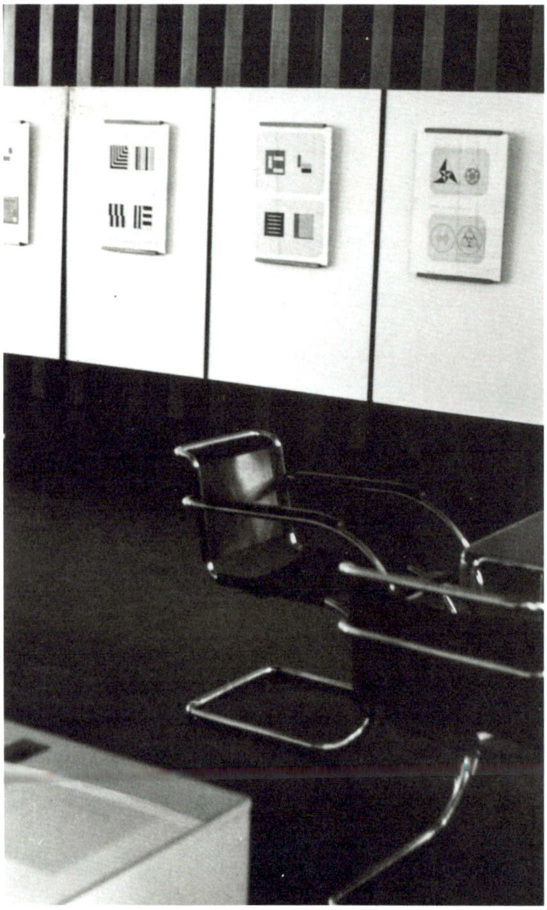

Fig. 67 Marianne Brandt, ashtray with triangular lid opening MT 36, 1924, donation by Karl Kasten, Dresden, 1977

Fig. 68 Exhibition of Konrad Püschel at the canteen of the Bauhaus Building, 1981

at the Hochschule für angewandte Kunst in Berlin-Weissensee.

The Marianne Brandt collection of artistic and design works and documents was handed over to the Bauhaus Dessau Foundation collection in successive installments and from various sources. Thus, on October 9, 1989, a gift of Brandt's works was made through the regional art center in Karl-Marx-Stadt, while in November 1989 another set of items was sold by Lieselotte Lange from Kirchberg.

The estate left behind by the Bauhaus student and worker consists of around 800 graphic works, paintings, drawings, objects, photographs, collages, and pieces of correspondence.

The Müller residence

The furniture from the Müller residence in Dessau represents a unique legacy with a special connection to Dessau. Its history begins in 1925, when Frieda Stepel, a young Dessau woman interested in art and music, first became aware of the Bauhaus, which had recently moved to Dessau. She first visited the school in 1927. In 1929 she decided to have her house in the town's northern suburbs furnished by the Bauhaus. With this in mind, she sought advice from Karl Bökenheide, director of the Bauhaus carpentry workshop. The process by which she subsequently filled her house with furniture and textiles from the Bauhaus can be reconstructed from numerous extant documents. Her home's furnishings initially comprised a music cabinet, a bookcase, and two chairs designed by Josef Albers. In 1930 she acquired a writing table, a cabinet with wooden doors and another with glass doors, three little nested tables, two armchairs, and a high-backed chair. Another visit to the Bauhaus Dessau, now accompanied by her boyfriend Otto Müller, was aimed at expanding their future joint household. In 1931, Frieda Stepel became a member of Friends of the Bauhaus. Following their marriage in 1932, the young couple Frieda and Otto Müller moved into a five-room apartment in the north of Dessau. Almost the entire apartment was now furnished with Bauhaus pieces. In the end there was a music room, a library, a dining room, a bedroom, and a kitchen.

A first set of documents and furniture was bought from Frau Müller in 1989, followed by a second group purchase in 1990. In 1996, after her death, the Bauhaus Dessau Foundation received further Bauhaus furniture from the same apartment as a donation as the result of an estate regulation made in 1994.

The Walter Allner collection

Dessau-born designer and artist Walter Allner studied at the Bauhaus Dessau from 1927 to 1930. After his studies he worked as a graphic designer, including as an assistant to Dutch typographer Piet Zwart. From 1933 to 1945 he lived and worked in France, then in Switzerland and from 1949 in New York, becoming a US citizen in 1957. Allner was highly productive as a graphic designer: he worked for many years as art director of *Fortune* magazine and was a member of many national and international graphic design associations. Along with his extensive work as a graphic designer, he also devoted himself to painting and graphic art.

Walter Allner resumed contact with his hometown and place of study on February 13,

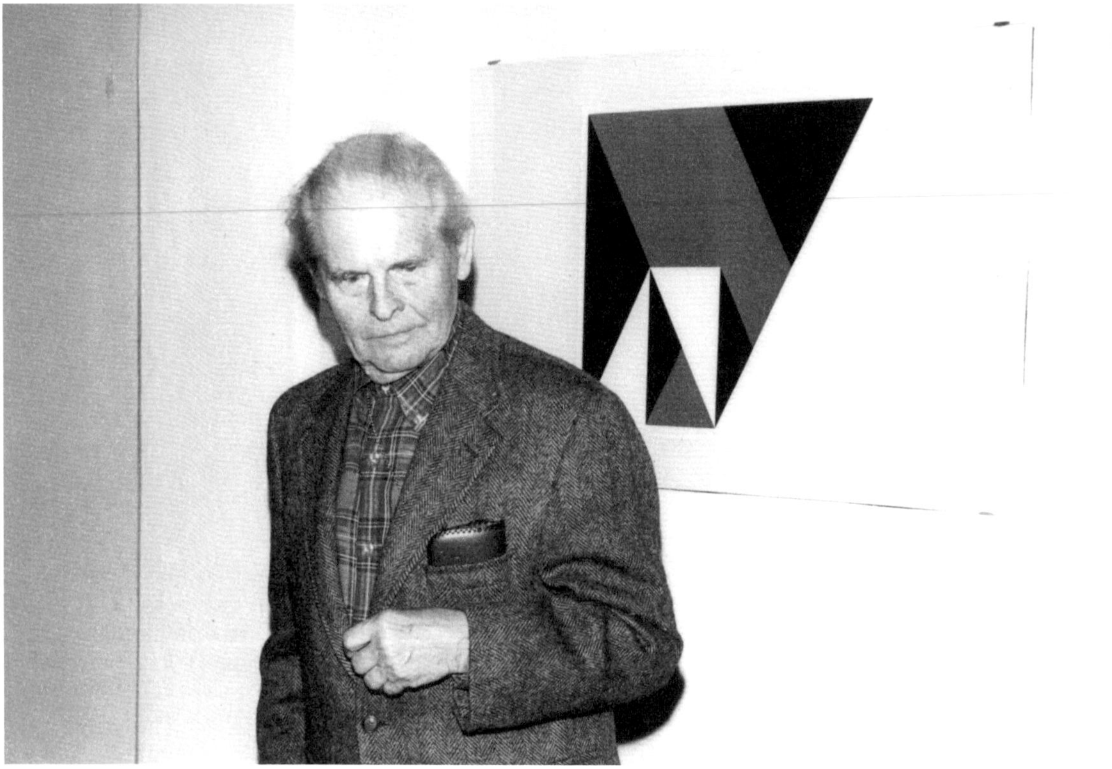

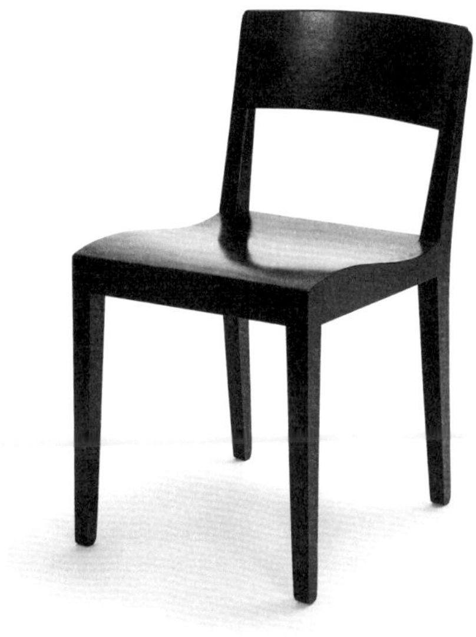

Fig. 69 Walter Allner in the Bauhaus Building, November 1989
Fig. 70 Martin Decker, (design) chair ti 201 from the apartment Müller, 1928 (draft), maple, stained

1978 with a letter to the then mayor of Dessau, Thea Hauschild. In the same year he donated a first painting to the WKZ Bauhaus Dessau. Several visits to Dessau and Weimar ensued, and Allner began a long-standing correspondence with the WKZ's director, Georg Opitz, continued after his retirement by Lutz Schöbe. Walter Allner's network, as documented in the surviving correspondence, included Herbert Bayer, Konrad Püschel, Dora Fieger, and Heinz Hirdina, among others. In 1985 he came into contact with journalist Michael Grüning, who exploited his connections at the East German Ministry of Culture to begin making a film about Walter Allner shortly afterward.

Walter Allner regularly sent prints of his own designs, such as title pages of *Fortune* magazine, to the Bauhaus Dessau. He proposed that this material be used as the basis for an exhibition at the Bauhaus Dessau. Following a visit by Michael Grüning to Walter Allner in New York, Grüning wrote on May 22, 1989 to the director of the Bauhaus Dessau, Rolf Kuhn, announcing a further donation of typographical and other works. Grüning also recommended putting on an exhibition to coincide with the artist's eightieth birthday that autumn. In August 1989 the Bauhaus Dessau accepted the recommendation and set about organizing the exhibition within a tight time frame. On November 3, 1989, amid all the protests and turmoil of the Peaceful Revolution and only a few days before the fall of the Berlin Wall, the exhibition "Walter Allner: Graphic Design from the USA" was opened in the presence of Allner, who had been invited as a guest of the East German Ministry of Culture. He had produced a screen print in a limited edition of 100 copies which was available for purchase during the exhibition.

Besides the extant correspondence from 1978 to 2006, the Walter Allner collection contains three paintings, several screen prints, and around 100 prints.

Conclusion

Between 1977 and 1990, the Dessau Bauhaus collection grew to around 6,000 objects. It was initially accommodated in two small rooms in the basement of the workshop wing. Three larger rooms on the ground floor were added in 1984, followed by additional rooms at the basement level from 1987. The objects were secure, but not temperature-controlled. At times, construction work and careless handling of materials during removal gave cause for concern. Air conditioning was finally installed in 2000.

From 1987, the collection was strengthened through the employment of new staff: architect Luise Schier bore particular responsibility for architecture-related holdings (she inventoried the estates of Carl Fieger and Hannes Meyer), while archivist Ines Hildebrand and furniture restorer Rüdiger Messerschmidt were placed in overall charge of archival work.

The collection was not sheltered from the winds of change that swept through East Germany in the autumn of 1989. In the same week in November 1989 that saw the opening of the Wall in Berlin, the Bauhaus Dessau hosted an international seminar from which the idea of an Industrial Garden Kingdom (Industrielles Gartenreich) was born—an idea that endured beyond the process of reunification and would guide the Bauhaus Dessau (from 1994: Bauhaus Dessau Foundation) throughout the next decade.

In 1990 the future of the Bauhaus Dessau as a "cultural lighthouse" was secured by the Federal Republic of Germany and the newly established state of Saxony-Anhalt. This not only guaranteed the continued existence of the collection; it also led to improved storage conditions. The government of Saxony-Anhalt, in particular, earmarked funds for further acquisitions, the most important and extensive of which was undoubtedly the Bröhan collection. At an auction in London in October 1991, the government of Saxony-Anhalt successfully bid for around 250 pieces of European design and art history—many of them one of a kind—produced between 1890 and the late 1930s. With objects from the Wiener Werkstätte, the artists' colony Mathildenhöhe, the Deutscher Werkbund and the Dutch De Stijl movement, a new note was sounded in the collection. Gaps in the collection were filled with the purchase of steel-tube furniture based on designs by Ludwig Mies van der Rohe and Marcel Breuer as well as paintings, watercolors, and well-preserved prints by individual Bauhaus artists.

In 1994 the Bauhaus Dessau Foundation was established under the aegis of the Federal Republic of Germany and the state of Saxony-Anhalt. Its declared goal was to make "the message sent out by the Bauhaus of the 1920s, which lives on today as the Bauhaus idea," the reference point and yardstick for contemporary work.[196] The collection had been given a secure anchorage. Today it contains over 50,000 items.

196 "Satzung der Bauhaus Dessau Foundation," in: *Ministerialblatt für das Land Sachsen-Anhalt* 15, no. 12, Magdeburg, March 29, 2005, 175–176.

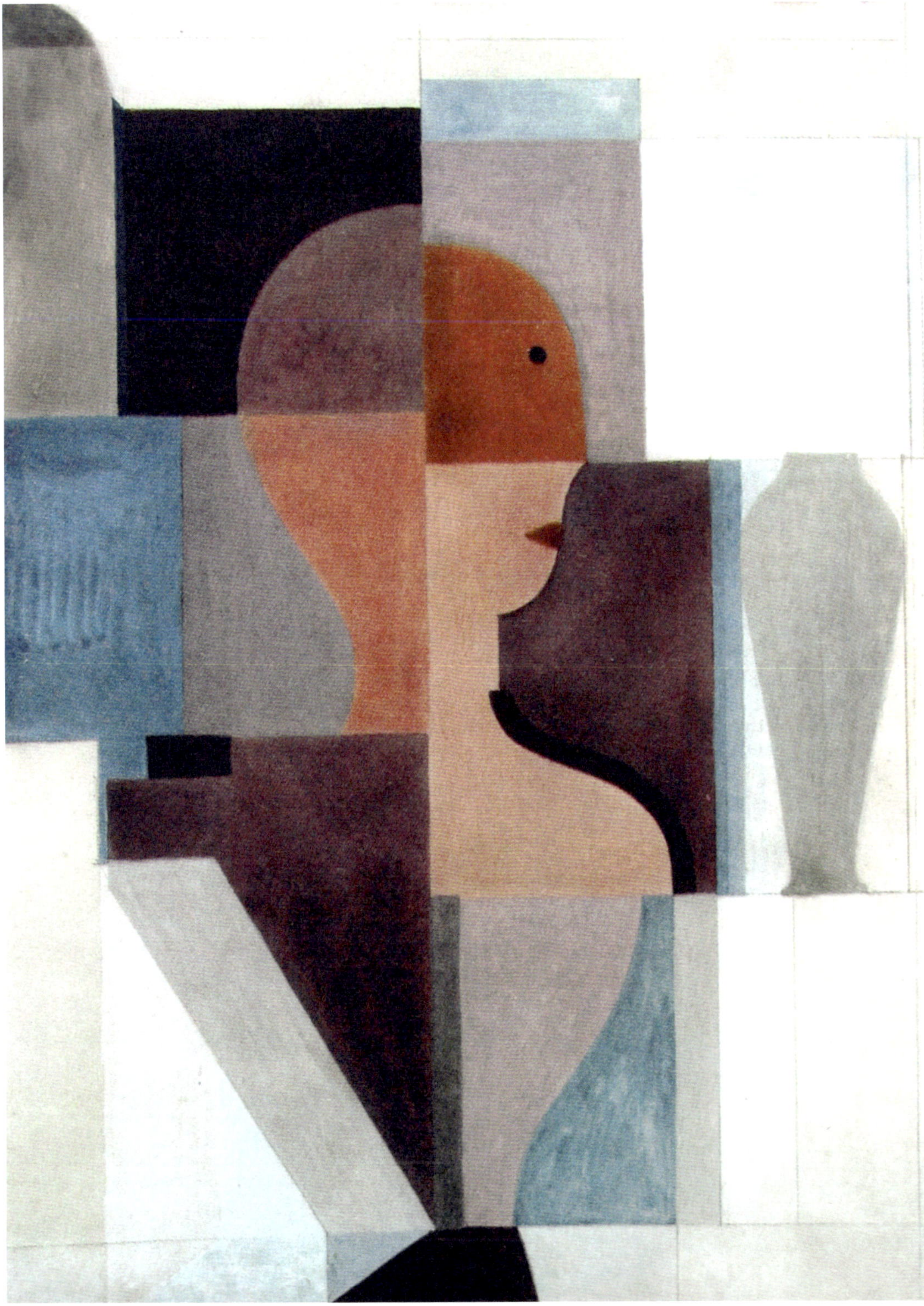

Fig. 71 Oskar Schlemmer, *Geteilte Halbfigur nach rechts* [Split half-length figure to the right], 1923, gouache over pencil on laid paper

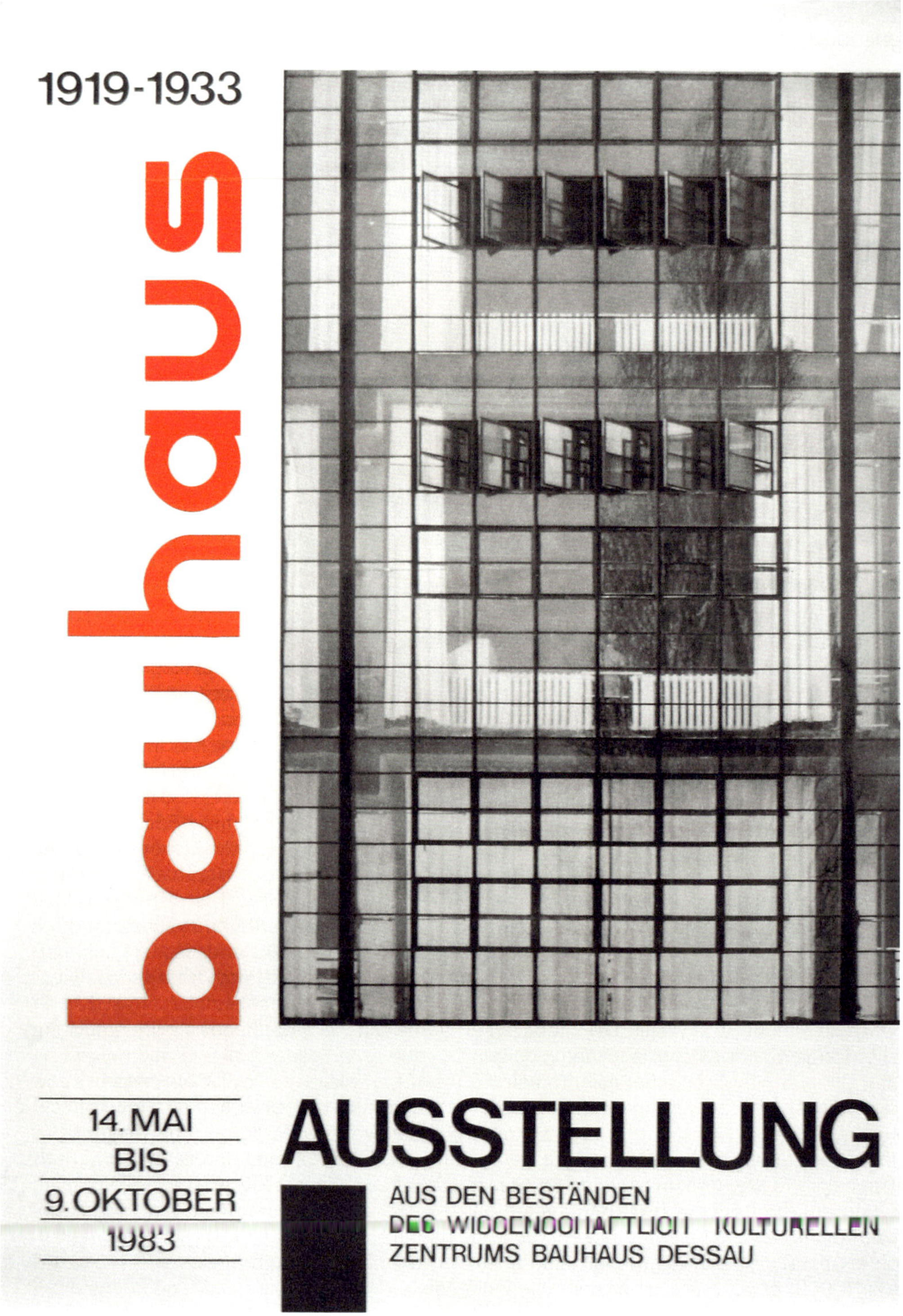

Fig. 72 Poster of the exhibition of the WKZ Bauhaus Dessau, 1983

5 WKZ Bauhaus Dessau/ Bauhaus Dessau Exhibitions from 1977 to 1990 with Exhibits from the Collection

12/4/1976 – April 1979
Das progressive Erbe des Bauhauses und die Entwicklung von Städtebau, Architektur und Formgestaltung in der DDR

12/17/1977 – 3/26/1978
Bauhaus-Grafik

6/17/1978 – 9/15/1978
Carl Fieger – Leben und Werk

12/17/1978 – March 1983
Werkstattarbeiten des Bauhauses

Oct. 1979 – Sept. 1986
Bauhaus Weimar – Dessau – Berlin

9/13/1980 – 10/5/1980
Arbeiten aus den Werkstätten des Bauhauses Weimar, Dessau, Berlin 1919–1933
Exhibition in Bytom, Poland

11/20/1980 – 11/30/1980
Bauhaus Weimar, Dessau, Berlin 1919–1933
Exhibition in Warsaw

6/20/1981 – August 1981
Konrad Püschel – Studienarbeiten am Bauhaus Dessau 1926–1930

11/15/1981 – 12/9/1981
Reinhold Rossig

12/19/1981 – 2/28/1982
Carl Marx – Malerei, Grafik

3/16/1982 – 4/9/1982
Bauhaus Weimar, Dessau, Berlin 1919–1933
Exhibition in Budapest

5/14/1983 – 10/2/1983
Bauhaus 1919–1933
Exhibition with works from the Bauhaus Dessau collection as illustrations

11/12/1983 – 1/17/1984
Gyula Pap – ein ungarischer Bauhausmaler

1/1/1984 – 1/14/1984
Bauhaus Weimar, Dessau, Berlin 1919–1933
Exhibition in Prague

April 1984 – Sept. 1984
Werkstattarbeiten und freie Grafik aus der Bauhauszeit

3/8/1985–3/28/1985
Bauhaus Dessau 1926–1932
Exhibition in Bari, Italy

8/3/1985 – 9/15/1985
Bauhaus Textiles (tessitura del bauhaus)
Exhibition in Pesaro, Italy

12/14/1985 – 2/16/1986
Bauhaus Textiles (tessitura del bauhaus)
Exhibition in Capri, Italy

5/16/1985 – 6/23/1985
Bauhaus Dessau 1925–1932
Exhibition in Kastrup, Denmark

6/28/1985 – 8/11/1985
Bauhaus Dessau 1925–1932
Exhibition in Randers, Denmark

Sept. 1985 – 11/28/1985
Antifaschistische Grafik und Malerei der Bauhäusler Franz Ehrlich und Reinhold Rossig

8/14/1986 – 10/21/1986
Carl Marx – Malerei und Grafik

12/10/1986 – June 1988
Bauhaus 1919–1933
Permanent exhibition

1/31/1987 – 5/17/1987
Zur Entwicklung des Stahlrohrstuhls

9/12/1987 – 3/20/1988
Franz Ehrlich 1907–1984. Kunst und Gestaltung

10/5/1988 – 11/27/1988
Albert Hennig – Malerei, Grafik, Foto

6/20/1989 – 7/31/1989
Hannes Meyer. Plannachlass

Nov. 1989 – Dec. 1989
Walter Allner

1/31/1990 – March 1990
Bauhaus Dessau
Exhibition in the GDR Cultural Center in Paris

3/27/1990 – 4/22/1990
Wilhelm Wagenfeld zum 90. Geburtstag

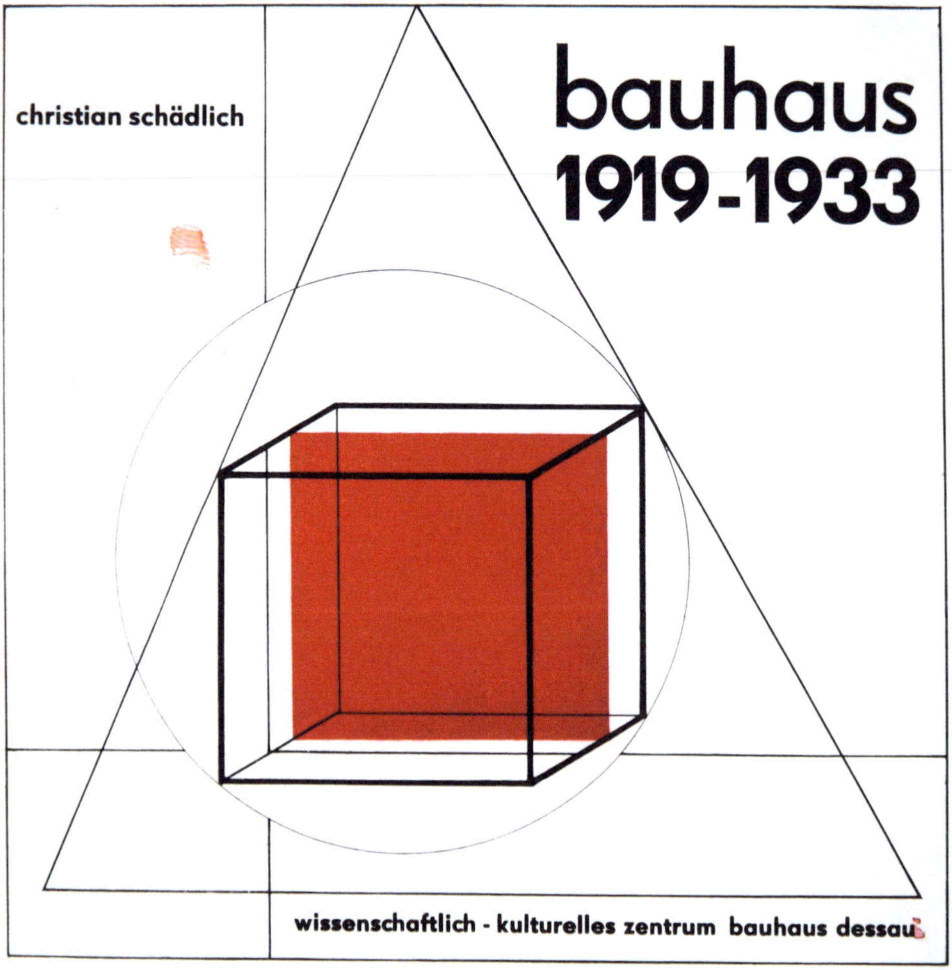

Fig. 73 Cover of the brochure of the WKZ Bauhaus Dessau: Christian Schädlich, *bauhaus 1919-1933*, 1983

Image credits

Fig. 1 © Bauhaus Dessau Foundation, Inv. no. I 17225,1-5 D
2 © Photo: Wolfgang Thöner (2004)
3 © Federal Archives (Image 183-27387-0001), Photo: Klein
4 © Photo: Wolfgang Thöner (2018)
5 © Photo: Wolfgang Thöner (1999)
6 © Private archive
7 © Bauhaus Dessau Foundation, Inv. no. I 2294 G / Image by Google
8 © City archive Dessau-Roßlau, Photo: unknown
9 Fig. from: City of Dessau (ed.), *Dessau,das Bauhaus und die Familie Harksen*, Dessau 2004, Photo: unknown
10 Fig. from: City of Dessau (ed.), *Dessau, das Bauhaus und die Familie Harksen*, Dessau 2004, Photo: unknown
11 © Bauhaus Dessau Foundation, Püschel estate, Inv. no. I 18584/24 F, Photo: unknown, © (Püschel, Konrad) Community of heirs of Konrad Püschel
12 © Zentralinstitut für Gestaltung
13 © Albers, Josef. The Josef and Anni Albers Foundation / VG Bild-Kunst, Bonn 2019
14 © Anhaltische Gemäldegalerie Dessau, Photo: Hajo Rose, © (Rose, Hajo/Mies van der Rohe, Ludwig/ Feininger, Lyonel) VG Bild-Kunst, Bonn 2019
15 © Anhaltische Gemäldegalerie Dessau, Photo: Hajo Rose, © (Rose, Hajo) VG Bild-Kunst, Bonn 2019
16 © Bauhaus Dessau Foundation, Püschel estate, Inv. no. I 9944 F, Photo: unknown
17 © Bauhaus Dessau Foundation, Püschel estate, Inv. no. I 11555 F, Photo: unknown
18 © Bauhaus Dessau Foundation, Püschel estate, Inv. no. I 9931 F, Photo: unknown
19 © Bauhaus Dessau Foundation, Püschel estate, Inv. no. I 11561 F, Photo: unknown
20 © Bauhaus Dessau Foundation, Photo: unknown
21 Photo: unknown, © (Gropius, Walter/Brandt, Marianne) VG Bild-Kunst, Bonn 2019
22 © (Pap, Gyula) VG Bild-Kunst, Bonn 2019
23 © Photo: Hajo Rose, © (Rose, Hajo/ Brandt, Marianne/Mies van der Rohe) VG Bild-Kunst, Bonn 2019
24 © Stiftung Bauhaus Dessau SBD, I 43083 F, Photo: Hajo Rose, © (Rose, Hajo/Brandt, Marianne) VG Bild-Kunst, Bonn 2019
25 © (Reichardt, Margaretha (Grete)) Kaiser, Gisela
26 © Galerie am Sachsenplatz
27 © (Ehrlich, Franz) Community of heirs of Franz Ehrlich
28 © Photo: Ulrich Windoffer, © (Marcks, Gerhard) VG Bild-Kunst, Bonn 2019
29 © Bauhaus Dessau Foundation, Inv. no. I 43162 F, Photo: unknown, © (Rose, Hajo) VG Bild-Kunst, Bonn 2019
30 © Photo: Ulrich Windoffer, © (Ehrlich,Franz) Community of heirs of Franz Ehrlich
31 © Photo: Hajo Rose, © (Rose, Hajo) VG Bild-Kunst, Bonn 2019 © (Ehrlich, Franz) Community of heirs of Franz Ehrlich
32 © Photo: Ernst Goldberg, © (Ehrlich, Franz) Community of heirs of Franz Ehrlich
33 © Photo: Hajo Rose, © (Rose, Hajo) VG Bild-Kunst, Bonn 2019 © (Ehrlich, Franz) Community of heirs of Franz Ehrlich
34 © Bauhaus Dessau Foundation, Inv. no. 11295 F, Photo: Ernst Steinkopf
35 © Bauhaus Dessau Foundation, Inv. no. I 2581/2 D
36 © Bauhaus University Weimar, Archiv der Moderne, Photo: unknown, © (Gropius, Walter) VG Bild-Kunst, Bonn 2019
37 © Bauhaus Universtity Weimar, Archiv der Moderne, Photo: unknown, © (Gropius, Walter) VG Bild-Kunst, Bonn 2019
38 © Bauhaus DessauFoundation, Photo: Peter Kühn, Dessau
39 © Bauhaus Dessau Foundation, Photo: unknown, © (Gropius, Walter) VG Bild-Kunst, Bonn 2019
40 © (Brandt, Marianne) VG Bild-Kunst, Bonn 2018
41 © (Gropius, Walter) VG Bild-Kunst, Bonn 2019
42 © Bauhaus Dessau Foundation, Photo: Peter Kühn, Dessau (1987), © (Gropius, Walter) VG Bild-Kunst, Bonn 2019
43 © Bauhaus Dessau Foundation, Photo: Peter Kühn
44 © Bauhaus Dessau Foundation, Photo: Peter Kühn, © (Gropius, Walter) VG Bild-Kunst, Bonn 2019
45 © Photo: Wolfgang Thöner, © (Gropius, Walter) VG Bild-Kunst, Bonn 2019
46 © Photo: Wolfgang Thöner, © (Gropius, Walter) VG Bild-Kunst, Bonn 2019
47 © Photo: Wolfgang Thöner, © (Gropius, Walter) VG Bild-Kunst, Bonn 2019
48 © Photo: Fritz Barthel
49 © Bauhaus Dessau Foundation, Inv. no. I 682 G, © (Feininger, Lyonel), VG Bild-Kunst, Bonn 2019
50 © Bauhaus Dessau Foundation, Inv. no. I 680 G, © (Brandt, Marianne), VG Bild-Kunst, Bonn 2019
51 © Bauhaus Dessau Foundation, Inv. no. I 705 G, © (Rose, Hajo) VG Bild-Kunst, Bonn 2019 / Image by Google
52 © Bauhaus Dessau Foundation, Inv. no. I 853 T, © (Reichardt, Margaretha (Grete)) Kaiser, Gisela
53 © Bauhaus Dessau Foundation, Inv. no. I 462 G / Image by Google
54 © Bauhaus Dessau Foundation, Inv. no. I 348/3-7 M
55 © Bauhaus Dessau Foundation, Inv. no. I 14307 G, Photo: Erich Consemüller, © (Consemüller, Erich) Consemüller, Stephan, © (Gropius, Walter) VG Bild-Kunst, Bonn 2019
56 © Photo: Wolfgang Thöner, © (Gropius, Walter) VG Bild-Kunst, Bonn 2019
57 © Bauhaus Dessau Foundation, Inv. no. I 67 G, © (Rossig, Reinhold) Ross, Rowland / Image by Google
58 © Bauhaus Dessau Foundation, Inv. no. I 6184/5 G, © (Rossig, Reinhold) Ross, Rowland / Image by Google
59 © Bauhaus Dessau Foundation, Inv. no. 452 G
60 © Bauhaus Dessau Foundation, Inv. no. 33405 G, © (Ehrlich, Franz) Community of heirs of Franz Ehrlich / Image by Google
61 © Bauhaus Dessau Foundation, Inv. no. I 12880 F, © (Ehrlich, Franz) Community of heirs of Franz Ehrlich, Photo: Friedrich Weimer, © (Weimer, Friedrich) Deutsche Fotothek
62 © Bauhaus Dessau Foundation, estate Fieger, Photo: Ernst Steinkopf, © (Gropius, Walter) VG Bild-Kunst, Bonn 2019
63 © Bauhaus Dessau Foundation, Inv. no. 17363 / Image by Google
64 © Bauhaus Dessau Foundation, estate Püschel, Inv. no. 11590 F, Photo: unknown
65 © Bauhaus Dessau Foundation, Inv. no. I 1687 F, © (Peterhans, Walter) Museum Folkwang, Essen, © (Meyer, Hannes) Community of heirs of Hannes Meyer, © (Wittwer, Hans) Wittwer, Sandra / Image by Google
66 © Photo: Wolfgang Thöner, © (Gropius, Walter) VG Bild-Kunst, Bonn 2019
67 Bauhaus Dessau Foundation, Inv. no. I 104 M, © (Brandt, Marianne (born Liebe)) VG Bild-Kunst, Bonn 2019, Photo: Binsack, Gunter, 2018
68 © Bauhaus Dessau Foundation, Püschel estate, Inv. no. 11037 F, © (Püschel, Konrad) Community of heirs of Konrad Püschel, © (Gropius, Walter) VG Bild-Kunst, Bonn 2019
69 © Photo: Wolfgang Thöner, © (Gropius, Walter) VG Bild-Kunst, Bonn 2019
70 © Bauhaus Dessau Foundation, Inv. no. I 7560 M, Foto: Esther Hoyer, 2018
71 © Bauhaus Dessau Foundation, Inv. no. I 7420 G / Image by Google
72 © Bauhaus Dessau Foundation
73 © Bauhaus Dessau Foundation

Cover: Hajo Rose, *Montage Selbstporträt* [montage self-portrait], 1930/31, exposure from two negatives (Photograph of the portrait: Chanan Frenkel). Acquired from the first Bauhaus-Verkaufs-ausstellung [sales exhibition] of Galerie am Sachsenplatz Leipzig, 1976, © Stiftung Bauhaus Dessau, Inv.-Nr. I 771 F / Image by Google

Colophon

Bauhaus Dessau Foundation
Edition Bauhaus 54

Edited for the Bauhaus Dessau Foundation by Wolfgang Thöner and Claudia Perren

Text: Wolfgang Thöner
with Christin Müller-Wenzel

Bauhaus Dessau Foundation
Director Claudia Perren
Gropiusallee 38
06846 Dessau-Roßlau

Concept: Wolfgang Thöner
Coordination, concept and management: Caroline Jansky
Design: Hannes Drißner, based on a preliminary concept by Katharina Köhler
Proofreading/editing: Michael Pilewski
Translation German > English: Robert Savage
Printed by: Gutenberg Beuys Feindruckerei GmbH

This publication is indexed in the Deutsche Nationalbibliografie of the German National Library; detailed bibliographic information is available online at www.dnb.de

Published by:
Spector Books
Harkortstraße 10
04107 Leipzig
www.spectorbooks.com

Distribution:
Germany, Austria: GVA, Gemeinsame Verlagsauslieferung Göttingen GmbH&Co. KG, www.gva-verlage.de
Switzerland: AVA Verlagsauslieferung AG, www.ava.ch
France, Belgium: Interart Paris, www.interart.fr
UK: Central Books Ltd, www.centralbooks.com
USA, Canada, Central and South America, Africa, Asia: ARTBOOK/ D.A.P., www.artbook.com
South Korea: The Book Society, www.thebooksociety.org
Australia, New Zealand: Perimeter Distribution, www.perimeterdistribution.com

The Bauhaus Dessau Foundation is a non-profit foundation under public law. It is institutionally funded by the German-Federal Commissioner for Culture and the Media, the State of Saxony-Anhalt, and the City of Dessau-Roßlau. The Publication *The Progressive Heritage of the Bauhaus* is gernerously funded by:

EvS
ERNST VON SIEMENS KUNSTSTIFTUNG

ISBN 978-3-95905-278-8

Die deutsche Ausgabe von *Fortschrittliches Bauhauserbe* erscheint bei Spector Books unter der folgenden ISBN 978-3-95905-277-1

First edition
Printed in Germany